northern pride

the very best of northern
architecture from
churches to chip shops

northern pride

the very best of northern
architecture from
churches to chip shops

John Grundy

GRANADA

First published in Great Britain in 2003
By Granada Media, an imprint of André Deutsch Limited
20 Mortimer Street
London W1T 3JW

The Tyne Tees Television production *Grundy's Wonders* is written and
presented by John Grundy and produced by Steve Robins.

A catalogue record is available from the British Library

ISBN 0 233 00003 8

Typeset by E-Type, Liverpool
Printed and bound in Great Britain

2 4 6 8 10 9 7 5 3 1

Contents

Introduction

North versus South

I'm a northerner, I have to make that clear from the start. I was born and brought up in Cumberland and lived my whole adult life in Durham and Northumberland (except for two exile years in the deepest of the deep south – Leicestershire). I love almost all of Yorkshire and I've even been known to say nice things about Lancashire so first and foremost, this book is going to be a celebration of the built environment of the north of England.

But the first questions that need to be asked are, what is the north and where does it start? I suspect that there are people in London and the South East who think that Birmingham's in the north but this book's not about Birmingham. Good gracious no. There are lots of other people who would include Cheshire and Derbyshire as the north but not me. I class them as being in the Midlands – north Midlands admittedly but not really the north. No, this book is about the buildings of Yorkshire and Lancashire, Durham, Cumbria (in fact I'm so old-fashioned that most of the time I'm going to call them Cumberland and Westmorland) and Northumberland. This book is about the real north.

So what's it like, the real north?

Well, if you only read what southerners think about the north, it's a rather backward place where nothing terribly important has ever happened – at least not until it began to make lots of money with its industry in Victorian times and even that had the effect of leaving it dirty and ugly. To outsiders it's poor, of course, all of the money is thought to have oozed south in some rather mysterious way and, needless to say, it's not really and truly civilised. This seems like a rather exaggerated description, but the more you read, the more you come across attitudes like these.

For example, in the mid 18th century, Hugh Smithson was a southerner who'd married the heiress to the great estates of the Percy family in Northumberland. He'd also been a very useful politician so he was rewarded, by a grateful government, with the title of First Duke of Northumberland. In the 1770s he had a shooting box built – well actually it's quite a big pretendy castle called Kielder Castle – high up near the headwaters of the River Tyne. He described the people who lived there as being:

> 'quite wild ... the women had no other dress than bed-gown and petticoat. The men were savage and could hardly be brought to rise from the heath ... They sang a wild tune, the burden of which was "Ourina, Ourina, Ourina". The females sang, the men danced round and at a certain point they drew their dirks which they always wore.'

Fifty or so years later, in 1848, the historian, Thomas Babington Macaulay, retold the story and made it sound even worse. He said that the hills around Kielder Castle were inhabited by 'a race' who were 'scarcely less savage than the Indians of California'. He told how you could see 'half-naked women chanting a wild measure while the men, brandishing dirks, danced a war dance'.

Half-naked women and rough chaps

Now, I've spent a lot of time around Kielder, in hopes I have to admit, of seeing half-naked women chanting wild measures but sadly I've seen none and you can understand why, since the only savage dance is that performed by people slapping themselves to try and get rid of clouds of incessant midges. What the Duke was seeing wasn't savages, it was folk music and country dancing, probably performed to the mournful but delicate beauty of the Northumbrian pipes; and what he was being was a southerner misunderstanding and stereotyping the north.

He wasn't alone. Nikolaus Pevsner, who was a refugee from Nazi Germany and the author of *The Buildings of England*, published his volume on Northumberland in 1957 and wrote this about the county:

> 'Rough are the winds, rough the moors, rough the miners, rough the castles, rough the dolerite cliffs by the Roman Wall and on the coast, rough is the stone of the walls which take the place of hedges, if you compare it with walling in the Cotswolds and rough even seems the smoother and more precisely worked stone under the black soot of Newcastle.'

Bearing in mind that there are barely any miners any more (and those that remain are said to be jolly nice chaps, not at all rough) and that Newcastle has been thoroughly de-sooted since that was written, it still gives an impression which is a bit less than comfy or civilised. And that's typical. You read almost anything by outsiders talking about the north and words like 'rough' and 'poor' and 'backward' and 'blackened' and 'remote' and 'wild' litter the pages.

An empty land?

That is, of course, if they mention the north at all. When I was thinking about writing this book, I had a little romp through the indexes of a lot of my architecture books to see which buildings the experts considered important and, do you know, it was often a really irritating and quite depressing experience. The same few buildings kept on reappearing and in many of the books the north was almost unrepresented – as if it was an uninhabited waste.

A few years ago I was involved with some friends in writing another book (about the buildings of Northumberland). We'd only just started and we got a letter from our editor who had just driven from Edinburgh down to London. She'd driven through Northumberland on the A68 which is admittedly a very beautiful road through the rural heart of the county but she wrote, 'What a beautiful county, but where are the buildings?' We put her right of course, she soon learnt that there were lots and lots of fascinating buildings, but this was the sort of attitude I found in my architecture books as well. One book called *The English House* mentions 220 different English houses in the index but only 15 of them were in the north and even then most of those were in Yorkshire. Yorkshire gets a slightly different treatment by southerners because it's big and loud and they've heard of it, but there was only one house mentioned in Cumbria (Levens Hall in Westmorland), one in County Durham (Lumley Castle), a couple in Northumberland and three in Lancashire. There was a clue on the jacket of this book about English Houses as to why the north was so poorly represented. It said:

> 'England's country houses owe their existence to England's unique history: to the fact that after the Middle Ages the nobility had no need to defend strongholds; to five hundred years of internal peace.'

It's all very well to talk about 'five hundred years of internal peace' but unfortunately it just isn't true of large parts of the north where 'after the Middle Ages', for another couple of hundred years, there wasn't much internal peace; where because of the proximity of the Scottish Border the nobility still lived in the fear and reality of war. What that has meant for the 'English Houses' of the north is that they are often very different from country houses elsewhere (as we will see later in this book). It's as if the writer of my 'English Houses' book is writing about an England that doesn't include the north. She is writing about the south in fact and those few bits of the north which resemble it. She's writing about broad and peaceful pastures and the north only gets a mention in exceptional circumstances.

Loads of my books turned out to be like this. Looking at them with my new eyes I didn't know (considering my intense local patriotism) why I'd bought them. One classic text (*The English Country House* by Sacheverell Sitwell) had no northern examples at all. Books on churches, country houses, manor houses and villages, they almost all focus on typical 'Englishy' scenes, select the few northern examples which are so great they can't be ignored and include a few others in an almost embarrassed sort of way before returning happily to the shires. I got really grumpy reading them.

A dirty land ...

Another writer who expresses a very common southerner's view of the north is the 19th-century novelist Elizabeth Gaskell who was born in Chelsea (deep south), brought up in Cheshire (north Midlands) but moved to Manchester when she was married at the age of 22. Margaret Hale, the heroine of her novel, *North and South*, has a similar background. She's been brought up in a pretty little village down south where there are lots of apple trees and the villagers wear smocks but she has to move with her minister dad to Manchester (which is called Milton in the book). It's a bit of a shock.

> 'Quick they were hurled over long, straight, hopeless streets of regularly-built houses, all small and of brick. Here and there a great oblong many-windowed factory stood up, like a hen among her chickens, puffing out black "unparliamentary" smoke.'

Margaret's mother is utterly cheesed off at the prospect of moving to this bleak northern city.

'"Oh Margaret! Are we to live here?" asked Mrs Hale in blank dismay. Margaret's heart echoed the tone in which the question was put.'

A ghastly land

Of course, Elizabeth Gaskell was writing a long time ago, in Victorian times. Nobody would still be talking about the north in these negative ways nowadays, would they?

Oh, wouldn't they. I've just been reading (early in 2003) an article in my local newspaper about a new exhibition to be opened in the Baltic Centre for Contemporary Art in Gateshead and I find myself confronted by the views of the London art critic, Brian Sewell, who's quoted as saying 'It's absolutely absurd to arrange a major exhibition of fundamental importance to the understanding of what happened to art in the second half of the 20th century and deprive London of an immediate view.' The article goes on to quote an earlier comment of his in which he apparently said, 'Gateshead is a self-inflicted wound. Bomb it, then you will change it. It is an awful place. Most of the north is awful.'

I realise that I'm being grumpy and paranoid and I'm sure there are loads of other southern writers who've been thoroughly praise-worthy in their representation of the north, but I've found, on the whole, that the attitude of outsider writers has been that the north is wild and rather backward, isolated, unimportant in terms of things that really matter, lacking in buildings of real quality and too often dirty and ugly.

So, how true is this picture? To test it I'm going to start off by looking at five buildings which might be thought of as typical 'northern' buildings – one in each of our counties – and see what they tell us about our region and its history.

chapter **o n e**

Five of the Best

One: Northumberland

Wildness galore

The first of my buildings explores the idea of 'wildness' and 'rough-ness'. I'm not going to deny that this is at least partly true. The wildness is partly true, bits of the north are still as wild as anything. The old county of Northumberland, for example, before the more populated bits of it were taken away and turned into Tyne and Wear, was the fifth largest county in England but in terms of population it was about twenty-ninth or thirtieth and even then 90% of its population lived within ten miles of the River Tyne. The rest was, and still is, wonderfully empty. Villages are few and far between, farms are big and therefore infrequent, towns are small and the moors are vast. The enormous Northumberland National Park has a human population of about 2500. And Northumberland doesn't stand alone. The North York Moors, the Durham Pennines, the Lakes, the Yorkshire Dales, the Trough of Bowland ... the list goes on ... as much wildness as you could possibly want. I once stood on Blackstone Edge, on the moors between Rochdale and Halifax, in the driving rain, in a place which I knew had an ancient human history because I was standing beside the clear and outstanding remains of a Roman road that followed these bleak heights, in a scene of almost transcendental isolation and I wondered if there was anyone else left in the world. That's how wild the north can be.

The Bastlehouse

But my first building is one which I filmed recently in one of the wildest bits of the north, high, high up in the Cheviot Hills near the border with Scotland. It rejoices in the name of Shittleheugh which is rather a risqué name but we Grundys have never been afraid to live life near the edge, so I'll say it again. Shittleheugh. Shittleheugh is a ruin, dramatically sited on a bare hillside, deep in rough grass and bracken, well back from any road and visited in the main only by sheep which rather disdainfully ignore any humans who turn up. There are old and very atmospheric stone walls round about and one gnarled hawthorn tree. It's a single rectangular building about 40 feet long and perhaps 20 feet wide. It has been a two-storey building and the gable ends stand, quite impressively, to full height but the side walls are only about six feet high. In one of them, though, there is still a doorway with its lintel intact and the remains of a tiny porch in front of it. Inside there's nothing but a jumble of fallen stones and, in two of the walls, very deep, narrow, slit windows.

All of this is very atmospheric but none of it is the really remarkable thing about this small ruined building. The really remarkable thing about it is the stonework it's built of. Its walls are extraordinary. They are over four feet thick and built of huge boulders of untreated stone, laid roughly, but only very roughly, in courses. Some of the stones are truly enormous, five and six feet long and two or three feet thick. In between the biggest stones small slivers of stone are hammered in to fill in the chinks (a process known as *galetting* should you be interested) and deep in the cracks you can see that the stones are held together with pinkish lime mortar. The effect of these walls, close up, is overwhelming and to be honest, barbaric. What sort of people, you can't help asking, lived in this building and what sort of lives did they lead?

Shittleheugh is an example of a class of building called 'bastlehouses' which are unique to this isolated area of the Anglo-Scottish border. I really mean unique. There's nothing like them anywhere else. What makes them unique is a combination of different qualities they have – each of which is shared by other types of building elsewhere but only bastlehouses have them all. They are massively built of stone (as we've seen) and they were intended to be defensible, to keep their occupants safe from attack. Their occupants were of two kinds – animals and human. The ground floor of bastlehouses was given over to animals while the people lived upstairs. Often in these bastlehouses the only way to get upstairs was by a ladder which could be pulled up after you. The ladders have long gone but in many of them the upper doorway remains hanging and unapproachable.

In Cumberland and Northumberland there are several hundred of these bastlehouses surviving to some extent or other and there were probably several hundred more which have disappeared and been replaced by more convenient farmhouses ... for that is what they were ... they may be very odd but they were in essence just farmhouses. They were built from the latter part of the sixteenth century until a couple of years before the English Civil War – between about 1570 and 1640. In the south at that time Longleat and Burghley House were being built. In Kent, thousands of beautiful half-timbered farmhouses and manor houses were already a century old and becoming mellow with age. Shakespeare lived and died within these dates, but here, on the English border, people were living in one-roomed bastlehouses.

Four hundred years of war

These unique bastlehouses are here because they were necessary. The region we know of as the north was first made a border zone between the north and south of this island by the Romans but from the 1100s, when the present national border was first established, the north acted as a buffer between Scotland and England. It was a violent buffer, a scene of almost continuous warfare. There were a few quietish times – the 1200s on the whole was a quietish time – but in 1296 Edward I adopted an aggressive new policy of interference in Scottish affairs. He started a war which went on intensely for 300 years. It lasted officially until 1586 when the newly crowned James VI came to an agreement with Elizabeth I, but to a lesser extent it continued for far longer than that. For example there was a battle between Scottish raiders and English pursuers at the village of Crookham as late as 1685. So some people, and I'm one of them, tend to call this the *400*-year war.

You can't be at war for hundreds of years without it having a terrible effect on the landscape and the people who lived in it. This is why the north as a whole is the ultimate 'castle country' of England.

At the time when these castles were being built – in the 13th to the 15th centuries – the north was anything but backward and remote. In fact, with Scotland as our chief enemy, the north was at the centre of political power, vital to the safety of the Kingdom. northern Lords like the Percies of Alnwick and Warkworth or the Nevilles of Raby Castle were among the powerful people in the country. The Bishops of Durham in their superb castle beside their cathedral were even known as 'Prince Bishops' and given massive additional powers by the king in order to help keep control of this vital northern border. They could raise troops, administer justice, even mint their own money. Kings and king-makers were constantly traipsing all over the place, Parliaments were even held up north, but with the war going on for so long, eventually control and discipline broke down and warfare became like an epidemic, no, it became endemic, which means that it was always present. Even when the two governments were officially at peace the war was continued at an unofficial level by local chaps who'd never known anything else. By the mid-1500s, on the borders, a class of men called 'reivers' had emerged who lived by raiding, cattle rustling and sheep stealing.

The Border Reivers

(The word 'reive' was an old Border word meaning to steal. It survives in English in the word 'bereave'. Another old Border word was 'mail' which was a word for rent. The Border word for an illegally imposed rent was 'blackmail'. So the warlike borders have left us two words – 'bereave' and 'blackmail'. Does that say something about what life was like up here!)

The reivers didn't usually attack in full-scale armies but in bands which raided across the border into the next country or across the ridge into the next valley. It was all terribly indiscriminate violence. The distances could be tiny or they could be huge. Scottish raiders were quite likely to raid as far south as Yorkshire and Lancashire;

English raiders went as far as the gates of Edinburgh. Usually the raids were carried out by just a small group of men – men who all came from the same clan or 'name'. (on the border they didn't call them clans but 'graynes') If you're called Armstrong, or Dixon or Eliot, Hetherington, Graham, Fenwick, Dodd, Milburn or Robson or any of the old Border family names, it means that almost certainly your ancestors used to sneak around in little groups nicking cows from their neighbours. It should make you feel very proud.

Mind, the bands of reivers could at times be quite big. There's an account of a raid led in 1584 by a Scot called William Armstrong (or Kinmont Willy) who led a band of 300 reivers from Dumfriesshire into North Tynedale and stole 140 cattle, 60 horses, 500 sheep. Oh, and they also burned 60 houses and killed 10 men! Kinmont Willy was eventually captured by the English Warden, Lord Scrope, and imprisoned in Carlisle Castle. The two countries were officially at peace at the time so the arrest infuriated the Scots and caused an international incident which the Scots resolved by staging a dramatic rescue across the border. It was all very SAS-ish and involved a night-time raid on Carlisle Castle and it thrilled me as a little boy because it was the only time my home suburb of Stanwix (or Staneshaw as it's called in the poem) gets a mention in literature. The Border Ballad which celebrates the event says that after the rescue, when the alarm was given, the rescuers fled north across the River Eden and reached Staneshaw-bank (which I used to fail regularly to cycle up on my way home from school):

> They scarce had won the Staneshaw-bank
> When'a the Carlisle bells were rung
> And a thousand men, in horse and foot
> Cam wi' the keen Lord Scrope along

It didn't do them any good though, because the noble Scots were safely away. Indeed, Lord Buccleuch, the leader of the rescuers, found time to turn and issue a taunt to his pursuers

> If ye like na my visit in merry England
> In fair Scotland come visit me.

Now I suspect that there are elements of exaggeration in all of this. I'm pretty sure Carlisle Castle never held a thousand men and the figures for the raid on Tynedale sound huge, but the essence is right. By the end of the 1500s the borders were a wild and dangerous place and that's why bastlehouses made their appearance. They were a response to savage but rapid raids. They were never strong enough to resist an attack or a siege by a full-scale army but, in the event of a reivers' attack, the owners of a bastlehouse could hope to drive their cattle into the stone-vaulted basement of the bastle, lock the door, pull up the ladder and sit it out behind their four-foot walls and their tiny barred windows long enough for the raiders to move on.

I've done an odd thing here, I hope you'll recognise. I've chosen as my first 'northern' building one which appears to support the southerner's view of the north as wild and backward. Shittleheugh is wild in every sense of the word and the life it reflects was savage, so by the end of the Middle Ages parts of the north were backward, uncivilised even, but the picture as a whole is more complicated than that and that leads me to …

Two: Cumbria

Great Art in the Wilderness: the Bewcastle Cross

Twenty miles west of Shittleheugh, equally near the Scottish border, but in Cumberland, is another place which seems at first glance to support all of those stereotypical views of northerness.

It's called Bewcastle and it's about 15 miles NW of Carlisle on the edge of moors as wild as anything on the border. It's a place oozing with the atmosphere of a warlike past. On the moors all around there are ruined bastlehouses and it's likely that some of the surviving farmhouses started life as bastlehouses as well and as if these weren't enough, Bewcastle itself has two castles. One is a Roman fort, an advanced station, an outpost seven or eight miles to the north of Hadrian's Wall (i.e. in enemy territory). It was destroyed violently at least twice but its ramparts are still visible and within them there is a dramatic crag of medieval castle, 30 feet high, 90 feet square, incredibly plain and forbidding. It was a Royal castle, never meant as a home but as a military barracks on the wildest and most dangerous part of the border.

Within the ramparts of the Roman Fort, the castle isn't alone. There's a farm and a vicarage and also a church – not very old in its present form, and rather plain. In its north wall there are no windows at all, which tells you something about the weather up here – but in its churchyard is an object that challenges a lot of the stereotypes about the north.

It's called the Bewcastle Cross.

The Bewcastle Cross has lost its top so it isn't a cross at all any more, it's just a square tapering shaft of stone 14ft 6in high, not counting the base it rests on and it's covered, on all four sides, with carving. On one of the sides there are some ancient runes which have been interpreted to show that the cross was erected at least partly in memory of an Anglo-Saxon king called Alcfrith, son of Oswi and he died round about the year AD 700. There may even be a carving of him at the top of one of the sides, the south side, with a hawk on his arm. Below him, carved in arched recesses, are first of all Jesus crushing a lion and an adder beneath his feet, and at the bottom, John the Baptist. They're quite well worn nowadays, these figures, as you would be yourself if you were to stand in all weathers in Bewcastle churchyard for over 1300 years. Not that you could, of course … but, though worn, the quality of these figures still shines out. They look, first and foremost, like men, like real people, realistic, convincingly human and natural.

Spiffing though it is, this south side is not my favourite. All of the other sides have brilliant decoration, vines and intricately carved knots and checkerboard effects and so on, but the east side is my favourite. It's made up of one single, scrolly vine stem which snakes its way from top to bottom of the shaft. The vine is 'inhabited' as they say in the text books; it has birds and beasts living in it – beasts near the bottom with long tails curled around the vine stem, and birds perched higher up. As you go from top to bottom of the scroll, each beast or bird is facing in the opposite direction to the one beneath it. It's an absolutely magnificent piece of design, it all is actually, the whole cross. I'm going to quote Nikolaus 'rough man' Pevsner again (*Buildings of England: Cumberland and Westmorland* this time)

'The quality is amazingly high … there is nothing so perfect and of a comparable date … in the whole of Europe.'

I hear you gasp. You stand amazed. Nothing so perfect … in the whole of Europe! And this is an outsider talking about a piece of northern design. Pevsner is talking about stone-carving here. He's saying that nowhere else in Europe at that particular time, round about the year AD 700, could you have found stonecarvers capable of doing carving of this quality, with the amount of skill that's found at Bewcastle. In most other places if you look at carved stonework of that period you see grotesque parodies of human beings, ungainly little dolls, but here, in Bewcastle, the people look like people and the vines and beasts look like vines and beasts and as well as that, the carvings are perfectly controlled, they fit perfectly and symmetrically into their spaces. That's another thing you don't find in the 7th and 8th centuries in other parts of Europe. And there's more! There's another thing. Whoever carved this extraordinary cross was aware of earlier art from all over the known world. The precursors of all the different decorative motifs on the cross come from the Mediterranean, from Egypt and Greece and Rome, early Christian art in southern Italy and southern France. It all comes together at Bewcastle.

How? Why? What on earth is something this civilised and refined doing in the wilds of the north? Answer me that.

Well … of course it wasn't the wilds of the north when the Bewcastle Cross was carved. There were Anglo-Saxon kingdoms here which covered the whole area of what we call the north nowadays and spread north into present-day Scotland as well and these kingdoms were the opposite of wild. They were at the very centre of the civilised European world and were producing great works of art, not just in stone carving but in every area of the arts. There are other stone crosses as great as Bewcastle at Ruthwell just over the present border in Dumfriesshire and (in rather fragmentary form) at Rothbury in Northumberland. At Holy Island the Lindisfarne Gospels were just the climax of a whole series of illuminated masterpieces that were created there and in the scriptorium of the Venerable Bede's twin monastery at Jarrow and Monkwearmouth in Sunderland. In literature, Bede himself was the greatest writer of his age, revered throughout Europe for the brilliance and the freshness of his work. I'll give you a sample of it. Bede never left the north and this is how he described the world he saw around him – not wild, not savage or backward but like this …

> 'The island is rich in crops and trees and has good grazing for cattle and draught animals; it also produces vines in some areas. Land and sea birds too, of various species flourish there, and it is famous for its rivers, with their abundance of fish, the salmon and the eel in particular … Because it lies almost beneath the North Pole, the nights are light in summer, so that often people watching at midnight are uncertain whether the evening twilight still lingers or morning dawn has already arrived …'

Doesn't it sound nice? I bet you wished you lived there. Oh! You do, it's called the north.

Benedict Biscop and others – Anglo-Saxon Tourists

But if Bede never left the north, many other Northumbrians did. Benedict Biscop, the rich Northumbrian nobleman who founded Bede's monastery in AD 681 went to Rome on six separate occasions. There and back. Not on Eurostar I might add, unless he called his donkey that, which is probably unlikely. No, he went on foot six times and each time he brought substantial quantities of loot back with him. He brought paintings and sculptures and books and he also … (and I don't want you to do this yourselves when you come back from holiday because it will only get you into trouble) … he also imported workmen from Italy and Gaul who re-introduced into Britain the sort of artistic and architectural techniques that the area hadn't seen since the Romans left. In particular he imported stonemasons and glassmakers who could create in the north the sort of stone churches he'd seen in Italy.

Other church leaders were doing the same. St Wilfrid, who founded the great churches at Ripon and Hexham at exactly the same time, was another monk who was never at home (ee yer niver at home, our Wilfrid, his mother used to say) and among the goodies he brought back with him from Rome was the kneebone of St Andrew (once again I would like to discourage you from copying him. Nowadays the importing of kneebones is frowned upon, and rightly so, by Her Majesty's Customs.)

This relic though, became the centrepiece of the church that Wilfrid built at Hexham where it remained for 600 years before being eventually stolen by invading Scots who took it home and made Andrew the patron saint of Scotland.

Hexham – a crypt with atmosphere

The churches, like Jarrow and Monkwearmouth, which survive from those days can seem to us, with the benefit of hindsight, to be quite rough and simple but at the time they seemed positively astonishing. Wilfrid's church at Hexham was considered by his contemporaries as the greatest church north of the Alps but sadly all that remains of it now is Wilfrid's throne, the Frith Stone, exquisitely carved from a single block of stone and decorated with delicate interwoven 'Celtic'-style carving – and his marvellous crypt – a network of tiny corridors and chambers and corridors built of Roman stones from nearby Roman sites re-used without any understanding of their original purpose. Stones are used upside down, inscriptions are used incomplete and out of context, bits of Roman decoration are totally misused. There's part of an inscription to the Emperor Septimius Severus built into the ceiling of one of the corridors. In one way it's all a little quaint but the overall effect is much more powerful than quaint – it's dark and deeply moving, enormously atmospheric. It was built to be a *relic chamber* – to display relics of ancient saints and there's a niche in the east wall of the main chamber where Andrew's kneebone would have been displayed in a jewelled reliquary, and on either side there are other niches for lamps to display the relic to its best effect – he was nothing if not a showman, Wilfrid. He knew the most effective way to sell his Christianity was to dramatise it a bit, make it exciting. Just imagine what it must have felt like to be down in that crypt in those days, in a darkness part lit by flickering oil lamps, surrounded by mysterious and ancient stones, in the presence of the kneebone of a man who had known Jesus.

Where a saint has trod ...

There's something about these monuments of the early north which somehow makes them greater than the sum of their parts. Holy Island is a good example. There's very little tangible survives on the island from those early Saxon days after the monastery there was founded in AD 635 by St Aidan, except some carved stones in the museum and a few fragments of the parish church. Virtually everything you see now is part of the building made by Norman monks after the original monastery had been abandoned for over 200 years in the face of attacks by the Vikings, but somehow the memory of Cuthbert and his fellow early saints seems to hang in the air and to be almost touchable. The Vicar of Holy Island told me once that he believed that the gap between heaven and earth was smaller at Holy Island and that the footsteps where a saint has trod can never be erased. That's true of Hexham too and despite the wildness that re-invaded the landscape in later centuries, it's certainly true of Bewcastle. To stand in front of the ancient cross, in that lonely place, is to feel the hairs stand up on the back of the neck.

Shivery.

All of these wonderful things (and I've only just touched the surface of them) were created here in the north because at that time, in the 7th and 8th centuries, far from being a remote backwater, this area was at the heart of things. It was on the front line that was pioneering the spread of Christianity in Britain. Its kings ruled over a rich and normally peaceful country and they took it upon themselves to convert the heathens who lived to the south of them. It lay (as it still does) on the major trade routes that existed between Europe and Ireland. It was in constant and fruitful contact with the rest of Europe and the people who lived here and the things they made were recognised by other Europeans as being of the greatest value. It's a pity it's not like that nowadays, isn't it.

All of this talk of fruitful international contact, European significance and Cuthbert leads me to ...

Three: Durham

The greatest church of them all

Durham Cathedral was built to house the body of St Cuthbert, which was a very remarkable body as bodies go. Cuthbert had died in AD 687 after a life divided between personal piety and useful contributions to his community. In his death he performed one final act of contribution to that community. He didn't rot. For some reason, 20 years after he died his fellow monks dug him up and found his body still uncorrupted. You can briefly discuss among yourselves why they would do this or how convenient it was for them that this miracle had occurred – because a miracle was what it was immediately seen as and Cuthbert was immediately venerated as a saint. The cynical among you might want to wonder how much dosh could be generated by the possession of a genuine saint in your monastery, the less cynical will recognise the tremendous sense of wonder that such an event might create.

Two hundred years later, in AD 875, after a series of raids by those nasty rough Vikings, the monks fled from Holy Island carrying with them as luggage a few bits and pieces just like you and I would have done were we to be attacked by Vikings. They took one of their two churches with them (the wooden one – for some strange reason they left the stone one behind … 'I'm not carrying that … I don't mind helping with a few bits of wood but that stone weighs …') and obviously they took the saint in his coffin. I say 'obviously' because he was their most valuable possession – spiritually as well as financially. They wandered about for a bit, preaching and converting and so on, until in AD 883 they settled in Chester-le-Street where they stayed there for another hundred years until AD 998 when they moved to Durham and began to build a church worthy to hold the body of a saint.

I'd like to just say, first of all, that they succeeded. There is no building greater than Durham Cathedral. A poll of world architects recently voted it the greatest building in the world and, though I haven't visited all of the others so I can't comment on them, I want to stress that in talking about Durham Cathedral we are talking about a building which is *seriously* good.

A genius with no name

I'd love to be able to tell you the name of the architect who designed it but his name's not known. We know the names of the Bishops he worked for, but not his; but whatever his name, he was a genius who helped transform the history of architecture. Durham was the first building in England to be stone-vaulted throughout. It was the first building in Europe to use rib vaults. The pointed arches that divide the nave vaults into sections are among the very earliest pointed arches in the world and that, too was an innovation that was to be hugely important in the invention of the Gothic style. So the unknown architect was a brilliant engineer/inventor but he was also a brilliant designer.

Durham is a work of genius inside, transforming the usually solid and weighty Norman style into something that soars. It's amazing how it's done. The piers of the nave, for example are massive. Their circumference is almost the same as their height – they are about 24 feet round and 27 feet high – which ought to make them look as solid and dumpy as anything. Imagine what you would look like if you were nearly the same circumference round the middle as you are high. I'm 5 feet 8 inches tall; imagine if I had a waist of, say, 5 feet. A roly poly you would say – solid and dumpy – but the piers at Durham look nothing like that. This is partly because the line of the piers continues to soar upwards through the triforium and the clerestory and on into the beautiful stone vaults that cover the whole building so that the piers are just part of the whole breathtaking composition. But the decoration of the piers themselves helps to take away the dumpiness as well. They have extraordinary incised carvings on them – zigzags and diamonds and lozenges and spirals which are deep and bold and energetic, creating an image of life rather than solidity. They look absolutely wonderful.

Durham looks wonderful from outside too, partly because of its three lofty towers, and the beauty of its stone, but mainly because of its extraordinary situation. It's built on a deep meander of the River Wear and by some miracle or accident the steep banks of the river which almost surround it have never been built on and have been left covered with trees so that almost wherever you look from the church floats above the tree tops and the river much as it must have done 900 years ago when it was first built.

So what does that give me so far, in my initial survey of the buildings that make the north what it is – two masterpieces of European significance and one wild, savage and primitive little ruin. Not much of a pattern emerging so far and I can warn you that the situation will get no clearer when I move on to ...

Four: Yorkshire

A seat of power

A few miles north-east of the City of York is Castle Howard which is the country seat of the Earls of Carlisle. It's big. It's very big. It is in fact enormous though it isn't the largest country house in England, that honour goes to another Yorkshire mansion called Wentworth Woodhouse near Sheffield.

The Earls of Carlisle are a branch of the great Howard family which has been so important in the history of England but this particular branch originated from further north, indeed less than a hundred years before Castle Howard was built, there were Howards living in Naworth Castle near Brampton in Cumberland – in particular a remarkable soldier and administrator called Lord William Howard who was trying desperately to control the warlike border and administer justice in a ravaged land.

But there's nothing ravaged or warlike about Castle Howard. It might be called a castle but this is the classic English country house, magnificently placed in a landscape of rolling meadows, well-placed woods and man-made lakes. Dotted around the landscape are the usual array of kitchen gardens and bridges and lodges and temples and ...

... what am I saying? The usual array! There's nothing 'usual' about the array to be found at Castle Howard because this house and this landscape were the product of two of the most powerful and unusual minds in English Architecture.

Vanbrugh and Hawksmoor

Sir John Vanbrugh, to be honest, wasn't an architect at all. He was a playwright and a soldier and goodness knows what else but until he started to work on this house for the third Earl of Carlisle he doesn't appear to have had anything to do with building at all. It's all a bit mysterious and really quite amazing that a man with no training and no experience at all should be given the job of building one of the most important buildings in the country for one of the most important men (his client was the First Lord of the Treasury). What's even more mysterious and even more amazing is that out of this total lack of experience he produced a masterpiece, one of the greatest houses in the whole of Europe.

Mind you, he was helped by a genuine and hugely experienced architect called Nicholas Hawksmoor and it's not at all clear who did what. As an 18-year-old Hawksmoor had been Sir Christopher Wren's clerk of works on St Paul's Cathedral and in the Castle Howard duo he was almost certainly the practical man who kept the building up and got things done, but he was also a superb designer in his own right.

Who did what might be the issue in more academic books about the history of architecture but it's not the issue here. The issue here is that these two men produced a house and an attendant landscape which is truly extraordinary.

The Baroque style

The style it's all in is called the 'Baroque Style'. The style originated in Italy in the second half of the Renaissance. It was a style which took the details and the rules of the Classical style – all of the restrained and controlled rules of Ancient Greece and Rome – all of the Classical Orders of architecture, the Doric, Ionic and Corinthian orders – and twisted the lot into new and exaggerated shapes, breaking the rules, squashing things up, making it all a bit more energetic.

That's what Vanbrugh and Hawksmoor did at Castle Howard. It's all spiffingly overblown and exaggerated. Their arches have massive keystones, there are grotesque carved masks all over the place. My favourite is a gateway into the Kitchen Gardens which is called the Satyr Gate. It's just a pedestrian entrance so it isn't actually huge but its scale is gigantic. It has an enormous keystone and the columns or pilasters that frame the opening look as if they've been pegged in place by great big stone hoops. The tops of the pilasters, where the capitals should be, are carved with two huge grotesque masks, great hairy faces leering down at you as you walk through the door. It's a marvellous thing but to be honest the house is even better. It has the same grandeur of scale but without the grotesque quality. The entrance hall is massive, its fireplace, super massive, its domed ceiling … Well, you get the idea. In domestic architecture Vanbrugh went on to produce the first great masterpiece of the English Baroque and one of the most astonishing houses in the world …

… in Yorkshire …

… in the north!

So what makes that surprising? Why am I sprinkling exclamation marks beside a statement like that as if nobody could seriously be expected to believe such a thing was possible? I suspect that Vanbrugh himself wouldn't have been the slightest bit surprised to have produced a masterpiece in the north. A few years later in his career he built another stupendous house at Seaton Delaval on the coast near Newcastle which is, if anything, even more wild and exaggeratedly restless than Castle Howard. My old friend, Nikolaus 'wild-man' Pevsner described it as 'architecture for the storm and the driving cloud, for sombre ships and the battering sea' (which isn't a bad bit of writing for a German refugee who learnt his English in adulthood). When he was up here building it, Vanbrugh wrote admiringly about the north, comparing it favourably to 'the tame sneaking south'.

Do you know, I've always loved him for that. I'm going to write it again … 'the tame sneaking south'. Snigger, snigger … He was responding to the landscape and to the history and to the weather of course and though in both cases – at Seaton Delaval and at Castle Howard – he produced something which was superficially like a standard English Country House, in reality he came up with something wilder and distinctively northern.

OK, last but not least …

Five: Lancashire.

Victorian innovation

In the middle of Liverpool there's a Victorian office block. That seems a silly thing to say. In the middle of Liverpool there are hundreds of Victorian office blocks but on Water Street there's a

Victorian office building which is the perfect introduction to another aspect of northern architecture and that is … innovation.

It was built in 1864 by a very little-known man called Peter Ellis. I say 'little known' but in fact I know nothing about him at all except that he built this building on Water Street and another one on Cook Street, also in Liverpool, both of which are, in structure and design, way, way ahead of their time.

The building on Water Street is called Oriel Chambers and that's the better known of the two. Looked at from the front it's almost entirely made of glass, big sheets of plate glass, four storeys, in fact, of plate glass. There are thin stone columns between the windows made so fine that they are clearly intended to look like iron and there's a small, rather pathetic stone pediment over the top but the façade is really entirely dominated by glass held in place by incredibly fine strips of iron. There's even more glass than I've implied so far because three of the storeys are made up of rows of oriel windows, which means sticky-outy windows, each with three sides made of glass. Round the back, in fact round the back of both of these Peter Ellis buildings, the effect is even more extreme. The stone disappears entirely and we are left with walls apparently made just of glass.

Nowadays we take it for granted that buildings are made of glass, glass hung almost invisibly on steel frames, but in 1864 the idea was entirely revolutionary. Greenhouses had been around for a long time of course and they were getting more and more adventurous in scale as time went by. In 1851 the Crystal Palace had been built to house the Great Exhibition and that was made entirely of iron and glass – an utterly revolutionary building. But nobody had attempted to carry the revolution into the town. Nobody had thought to break free from the old Gothic or Classical traditions and produce buildings almost stripped bare of details – in fact nobody else really thought of it for another 20 years or so when the skyscraper builders of New York and Chicago began to invent a completely new sort of architecture – nobody that is, except Peter Ellis.

It might be a surprise that a virtual unknown should come up with such an innovative idea, but if the idea was going to come up at all, it's no surprise that it should happen in mid-19th century-Liverpool. South Lancashire (Liverpool and Manchester first of all of course, but Oldham and Bolton and Rochdale as well) is among the finest of all places to see Victorian architecture, especially Victorian commercial buildings and industrial buildings and the reason for this is quite simple – the Industrial Revolution.

Lancashire's been making stuff for a very long time. There were coal mines and cotton manufacturing in the Middle Ages, but in the 1700s everything changed and industry in the county took off at extraordinary speed and in millions of different and ingenious directions most of them, though, to do with cotton. If this was an essay about the origins of the Industrial Revolution I'd have to try and explain why it all happened but it's not and I'm pleased because I don't know why it happened.

Some things are fairly obvious. Liverpool, as a port on the west coast, was in a good position to take part in trade with the newly emerging power of America, so cotton was easy to get. That's one thing. Another thing (and I'd like you to keep this quiet; don't tell anybody) is that Lancashire's wet. It rains a lot and cotton benefits from a damp climate. The rain and the hills provide plenty of fast-flowing streams which can drive water-powered mills. There was masses of coal so that when steam power was invented the county was in a position to benefit from it …

But other things are less easy to explain. Why did it all come together in a few places? Why did so many brilliant people all suddenly emerge with ideas that revolutionised the way we did things? In the Lancashire cotton industry alone there were men like John Kay who invented the flying shuttle in 1733 and James Hargreaves who invented the Spinning Jenny in about 1765. There was Sir Richard Arkwright from Preston and Samuel Crompton from Bolton. These are the men who revolutionised the way that things were made.

It didn't just happen in Lancashire, of course. Brilliant inventors and entrepreneurs emerged at the same time all over the north and, if I'm being reluctantly honest, elsewhere as well – in Birmingham even and Coalbrookdale and especially in Scotland. But enough of this reluctant honesty, stick to the north. On Tyneside, men like George Stephenson brought about the birth of the railways, while Lord Armstrong forged a massive industrial empire out of hydraulic engineering. Middlesbrough emerged (in Prime Minister Gladstone's memorable phrase) as an 'infant giant' on the back of its massive iron deposits. The Yorkshire wool industry was a tremendous source of wealth and men like Sir Titus Salt turned it into startling towns and marvellous buildings.

But it was Lancashire that capped the lot. South Lancashire is the ultimate 19th-century landscape. Manchester and Liverpool in Victorian times rivalled London in importance. They were the places where the real money was made. At that time, for a while at least, the north was genuinely important.

To sum up ...

So there you are. Five buildings – Shittleheugh Bastle, Bewcastle Cross, Durham Cathedral, Castle Howard and Oriel Chambers. When you look at them together what do they say as an introduction to the buildings of the north?

- That sometimes they're wild and backward.
- That sometimes they're not.
- That sometimes the north leads the world.
- That on at least three separate occasions (7th century, Scottish Wars, Industrial Revolution) the north has not been a backwater but has been at the centre of national affairs.
- That it has wonderful buildings.
- That it is rich in variety.

chapter | **t w o**

Churches

Churches – is there a northern style?

I was very young when I started looking at churches. My father trawled me around them when I was still in nappies and I have done the same to my own family. When my own son was two and a bit I tried to leave him in the car with his grandma outside a church in the Eden Valley but he insisted on getting out and following me, saying earnestly, 'I'm very interested in churches.'

To do him justice, 28 years later he still is. And who can blame him because they are wonderful things, churches, and the north is wonderfully rich in them. I know that because I've visited hundreds of them, possibly thousands and I've hardly ever been disappointed. I have, on the contrary been thrilled, moved, astonished, amused, even shocked on occasion.

On the whole however – if you look at them altogether I mean, the north's churches superficially don't seem to be very different from the churches of the rest of the country.

They're built of northern stone of course which gives them a local character – but that doesn't make them one group, in fact it means that they're all different from each other. In South Lancashire, for example, there's dark red sandstone, in most of the Lake District it's slate but in the extreme south of the Lakes there are silvery coloured limestones that make the buildings and villages look almost white. That's also true of parts of southern and eastern Yorkshire where the churches are built of deliciously creamy limestones and further north there are the buff coloured sandstones of the North East. There is no single northern stone, then.

But is there a single recognisable northern style? Nah. I don't think there is. In fact all the styles that make up the history of English architecture everywhere are here and northern examples of each style look more or less the same as their equivalents elsewhere ...

The north's churches – as good as the best

Of course they can be as good as, or better than their equivalents elsewhere. There isn't a greater non-cathedral church in the country than Beverley Minster for example. It's breathtaking from outside, towering over the small-town glories of Beverley and inside it is just superb. It is mainly from the middle of the 13th century and of a richness that surpasses anywhere else I've seen. Every arch and pier is deeply carved with forceful but intricate mouldings. It's made of stone from floor to ceiling and the decorations are a total delight. The walls are lined with little stone medieval Yorkshire folk and I think it's fair to say that they were as mixed a bunch as you'd find on any Yorkshire street today ... and that, in my experience is pretty mixed.

Quality like this can be found all over the north. Hexham, Ripon, York Minster itself all provide evidence of how superb the Early English architecture of the 13th-century north could be.

And then there's Carlisle as well. As a Carlisle lad, I'm not going to pass up the opportunity to pour a bit of praise on Carlisle Cathedral's glories. The choir at Carlisle was burnt down in 1292 and immediately rebuilt. You wouldn't expect that to happen. The Scottish wars had just started and you'd think it would seem a bit risky to be putting good money into new churches right on the Border itself, but at Carlisle they immediately rebuilt the choir in a brilliant Decorated Gothic style. The east window alone is a staggering tour de force, 51 feet high and with the most beautiful flowing tracery. As a Carlisle schoolboy I was immensely jealous of the reputation of this window and liked to consider it the pinnacle of its style and I would get really irritated if people claimed that Selby Abbey in Yorkshire was greater. Now I'm not so sure. Now I don't care as much. The north has two glories to be proud of and there's another of course, and another and another … lots of wonderful churches.

A peculiarly northern power?

But are they local, local in style? Are they northern? Sometimes I feel I can sense a northern spirit. Durham Cathedral is so powerful that I find myself wondering whether its power comes from the location, the stone it's made of, the history that brought it into being. Of course it could just be that it was designed by a great architect but it does, somehow, seem more than that. Another Norman church which gives me similar feelings is Lastingham in North Yorkshire, deep in the southern side of the North Yorks Moors. It was originally founded by an Anglo-Saxon saint called St Cedd. He was a proper old saint, St Cedd, because he's reputed to have fasted a lot – making do for days on a little morsel of bread, an egg and a little watered milk. Not unlike my own frugal eating habits, I may add, except that I'm never given eggs. He died in AD 664 and there's no sign of his original church, but 400 years later, in 1078, monks from York built a monastery on the site. Part of the church that they built survives, but underneath it is the crypt that they built to hold Cedd's tomb and that is still absolutely complete. It is stupendous, unique. There's nothing like it, nothing so powerful anywhere else in the country. It has very short but very massive stone piers and the oppressively low stone vaulted roof rises out of them in a vision of powerful arches. It's like a mythological gnomes' castle. Here be ye dragons, you can't help feeling. In this low, dark and claustrophobic space, the effect is overwhelming and emotional.

I would like to think, I sometimes *do* think, that a power like that at Lastingham is a peculiarly northern power, an intensity born of the landscape, the weather and the history, but logically I suspect that I'm going too far and I'm just being seduced by the power of the Norman style all over the country.

However, I have been thinking about this, as I'm sure you would hope I have and though I have reached the conclusion that it is impossible to place the finger on a single northern shape to church architecture I think it is possible to see a lot of different sorts of churches in the north that you won't find elsewhere.

Some Northern Specialities

1. ANGLO-SAXON ARCHITECTURE

A period in which we are especially rich as I pointed out in Chapter one. There is in fact, a recognisable northern style of Anglo-Saxon church which is quite distinct from those further south. The best surviving example of the style is at Escomb, near Bishop Auckland in County Durham.

It's a remarkable survival, the 7th-century church at Escomb. Situated in the middle of a big circular churchyard which is probably as old as the church, and surrounded entirely by 1960s' council houses, it is one of only three absolutely complete Saxon churches in Britain and it is quite different from the other two. It is built of Roman stones, snaffled from the nearby Roman Fort of Binchester and it's very narrow, quite long and very high and these proportions are thought of as typically Northumbrian. Jarrow is the same and so was Monkwearmouth and so were loads of the Saxon churches in present-day Durham and Northumberland, but churches further south, in Kent for example, are shorter and wider. The details of northern Saxon churches are different too. One of the features that textbooks always mention as a way of recognising Saxon churches is the *quoins* or corner stones of the building. Anglo-Saxon churches, the books say, have *long and short quoins* – which means that the corner stones alternate between one laid horizontally and one laid vertically. It's a sure sign of Saxon-ness, they say. Not in the north. Only one Saxon church in the north of England (Whittingham in Northumberland) has long and short quoins. I have no idea why this should be the case. Perhaps it was chance, fashion, taste. Perhaps the builders that Benedict Biscop brought back with him from Gaul to Jarrow were copying a local style from back home. Whatever the reason, the Anglo-Saxon style up here developed differently. A northern style in fact and though the north's Saxon churches don't quite fit the national pattern, they are among our treasures that deserve to be explored:

Grundy's Twenty-Five Favourite Anglo-Saxon and Viking Church Sites in the north

Beverley Minster (Yorks). Only the 7th-century throne or Frith Stool survives from St John of Beverley's original church. The pilgrimage must be made though because of the man and his history.

Bewcastle (Cumberland). See Chapter one. The masterpiece of English Anglo-Saxon stonecarving.

Billingham (Co. Durham). West tower and doorway. Substantial chunks of Saxon nave – all in an extremely industrial setting.

Brompton in Allertonshire (Yorks). Fascinating Viking (hogback) tombs each complete with carvings of two muzzled bears.

Bywell (Northumberland). Two churches (St Andrew and St Peter) both impressively Saxon in a gloriously rural setting.

Corbridge (Northumberland). Saxon tower with re-used Roman arch as the tower arch. Hugely atmospheric.

Durham Cathedral (Durham). Some fragment of Saxon Cathedral in SE corner of cloister. In the Monks' Dormitory a wonderful collection of carved stones. In the treasury extraordinary survivals of St Cuthbert himself. Possibly the only place in Europe where the centre of a saint's cult has so many mementoes of the saint himself.

Escomb (Durham). Tiny, surrounded by an ancient churchyard and a ring of council houses. One of the most perfectly preserved of all Saxon churches. A must.

Gosforth (Cumberland). After Bewcastle, the finest surviving cross – but a Viking one. Loads of other ancient bits and pieces in the church.

Hexham (Northumberland). Of St Wilfrid's great 7th-century church, only his extraordinary crypt and his beautiful throne (Frith Stool) survive. But they are of marvellous power and this is an extraordinary church.

Holy Island (Northumberland). Nothing survives of the monastery of St Aidan and St Cuthbert except some beautifully carved stones in the museum, possibly a few fragments of the parish church and the most powerful atmosphere imaginable.

Jarrow (Durham). The Venerable Bede's church is still wonderfully complete though enlarged. Along with the excellent Bede's World museum next door it is a necessary visit.

Kirk Hammerton (Yorks). A relatively complete Saxon church.

Ledsham (Yorks). Even more complete and built of beautiful big blocks of stone. Its doorway is restored but dramatically decorated with Saxon carving.

Leeds (Yorks). St Peter's church contains the finest of all Yorkshire crosses, big, richly decorated, spectacular.

Long Marton (Westmorland). 11th and 12th centuries. The West doorway has fascinating and barbaric carvings of winged beasts over it.

Monkwearmouth (Durham). Sunderland's half of the twin monastery shared by Jarrow, founded by Benedict Biscop in AD 681. The lower half of the tower is of that date and used to be a porch until it was raised into a tower in the 10th century.

Nunburnholme (Yorks). Another fascinating carved Viking-age cross – among my favourites. Quaint and almost cartoon-like.

Otley (Yorks). Yet another cross or bits of crosses inside the church – of superb quality, including the best carving of a dragon I have ever seen.

Penrith (Cumberland). In the churchyard, the Giant's Thumb (a Viking cross) and the Giant's Grave (two Viking crosses and four Viking hogback coffins). That's a lot of Viking things for one graveyard.

Ripon (Yorks). St Wilfrid's other church, his first in fact, founded in about AD 670. As at Hexham the only thing to survive of the original church is the labyrinthine crypt inspired, it is said, by Wilfrid's visit to the catacombs in Rome.

Rothbury (Northumberland). Rothbury in Anglo-Saxon times had two churches back to back with a tower between then. All that's left is a fragment of a cross now used as the base of the font. On it, on one side, hands reach up through the clouds to a Christ seated in majesty who looks for all the world, in his toga, with his rolled-up scroll in his hand, like a Roman magistrate. A civilised-looking God and a useful reminder that 'The Dark Ages' weren't really all that dark.

Seaham (Durham). The cliffs and beaches around it have been rescued from industrial pollution, the hall next door where Lord Byron got married has been restored to pristine state and through it all this beautiful little Saxon church 'has survived unharmed.

Whalley (Lancs). A beautiful place full of historical interest so well worth a detour to the churchyard to see the best collection of Saxon stones in Lancashire.

Whittingham (Northumberland). Not a lot survives – half the tower and some masonry at the west end of the nave – but worth a visit to muse upon the Reverend Goodenough who, in 1848, had already blown up half the tower and had the rest packed with gunpowder to finish the job when his parishioners decided that they didn't want his new Victorian church as much as their old one and stopped him.

It isn't just the Anglo-Saxon churches which are different in the north. Each bit of the north has regional differences and it is possible to answer the question 'If I went to such and such a part of the north, what sort of churches could I see that I wouldn't be able to see anywhere else?' That's the question I'm going to answer next.

2. North Lancashire's parish churches.

What are they like, the traditional parish churches of North Lancashire?

Well, Sir William Addison who wrote a book called *Local Styles of the English Parish Church* described them as 'low and broad-beamed'. He went on to describe a typical north Lancashire church as 'a long low building with a squat battlemented tower and with good plain woodwork inside.' I think he's got it just about right. Hawkshead, Cartmel Fell, Heysham, Mitton, Chipping, St Michael's on Wyre and many more all have this quality. It's as if someone has been sitting on them as they were being built to keep them low. They're often built on mounds but they still hug the ground as if they're wary of the winds. The towers aren't high but they're usually very solid and heavy. The walls are thick. These churches are in fact, immensely satisfying buildings which look as if they were just meant to be, as if they're a part of the natural landscape. Sir William goes on to suggest that they're like this because they reflect the wild, rugged and intractable character of the people who built them – no-nonsense Lancashire folk building no-nonsense Lancashire churches. What do you think? I don't know.

The style spreads beyond the Lancashire borders in fact, into parts of Yorkshire and through Westmorland into Cumberland. The day before I wrote this section of the book I spent a day in Wensleydale and Wharfedale (little walk, pub lunch, couple of churches, lush landscape, cinnamon toast and a cup of tea, back in time for the football results. We know how to live, we Grundys) and the same style was to be found there – at Wensley, Blubberhouses and Burnsall. Those were the ones I saw yesterday and though they're all different from each other, they share this quality of broad solid roughness. They all have a simplicity as well – strong simple carving on the arches and piers, simple window shapes and simple tracery and beautiful, worn and simple woodwork.

Further north, Kendal and Crosthwaite in the Lake District are both huge parish churches but they share the same quality. Grasmere does as well and so does Beetham, Appleby's another … in fact dozens of churches towards the northern and western parts of our region share a shape. Not exactly a style, but a feeling. I don't know whether you could measure it and pin it down statistically but once you've seen it you recognise it. You couldn't help but do so.

3. South Lancashire's 19th-century collection

The old churches of South Lancashire are more like the churches of Cheshire (deep south) so we'll say nowt about them, pretend they don't exist, but the area is remarkable for one particular period of church building – the 19th century. I'm not going to pretend that there's a unique Lancashire style of 19th-century building, just that it is the place to go if you want to see some of the best, the oddest, the wildest and the most beautiful 19th-century churches in the country.

Even before I describe them I think if should be fairly obvious why there's so many 19th-century church goodies. There are two reasons:

the population was expanding fast and hundreds of new churches were needed to serve the new population; and secondly the interest in innovation that caused the industrial wealth led to new and innovative churches as well.

None more so than a group of churches built about 1812 and inspired by a man called John Cragg who was the owner of the Mersey Iron Foundry. He was fascinated by the possibilities of iron as a new building material and he persuaded the architect Thomas Rickman to build him a couple of churches using as much iron as possible. They are both in Liverpool: St George, Everton and St Martin in the Hamlet, Toxteth. They really are odd but surprisingly attractive. They're both tall, rather brittle churches in a typical early 19th-century style but they have iron windows with iron tracery, iron roof beams, iron roof panels, partly iron outside walls, iron galleries on iron beams, iron arches. I think they're unique but I may be wrong.

The interest in unusual materials resurfaced later in a number of churches built by a man called Edmund Sharpe. Sharpe was born down south (Cheshire) and he was one of the great intellectuals of 19th-century architecture, writing books which gave people a far greater understanding of medieval styles but his two main churches in Lancashire are very different to his writing. They're built of terracotta. Again, he was persuaded by an industrialist, a colliery owner called John Fletcher who had started making firebricks and terracotta with the colliery clay from his mine. He wanted Sharpe to show as many ways of using the stuff as possible (obviously as a form of advertising) and the churches (St Stephen, Lever Bridge, Bolton and Holy Trinity, Fallowfield, Manchester) are almost entirely of terracotta, inside and out. Even the seats and the organ case are made of terracotta at Bolton. They were very unpopular when they were built in 1845/6 (though they were cheap) but they seem fascinating to me nowadays.

I'd hate to give you the impression that South Lancashire's 19th-century churches were just curiosities though. There are hundreds of beautiful ones. Lots of them are Roman Catholic. Lancashire was one of the main centres for the survival of Roman Catholicism after it had been banned by Henry VIII and when it became properly legal to be a Catholic again in the 1830s the county's Catholic landowners encouraged the building of loads of churches, some of them beautiful, rich, adventurous. My favourites are at Barton on Irwell (by A.W. Pugin) and in Chorlton-on-Medlock, Manchester (by Joseph Hanson) but there are hundreds worth exploring. They tend to be a bit over-decorated for some tastes, but not for me. Pile it on is what I say.

Wherever you go in the country you find that while there may be a few Victorian churches by famous architects with national reputations, the bulk are by local chaps with no more than a local reputation. At their best they can be just as good as the famous ones. In the North West the best of the rest were a couple called Austin and Paley (especially Thomas Austin) whose practice was in Lancaster and I know about them because they did a pile of beautiful village churches in Cumberland and Westmorland which I used to visit when I was younger, but they are to be found all over Lancashire. It doesn't even seem worth listing them for you because they're never disappointing. Local chaps who transformed their local scene.

But finally, Lancashire isn't only graced by local architects. There are great works by nationally known architects as well. St Augustine in Pendlebury on the northern edge of Salford was built in 1871 by G.F Bodley and is one of the most beautiful Victorian churches in the country ... in the world ... in the univ ... etc.

4. The North's Defensible Churches – Northumberland and Cumberland.

Stop me if I've said this before but the Border country has had a pretty wild history. Ravaged by William the Conqueror in the 'harrying of the north' just after 1066 it only recovered slowly. It experienced a relatively brief period of peace during the 13th century before being plunged back into war at the end of the century – a war which was to last almost 400 years. Not good conditions for building churches. There were a few quite impressive churches built, mainly under the protective walls of great castles – Carlisle Cathedral of course and at Norham and Warkworth, Alnwick and of course within the safety of the city walls in Newcastle. There were a few great Abbeys which managed to be built and survive, though constantly under threat of attack. Beside these, the 13th-century 'window of peace' allowed most of the other finest churches to be built, but in the 1300s and 1400s hardly anything was built at all. Why?

Because by that time it was nasty up here.

Blood and desecration

In the grounds of Lilburn House, a 19th-century mansion in north Northumberland, there's a ruined church. It stands to only a few feet high, though there is enough surviving masonry to see (a) that it was beautifully built and (b) that it was built in the 12th century with an extra little chapel added in the 13th century. It's ruined, the story goes, because it was desecrated by blood shed during some Border conflict and its priest was murdered at his altar so the church was abandoned and has never been used since. It's a fate that must have been feared hundreds of times during the border wars and one which must actually have happened many times too. Lanercost Priory, for example, was attacked and partially destroyed by whole armies on loads of occasions – there's a savage account of the invasion of 1296 written by a chronicler from Lanercost Priory who records that Hexham and Lanercost were both burnt, 200 people ('a herd of little scholars') were blocked into the school at Hexham and burnt to death, a nunnery with all of its inmates was destroyed at Lambley in the Tyne valley. There were more attacks the following year, 1297, by William (Braveheart) Wallace and in 1311 by Robert the Bruce. Brucey even sacked Holme Cultram Abbey despite his father being buried there.

As a response to all of these terrifying incursions it is no wonder that all over the Border country communities responded to the fear by building defences into their churches.

Keep your head down ...

If the community was quite big and well-to-do, if it was a monastery for example, then it could afford relatively sophisticated defences. Sometimes the best possible defence was situation. Brinkburn Priory near Rothbury was so deeply buried among trees in the narrow valley of the River Coquet that it hoped to escape notice. Blanchland was another abbey which hoped to escape attack because of its isolation (though there they made the mistake once of celebrating their escape from an invading army by ringing the church bells too soon! Bad mistake!)

... or build some walls

Tynemouth Priory, on the other hand couldn't help but be noticed on its headland overlooking the sea at the mouth of the Tyne. But the situation there, of course, had its own defences – almost sheer cliffs on three sides. The builder monks didn't trust the natural protection, though, and provided walls on top of the cliffs, and on the unprotected landward side of the site they turned their house of God into a fortress. One of the monks who had come up from the community's mother church at St Albans wrote home to his brothers down south and described it like this:

> Our house is confined to the top of a high rock and is surrounded by the sea on all sides but one. Here is the approach to the monastery through a gate cut out of the rock, so narrow that a cart can hardly pass through ...

But the best place to see how much protection monks felt they needed is a little-known priory deep in the heart of the Duke of Northumberland's Hulne Park. You'll have to walk to it, mind, since no cars are allowed in the park, and you'll have to be out by dusk otherwise you turn into a peasant or something; but if you're prepared to walk four or five miles through the most beautiful unspoilt farmland in England and follow unsignposted roads and tracks with the confidence of Minnehaha or Davy Crockett, you'll come to Hulne Priory which is the most wonderful ruin. It belonged to the Carmelites or White Friars and it is both the earliest and one of the finest surviving friaries in England. It's gloriously romantic inside but initially you won't be struck by the harmony of its religious architecture because you won't be able to see it. What you will see instead (just like any Scottish invader would have seen) is its curtain wall, its boundary wall which still stands entire on all four sides to a height of 12 feet, completely plain and forbidding and quite unbroken except on the south side where an even plainer and even more forbidding gatehouse with an almost frighteningly tunnel-like entrance was the only point of access.

As if that wasn't enough, inside the precinct is another mighty tower with hugely thick walls and all of the usual defences (battlements and vaulted basements and so on). It was built in 1486 as a residence for the Prior and, of course as a last line of defence if the outer walls of the monastery were breached.

All over the area men of God seemed to put less trust in God for protection than they did in stone and mortar. The monasteries at Holy Island, Carlisle and Lanercost all had defensible towers within the walls and in each case they were clearly the residence of and intended for the protection of the top man. Isn't it unusual, boys and girls, that even in those days the bosses looked after themselves first of all?

Vicars' peles

Outside the monasteries the situation wasn't very different. Vicars built towers for themselves, or at least parishes built towers for their vicars. They weren't church towers but separate fortified towers to live in. They were often called 'vicars' peles' because they were the pele towers belonging to the vicars, obviously enough. The word 'pele' comes from the same source as 'paling' or 'palisade' and may have originated in wooden fortresses that were found in the area but it became a word to describe a stand-alone stone tower. Excellent examples of vicars' peles still exist all over the place – at Corbridge, where the 14th-century tower is almost perfectly unaltered and preserved tight in against the churchyard wall – at Croglin and upper Denton in Cumberland; in Northumberland at Alnham and at Elsdon where the tower is a cut above the rest. It is big, strong, probably rebuilt as late as the 16th century, so long did the danger remain in a place like this, high up, near the border, in the middle of the Cheviot Hills.

Fortifying the church itself

Elsdon Tower is just up the hill from the parish church, the Church of St Cuthbert, which stands, rather isolated in the middle of the village green. It's quite a curious church from outside with a fancy but rough bellcote over the west end and a few mismatched but genuine 14th-century windows in the chancel. Inside it's even odder. It's quite big and it has nice 14th-century arcades down the nave and spacious transepts on both sides. But amazingly the original aisles seem to have been demolished at some time, probably in the 1500s, and new, really thick nave walls built only about four feet away from the piers and arches, forming the narrowest church aisles you have ever seen. Literally. These aisles have got half vaults over them. That means that they have curved lean-to stone roofs which is an incredibly rare feature. The north wall has no windows in it at all and it is known that until 1835 when the church was restored, the south wall had no windows either. The nave was in fact a stone windowless box. It must have been incredible – but presumably safe, or safer; something of a refuge from attack, since that is the only possible reason for building such a structure. One of the piers of the church, the first one inside the door, is deeply scarred by scratches which have been interpreted as the marks made by defenders as they used the stone to sharpen the tips of their arrows.

Other churches went down the same or a similar line to Elsdon. Ingram in the Cheviots was another with windowless walls and at Ancroft near Berwick they went as far as to build a whole massive pele tower over the west end of the church. To do so they had to block up the original Norman doorway and they gave the tower a tunnel-vaulted ground floor, spiral staircase, immensely thick walls, tiny slit windows, in fact the whole panoply of castle architecture – within the walls of the church.

What a tower like this was meant to do is not quite clear. Whether it was like the vicars' peles, just for the protection of the priest, or whether it was a sort of community resource – a village hall of last resort where the whole population could pile in to seek refuge, is not at all obvious.

Other similar towers exist apart from Ancroft. Two of the best are in Cumberland. Newton Arlosh is a tiny little village nowadays living peacefully on the edge of the extremely peaceful Solway Firth but in the 14th century it was terribly exposed. Not only was it perfectly visible from Scotland a mile or two across the water but it was on the lands of the wealthy and desirable Holme Cultram Abbey so its church was built fortified with a mighty tower and nave walls up to five feet thick. The original door was less than three feet wide and the only windows were mere slits less than a foot wide. A few miles east, also on the Solway and if anything even more exposed because it lay near well-known fords (or *waths* as they were known) across the estuary, is Burgh by Sands, whose church had two towers, one at each end. The east one has been converted now into an odd sort of eastern vestry but it's still there and means that, almost uniquely, there is no east window in the church. The west tower has walls seven feet thick and a most remarkable survival at its base. The entrance into the tower is inside the church and it is protected by an extraordinary door, made entirely of iron. In Cumberland dialect it is described as a *yatt* and it is a dense lattice of thick, rough iron bars with massive bolts attached.

There are a number of other surviving yatts in castles and forti- fied houses but only one other church has one. It is at the village of Great Salkeld in the Eden Valley and to be honest it is an even more extreme example with the iron bars reinforced as well by massive oak planks and with the tower behind as much like a dungeon as the tower of a house of God.

Ancroft, Newton Arlosh and Burgh needed their defences because they were in very vulnerable positions, on flat, easy country close to the border. Bellingham in Northumberland was equally vulnerable, since it sits close to the junction of the North Tyne and Rede valleys, two of the most violent and dangerous parts of the Borders and regular routes for Scottish raiders into England. (The Rede Valley and North Tynedale had such a dreadful reputation for violence that in 1554 the Merchant Venturers of Newcastle passed a regulation which fined any of its members £20 if they took on an apprentice from either of these valleys.) Which makes it less of a surprise that as late as 1609 Bellingham felt the need to increase the defences on its church. Instead of merely adding a defensible tower, the medieval aisles were demolished and new side walls built with a new roof over the nave and south chapel. These roofs are like the roof of a castle dungeon – stone-vaulted with great heavy stone ribs making it even stronger – quite unique, as far as I know, among the churches of England.

This tendency to vault churches in stone, not for aesthetic reasons like you find in beautiful churches further south, but out of fear, is best expressed actually in Cumberland at the very remarkable Boltongate church on the edge of the Lake District which has the most wonderful stone vault over the nave. It is high and steeply pointed and there are chapels or transepts on each side which have the same sort of lean-to half-vaults as there are at Elsdon.

And finally ...

One other church which is stone-vaulted for protection rather than beauty – in fact probably the most powerful, even brutal example of all, is to be found in the church of St Gregory the Great at Kirknewton, just inside the Border to the north of Wooler. At one time the whole church was vaulted in stone, now only the vaults over the chancel and the south transept survive but they are remarkable enough. They rise almost directly out of the ground with virtually no side walls, so to stand in them is like standing in a stone tent. They are low and pointed and totally without decoration, but to one side of the chancel arch, just in front of the vault, is an astonishing carving. It's said to represent the Adoration of the Magi but in fact it looks like three very tough chaps in kilts and together with the vault behind, it creates a powerful image of the fear and danger of church life on the northern border. What it must have been like when the nave was vaulted in the same way, I can hardly imagine.

5. The Dale chapels of the Lake District

Your guide books and those books which list the best examples of churches and what not, have a tendency to overlook the small and the simple and the plain, indeed none of the churches I am about to discuss in this section gets a mention in the excellent catalogue called *England's Thousand Best Churches* and yet sometimes it is simplicity and plainness which are exactly what a building needs to fit perfectly into its environment.

In medieval times, the Lake District was still very wild, very remote and lightly populated. There were a few settlements, and a few medieval churches, even quite splendid ones, exist at Keswick (Crosthwaite), Kendal, Grasmere and most impressively in the extraordinarily beautiful monastic church at Cartmel in the Furness district.

Elsewhere, the great monasteries had big sheep farms in various places in the fells and there were a few isolated settlements but until the 16th century anything more than solitary farms and small clearings in the woodland were few and far between. However, in the 16th century two things began to change all of that. First of all the price of woollen cloth went through the roof and it became a far more economic proposition to farm the wool and make the cloth. Kendal, in fact became one of the most famous woollen towns in England (the town's crest is *pannus mihi panis* – which means 'cloth is my bread'; rather clever that seems to me. I've always been hugely impressed by people who could crack jokes in Latin) and its wool was famous all over the country and beyond. And secondly, the mineral wealth, especially the lead and the graphite that lurked within the Lake District hills began to get exploited. Both of these developments brought new populations of miners and sheep farmers into the hills and you know what miners and sheep farmers like to do most of all in their spare time – they like to go to chapel, so chapels began to appear all over the valleys.

By the 16th century the great periods of English church building were gone. The Gothic style had begun to run itself out. Henry VIII had booted out the Roman Catholics and the puritans were beginning to get a firm toehold in the old rock-face of the nation. Churches, in fact, tended to get simpler wherever they were built in the 16th and 17th centuries, but up in the hills especially, where the population was still small and the money scarce, they were simpler still.

Or maybe their builders just had good taste and recognised even way back then that this fantastically beautiful part of the country didn't need to be embellished with any fancy buildings and was better suited to something plain and simple. Because that's what they built – plain and simple little Dales chapels.

Do I have a favourite. I have three ... ooo, four ... no. Oh I just love them. Typically they're just a simple and single room without any division between the nave and the chancel. Typically too the windows are just completely plain, like house windows, though some of the chapels have simple Georgian, round-arched windows. Often they've been whitewashed which can look so beautiful against the green of the hills but many of them have been left as untreated slate, as rough and weathered as the hills that surround them.

Inside they tend to be just as simple. Often they're whitewashed inside as well. There are stone-flagged floors, plain and undecorated wooden furniture. Virtually no ornamentation. The best of them still have simple 17th-century or Georgian furniture and, in fact, because there wasn't much new money up here in the hills in the 19th century, because the populations had hardly grown at all, very few of the Dales chapels were much altered in Victorian times. That's one of their greatest charms.

Their greatest charm of all, though is where they are and how they sit in that landscape – tiny and white amidst the great hills. These are the ones that I would make my pilgrimage to. I am sorry if I have missed ones that you like just as much:

Matterdale and Martindale
Mungrisdale and Mosser
Uldale and Ulpha
Waberthwaite and Wythburn
Wasdale Head and Netherwasdale

And there's one other, which I have to mention separately because it isn't, strictly speaking, a dales chapel at all since it isn't in the Lake District dales, but it was built at about the same time and it's on a similar scale and it has a similar atmosphere – only more so. This one actually is in the old *1000 Best Churches* book and rightly so because it has wonderful qualities. It's the chapel called Ninekirk or St Ninians about a mile or so from Brougham, east of Penrith, on the banks of the River Eamont. It was built by a remarkable woman called Lady Anne Clifford, the countess of Pembroke, who lived at Appleby castle and restored houses and built churches all over Westmorland. She built Ninekirk in 1660 and it has all of the simplicity of the dales chapels but also the most beautiful interior – a perfect example of its date – a full complement of hand-made 17th-century oak furnishings set against the simplicity of white walls.

It's a walk to get there – actually it's a bit of an orienteering experience. We Grundys gave up twice before we finally hit on this tiny jewel in its overgrown churchyard – but it was worth the walk, well worth it.

6. Yorkshire's ruined Abbeys

Well, thank goodness for Henry VIII, that's what I say. If it hadn't been for him, if he hadn't asked the Pope for permission to divorce his first wife Catherine of Aragon who was not only his sister-in-law, and who had not only failed to provide him with a son but who was also rather plain and a bit older than him, then we probably wouldn't have had any ruined abbeys. The Pope of course said no, so Henry cut off all ties with the Roman Catholic church, started the Church of England, closed down all of the old monasteries, snaffled as much of their wealth as he could and left the buildings to rot.

Which is why we have ruined Abbeys, sublime survivals, almost all in wonderful situations, unrestored and unaltered by later generations, perfect time capsules of the styles of the past and absolutely oozing and dripping with history.

Because of this history, ruined churches, or more specifically ruined monasteries, are almost unique to Britain and they form one of the absolute glories of the British landscape. They exist all over the country but nowhere in more profusion or with such quality or amidst such beauty as in Yorkshire.

I have a personal favourite among Yorkshire's ruined Abbeys. It's called Jervaulx Abbey and it's in Wensleydale, close to the River Ure and surrounded by glorious countryside. It was founded by Cistercian monks in 1156. It's a bit unusual because it doesn't belong to the country, it's not an English Heritage site or National Trust or anything. It's still in private hands and therein lies much of its charm.

Instead of a ticket office it has an honesty box and postcards that you could steal if you were churlish enough to do so. And then, though it's all beautifully tended with spreading lawns, it hasn't been tidied up. There are still bits of stone lying everywhere to tempt the imagination. They peep out of the greenery and are allowed to get overgrown by flowers. There are no maps or instructions or guides

Hard men in a wild land

Yorkshire was ideal as a site for early monasteries because the monks were seeking to escape from the world, to enter into direct conflict with the devil who inhabited the wilderness and to carve out new empires in the emptiness. At one level they chose Yorkshire and the north because it was hard. The monk from St Albans who I quoted earlier, the one who was building Tynemouth Priory, had this to say about the north when he wrote back to his softy southern friends.

Day and night the waves break and roar beneath the cliff. Thick sea frets roll in wrapping everything in gloom. Dim eyes, sore throats are the consequence. Spring and summer never come here. The north wind is always blowing and brings with it cold and snow and storms in which the wind tosses the salt sea foam over our buildings and rains it down inside the castle.

Shipwrecks are frequent. It is a great pity to see the numbed crew who no power on earth can save, whose vessel, mast swaying and timbers parted, rushes upon rock and reef. No ring dove or nightingale is here, only grey birds which nest in the rocks and greedily prey upon the bodies of the drowned.

See to it dear brother that you never come to so comfortless a place.

This must be the north's first great tourism bad press, though monks arriving at the valley of the River Skell where they were to start Fountains Abbey in 1132 described it as 'more fit for wild beasts than men to inhabit' but visiting these places nowadays it's impossible to believe that when they chose the sites they weren't also aware of their beauty. The man responsible for the spiritual purity of the Cistercian Order of Monks, Bernard of Clairvaux, wrote about the beauty as well as the isolation. He said, 'You will find in the woods something you never find in books. Stones and trees will teach you a lesson you never heard from masters in school. Honey can be drawn from rock, oil from the hardest stone.' He knew that there was even more to be gained from the beauty than the wildness and the other monks learned his lesson. Wherever you go in the north; wherever the monks chose – at Whalley or Furness, Cartmel, Calder, Lanercost or Brinkburn or any of the sites in Yorkshire – they chose beautiful places to erect their beautiful buildings.

which means that you've either got to work out for yourself what the whole complex of building means or you've got to accept it for itself without worrying too much about being educated by it.

I love Jervaulx for its accidental and unexplained charms but I would have to acknowledge that there are even greater ruins to be found all over Yorkshire and the rest of the north. Just look at this list of the ones in Yorkshire alone:

Rievaulx	Roche
Fountains	Whitby
Byland	Eggleston
Kirkstall	St Mary's York
Easby	Kirkham

Cistercian simplicity

The most important monastery buildings in Yorkshire were put up by the monks of the Cistercian order who had arrived from France in AD 1132 to found Rievaulx Abbey near Helmsley. Cistercians were renowned for their belief in simplicity. They 'rejoiced in poverty' and their order had been founded as a reaction against the over-indulgent lifestyle of other orders like the Benedictines. Nearby Fountains Abbey was founded the same year as Rievaulx by rebel Benedictine monks who were impressed by the Cistercians and also wanted a return to simplicity.

Other Yorkshire Abbeys, Easby and Eggleston, were founded by Premonstratensian Canons whose beliefs were very similar to the austere Cistercians. The monks at Mountgrace Priory near Osmotherly went even further. They were Carthusians who believed in a life of total silence and total separation from the other monks so their monastery was a collection of individual houses where the inmates lived in permanent contemplation.

You can imagine, if you look at this lot, that men with beliefs like these weren't going to put up fancy buildings, and they didn't. The Abbeys of Yorkshire are among the most pure and simple buildings ever erected. There is a glorious, stripped back nobility about their abbeys which both reflects the character of the landscape and must have done a lot to create the character of it as well. All around North and West Yorkshire there are smaller churches either built by or inspired by the great abbeys and their character is the same as their parent buildings. North Yorkshire has wonderful parish churches but they are churches characterised by the same noble plainness as abbeys like Fountains. And you can't say fairer than that.

A taste for plainness?

So, there is no single northern church style as far as I can tell. There are lots of great northern churches, and they are built of northern stone but the churches of different parts of the north differ wildly from each other. Perhaps, apart from the hugely rich churches on the southern edge of Yorkshire and the Victorian wealth of South Lancashire, apart from those, perhaps there is a common taste for plainness and simplicity and perhaps that taste has grown out of the landscape itself and out of the harsh early history of this region. Just perhaps. I'm only guessing.

chapter three

Castles

Carlisle Castle

When I was little – this is a book about history after all – all those years when I was a boy growing up in Carlisle, I was entirely enthralled by Carlisle's castle. If I played in the park it towered above me, mighty buttresses supporting mighty walls. On my way to school the Norman keep was visible all the way. If I went to the library it loomed at the end of the street. As often as not if I drifted into town, I drifted into the castle too, or wandered under its walls. It was part of my life.

It is not, as castles go, a beautiful or romantic-looking one, in fact I recall one heretical writer claiming that it was so ugly that it held Carlisle back. It doesn't have picturesque glories and lofty battlements, instead it is solid, squat and dour, plain and workmanlike. It had to be. It had a job to do. It was built to guard the first major river crossing on the English side of the border and it was called into action on masses of occasions. In the first hundred years of the 400-years war it was besieged by full Scottish armies on at least nine occasions, in 1296 and 1297, in 1311 the army was led by Robert the Bruce who came again in 1315. Further attacks came in 1322 (R. Bruce again – what a pain that man was), 1380, 1385, 1387 and 1388. Sometimes they won, sometimes they didn't, but they were always made to work for the advantage by the massive solidity of the place.

So it isn't mellow and picturesque but I loved it nevertheless.

I loved it for all sorts of reasons. Edward I spent time there. Parliaments were held there on three occasions. Mary Queen of Scots was a prisoner there and was allowed to stroll along the 'lady's walk' on the edge of the outer moat. Richard III was there as Governor before he briefly became a king. Bonnie Prince Charlie came and forced the occupants to surrender (not many of them it has to be admitted) and after he had been forced to retreat, 96 of his men were packed into the castle's dungeons. These are fantastic names to be associated with a building on your doorstep. Can you wonder my romantic spirit was roused whenever I saw the place?

I loved its dungeons. I don't even know whether this story was true but when you visited the castle you used to be shown a ledge that ran around the dungeon in the basement of the keep. It was a slopey ledge a few inches above the floor and you were told that prisoners were attached to the wall above this ledge by spiked rings around their necks and forced to stand on the ledge. If they weakened and fell, the spikes could turn up and press into their throats. Isn't that a horrible idea? More certainly true and even more horrible was that the walls of this dungeon were worn smooth, glass-like smooth, slimey smooth, by the endless licking of prisoners' tongues desperate for the moisture that ran down the outside walls. There's something horrible to a child's imagination in a thing like that – an imaginary horror made worse by the sight of the disgusting smoothness of the stone.

There is another prison upstairs in the keep which I also loved. It's called McIver's Cell after a character in Walter Scott's 'Waverley' novels but the original of Scott's character was a man called Major MacDonald of Kippock, one of Bonnie Prince Charlie's men, who was captured at the battle of Falkirk because he was riding an English horse which carried him against his will into the English army. He was taken from this cell in 1746 to be executed on Harraby Hill (which was not only where all Carlisle executions took place but also … and how about this for a co-incidence, it was also *the place where my mother taught in a junior school!* Gasp). As if this romantic connection between his life and mine wasn't enough, the outer chamber to McIver's cell has the single best thing about Carlisle Castle – graffiti, ancient graffiti; 14th and 15th-century graffiti. I always wanted to do some graffiti but being a nicely brought up middle-class boy, never had the courage, but here, on the edge of the door, in the only part of the room which receives any direct light through the tiny window, centuries of Scottish prisoners have left their mark with ever-so lively carvings in the stonework. There are animals and crosses and fleurs-de-lys. There are obviously rude things that nobody ever mentioned when I was young. There's a Scotsman in a kilt. They all overlie each other as subsequent generations of prisoners have desperately sought some outlet for their feelings and creativity.

Oubliettes

They were lucky to have any outlets at all. Some of the castles in the north have dungeons that make Carlisle's seem like a holiday camp. ('Licking stones? Water? What to you think this is, laddy? Butlins?'). Cockermouth and Hexham are among those with 'oubliette' dungeons. 'Oubliette' is taken from 'oublier' which is French for 'to forget', in case you're wondering. An oubliette dungeon is a hole deep under the floor with a trap door at the top. The prisoner has to be lowered into it and is then left – forgotten – in the total darkness until someone remembers him, if they ever do. I was left down the one in Hexham once by a brutal and sadistic TV producer with no more company than a TV cameraman and everybody knows that they are animals. My, was I scared. The floor was 12 feet below the trapdoor and the walls sloped away from the trapdoor in an egg-shaped fashion so there was absolutely no prospect of getting out on my own. It wasn't nice.

There is a story about a prisoner in an oubliette just on the other side of the border, at Hermitage Castle (which is one of the grimmest buildings in the British Isles) who was left in the oubliette when an emergency called the castle's company away. When they got back he had eaten his own arm off. And very tasty it was, apparently.

A land of castles

I mention all of these gruesome thoughts as a reminder that these castles were built as practical objects, objects of fear not objects of beauty, but nowadays we tend to look on them in a different light. We revere them for their mellow beauties and their romantic associations. We love to visit them to get our souls stirred. Which is very lucky for those of us in the north who like a bit of soul stirring because we've got loads of them (lerds and lerds of them as we say in Newcastle).

I've done another of my little counts and I make it 83 full-blown castles and another 130-odd substantial tower-type things and that doesn't count the ones I've missed out – the demolished castles, the earthworks, the bastlehouses. If you put them all together that's lerds of castles if I'm not mistaken.

They're not evenly distributed of course. Lancashire hasn't many and the southern parts of Yorkshire haven't got many either. (Though in Conisbrough they have one of the most beautiful Norman keeps in England – exquisitely built and a work of architecture as well as a piece of fortification; and Pontefract was once astonishingly magnificent, before it was bashed about a lot in the Civil War. It had an enormous round keep which was a cluster of 13 round towers and there was in addition a ring of incredibly high towers built into the curtain wall. In old pictures it looks like something from a medieval fantasy.) Lancashire only has one proper castle and that's the one at Lancaster itself but that was probably enough because that one guarded the narrow entry into the county between the Pennine hills and the sea at Morecambe Bay and so the county was really given all of the protection it needed by the Lake District hills to the north and the castles of Cumberland. Lancashire, in fact was made safe by geology. It's relatively easy to attack England down the wide coastal plains of Eastern England and much more difficult to get to Lancashire by the mountainous west.

So most of the castles are further north, where they needed to be. First of all, there was a line of them guarding the Border itself (Berwick, Norham, Wark, Harbottle, Bewcastle, Naworth and Carlisle – that's roughly one every ten miles) and after that you just find them all over the place, just where they need to be – towering over towns, dominating vulnerable valleys, protecting the sea lanes (or possibly endangering the sea lanes), blocking major trade routes. From a castle point of view, the north's like a giant pinball machine. Any invader coming south would find their way blocked by one and then find themselves bounced from castle to castle. You want to avoid

Carlisle so you sneak off to the east – oops, there's Naworth; sneak west – there's Cockermouth; sneak past Carlisle and go straight ahead – there's Penrith. It doesn't seem to have been planned specifically like this but the effect is of protection in depth.

I suspect that in the Middle Ages the castles were even more of a presence than they might seem nowadays. In a world where roads were outstandingly bad and few and very far between, invading armies would inevitably be channelled along the routes that led to them and it would take a very clever commander to avoid them. Robert the Bruce did once. In 1322 he had a very cunning wheeze and, instead of trying to get south past Carlisle on the main agreed route over Shap, he sneaked round West Cumberland instead, crossing the Duddon Estuary and Morecambe Bay sands without having to deal with the big castles and led a lightning and devastating raid on Lancaster and Preston before sneaking back to Scotland.

... 57 varieties

Not only are castles numerous in the north but every conceivable type and period of castle is represented here too.

First of all there is a rich supply of the very earliest types of castle, the Norman Motte and Bailey castles. Skipsea in the East Riding of Yorkshire is a particularly impressive example and Elsdon in Northumberland and so is Liddell Strength, a large earthwork castle right on the border in Cumberland, by the side of the River Esk. Proper Norman Castles built in stone are everywhere too, and their main source of strength was the Keep. I was going to add, by way of added explanation, 'the stone tower in the centre of the castle', but at Richmond Castle in North Yorkshire the magnificent keep isn't in the centre at all, it's part of the outer wall and doubles its duties by acting as a gatehouse as well. You would think that it might rather weaken the castle having the main source of strength and the entrance as the same building and you might be right because the arrangement doesn't occur in any other Norman castle.

Usually, in fact, it wasn't even enough to have the keep in the middle of the castle. There had to be extra defences to it as well. Often that meant that the entrance was on the first floor but at

Newcastle's splendid keep (built in 1172 and a snip at £911 10s 9d) the only entrance is by a door into the *second* floor which is reached by a flight of very steep steps and protected by an elaborate fore-building. Bamburgh Castle, on the other hand, has a keep with a door on the *ground* floor which is almost as unusual – but Bamburgh was so well protected on its towering rock that it needed little else by way of protection.

13th- and 14th-century castles were inspired by returning crusaders who had seen the new techniques in fortification which were being invented by the Arabs in the Middle East. This meant mainly towers projecting outside the curtain wall to give flanking fire along the line of the wall. Inevitably the north grabbed every innovation it could. Warkworth Castle which was being built in about 1200 has a number of these towers and they may be the earliest in the north but before long towers like them are to be found everywhere in the region.

The next big development in the history of castles also occurred in the 14th century and that was the arrival of *quadrangular castles*. Ever since the time of the Normans castle builders had been putting extra buildings inside their castle walls, leaning extra apartments and great halls and so on against the inside of the curtain walls but gradually this process became a bit more regular and formal so that by the late 14th century what you get is four big ranges of buildings round a central courtyard and joined at each corner by massive corner towers. The ranges have windows on the inside, towards the courtyard, and they have windows high up on the outside. Because they have more windows, and because they look more regular and planned, they look a bit more like houses than most castles do, but they can still be fantastically strong. Bodiam Castle in Sussex is the first example that most of the text books turn to but there are lots of these quadrangular castles in the north and the really great example is in our region. It's Bolton Castle in Wensleydale in the North Riding of Yorkshire. It was the home of the Scrope family, big northern name (it was a Lord Scrope who chased Kinmont Willie and Lord Buccleuch after the escape from Carlisle Castle). Their castle absolutely dominates the northern side of Wensleydale. It is visible from almost everywhere, and close to it is tremendously impressive. Sheer, massive and unadorned. This is another of those castles that poor old Mary Queen of Scots was imprisoned in. She escaped from it in fact for about two hours until she was recaptured on the way to nearby Leyburn. Lumley Castle at Chester-le-Street is another quadrangular castle almost as great. Lumley was brilliantly altered internally in the early 18th century to turn it into a comfy house but it still has all of its castle-y qualities as well.

Castles as places to live in

And speaking of comfy houses, improved defences weren't the only developments that took place in castles over the centuries. Gradually they got more and more improved living quarters as well. Lots of people lived in castles and there had to be places to put them up, so one of the major improvements was to provide 'lodgings' for the various people who were needed to keep the place going. If you look at a plan, for example, of Alnwick Castle, you'll see that all of the towers around the walls have titles like Constable's Tower and Falconer's Tower and Abbot's Tower. So these towers did two jobs: they were fighting platforms and they were lodgings provided for the officials and their households – not their female households, mind you, oh, dear me no, no, no, no, no. There were no women, or virtually no women, in most medieval castles. In the Earl of Northumberland's household at Wressle Castle in Yorkshire there were 166 men and only nine women. The lord of the castle might have his wife, a daughter or two and a few female servants but all other women were left at home in manor houses and so the castles were entirely male affairs (if that's not a risqué thing to say under the circumstances). Life was very communal as well, at least in the earlier part of the Middle Ages, and great halls played a big part in castle life.

The Great Hall

In the early Middle Ages they were used for normal meals. Everybody, masters and servants, ate together in the Great Hall but gradually that situation changed and the hall was used mainly for the servants and for special occasions – and I do mean special. The Neville family, who were one of the greatest of all northern families, had castles in various places. Their main seat was at Raby Castle in Durham but when one of the family, George Neville, was made Archbishop of York in 1465, they had a feast at the Archbishop's Cawood Castle near York. The whole family was there (and there were loads of them) along with a whole raft of lords and bishops and knights and judges and assorted hangers-on. Including servers and waiters and cooks there were said to have been upwards of 2000 people involved over the several days of the feast. They ate 113 oxen, 6 wild bulls, 1000 sheep, 2000 geese, 2000 pigs, 2000 chickens, 4000 cold venison pasties, 12 porpoises and a bag of crisps. I was lying about the bag of crisps. They weren't that greedy.

Great Halls came fully into their own at special occasions like Christmas. The Earls of Northumberland, for example (at Leconfield and Wressle in Yorkshire) would elect a 'Lord of Misrule' to be in charge of the household over Christmas. He could be anybody from the household and he was allowed to do pretty much what he liked. He could pretend to be the Earl and extract the michael from him. He could issue phoney and whimsical orders which had to be obeyed and altogether he could indulge in 'merry disport'. I fancy that. It was the same at the Archbishop of York's castle at Cawood. There they elected a 'boy bishop' who could do pretty much the same thing. It all sounds great fun.

The Hall at Cawood has gone, in fact only the magnificent Gatehouse survives from the castle but we do have some magnificent surviving Great Halls in the north. Durham Castle, for example, which was the home of the Bishops of Durham, has a huge hall which was added in the 14th century and behind it, the original kitchens remain with splendid oak serving hatches, like school dinners but much posher.

The Bishops of Durham had another Great Hall, an even greater one than the one in Durham Castle. It is one of the greatest of all surviving medieval Great Halls and is in their other house, Auckland Castle at Bishop Auckland. It isn't a great hall any more because in 1665 it was turned into the Bishop's private chapel but it was built as a hall, probably by Bishop de Puiset in the 1190s. It's unusual because it's an aisled hall with two arcades of magnificently carved arches and piers and it must have been one of the most beautiful Great Halls in the country and now, since it was magnificently re-decorated in the 1660s it has become one of the most beautiful private chapels as well.

Naworth, near Brampton in Cumberland, the home first of the Dacre family and then of one of the branches of the great Howard family, is another castle with a whazzo Great Hall – long, tall, but sadly a bit bleak now. It was damaged by fire in 1844 and it's never quite recovered its atmosphere. It used to have four extraordinary heraldic beasts – big, big beasts, carved out of oak and brightly painted. There was a bull and a dolphin, a stag and a griffin. They dated from the 16th century and looked amazing but they've gone to the V & A Museum now which is sad – but behind this hall is a remarkable tower which more than makes up for the loss of the Great Hall's atmosphere. As the Middle Ages progressed, the owners of great castles seem to have got a bit cheesed off with life in the Great Hall and increasingly they retreated into more private quarters away from it, leaving the hall as the territory of the servants. At Naworth the owners retreated into a tower called Lord William's Tower after Lord William Howard, the greatest of the castle's owners, who lived there in the 17th century. His private tower is protected at the bottom by one of those amazing iron doors (yatts) which I mentioned when I was talking about fortified churches and upstairs there are some quite small but lovely rooms, culminating in a chamber with the most wonderful ceiling. It's a carved oak ceiling and it dates from about 1350. It has heavy, enormous beams covered with the most delicate and intricate Gothic carving and the effect of it in what is really quite a small room is almost overpowering. But exciting and intimate at the same time.

Warkworth – a castle within a castle

In my opinion, though, the most remarkable domestic addition to the inside of a medieval castle happened at Warkworth Castle in Northumberland at the very end of the 14th century.

Warkworth is the most wonderful castle, part of one of the greatest small towns in England. It lies on a hill in a loop, a complete meander no less, of the River Coquet. At the bottom of the hill is the parish church – a really good parish church, Norman and later. The town climbs up the hill between the church and the castle – two irregular rows of really nice stone houses with a couple of top notch pubs thrown in for good measure. The castle towers above this scene magnificently.

It dates from a variety of periods. There are a few chunks of Norman stonework and a whole heap of stuff from the 13th and 14th centuries including (as I've mentioned elsewhere) a pile of towers and an excellent gatehouse. It must have been a pretty posh castle even then because the remains of its chapel and its Great Hall show signs of being really magnificent. The Great Hall (which is ruined) has a porch with a brilliant carved lion over the door on the seriously posh porch.

But then, in the 1390s, the first Earl of Northumberland built a new castle within a castle for himself. At the north end of the castle was the original Norman motte, a steep-sided earthwork. It seems to already have had a tower on it but the first Earl started again and built a tower, a mighty and absolutely spiffing tower which soars above the rest of the castle. It looks superficially like a Norman keep but, far from being an extra piece of fortification, it's really more like a great house, brilliantly planned and beautiful to look at. In one compact building there's a second Great Hall and a second set of kitchens and chambers and chapels and all the other rooms that already existed elsewhere in the castle. I'm not sure why it was built really. There was a fashion for such enormous 'super towers' among the very rich at that time and perhaps the family used it as a more private house – as a place to retreat away from the more public castle. It obviously could act as a last line of defence in an emergency as well, but to be honest, when you really look at it, it looks like a big bit of showing off – I'm the bee's knees around here and I've got a bigger one than you have. So there.

Coping with gunfire – the last castles

Down south, by the 15th century, castle building had more or less ground to a halt. Domestic comfort was the order of the day, but up here in the north there was still a couple of centuries of warfare to go and there was still a powerful enemy across the border so developments in fortifications continued to be made. In fact some castles had not yet even been built. Lindisfarne Castle, wonderful romantic Lindisfarne Castle, wasn't even begun until the 1560s (though to be honest it was never really used in anger either. It was only attacked and taken once and that was because the Governor of the castle was so short of money and things to do that he was doubling up as the Island's hairdresser and while he was cutting the hair of the captain of a visiting ship, the captain, who was a Scot, pulled out a gun and seized the castle.) Lindisfarne was built, not really as a traditional castle, but as a large and elaborate gun emplacement. Instead of normal fighting platforms its roof was made up of a series of artillery batteries, and that's what most of the later developments to castles were for – to help cope with the invention of guns. Bamburgh Castle was the first castle in the country to be taken by soldiers with guns. That happened in the 1460s and from then on many of the north's castles had to be modified to cope with artillery attacks. Norham Castle and Harbottle Castle are two that I can think of with alterations made for gunfire in the 16th century but the most important new fortifications were made at Berwick.

Since 1482 Berwick has been an English town. In the three hundred years before then it was attacked and captured by the Scots at least 14 times. In fact it was the Scots (under the control of Robert 'Spiderman' the Bruce who besieged and captured it) who built the town's first walls. It didn't become safe from attack until Scotland and England united as one country in 1603 and even then its position was so dubious that until 1746 it continued to get a special mention in Acts of Parliament ('England, Scotland and Berwick-upon-Tweed') as if no one was absolutely sure who it belonged to. Because of this terribly insecure position, Berwick needed fortifications in the way that other towns need pubs – desperately – and in the 1500s it got a set which are almost unique in England.

Berwick was so important to the defence of the country that Henry VIII himself is said to have been involved in the design of the first set of new fortifications – a massive fort with walls over six metres thick which is now abandoned to the north of the present walls. The present walls were designed by an engineer called Sir Richard Lee. They were begun in 1558 and were based on new

Shittlehugh Bastle – rough stone and wild northern skies.

left The Bewcastle Cross, east side. Cumberland's
7th century masterpiece.

right Durham Cathedral –the world's finest building?

Baroque Splendour. Castle Howard and the Atlas Statue.

left Northern innovation, No 1. Cast iron and lots of glass.
Oriel Chambers, Liverpool.

right St Gregory the Great, Kirknewton, Northumberland.
The defensible chapel.

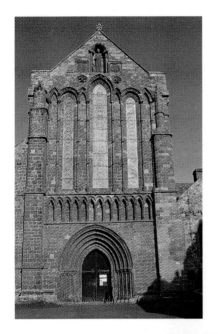

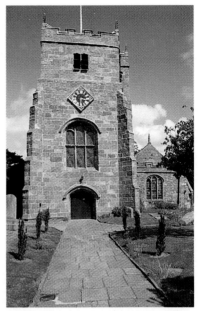

top left Windows of peace. 13th century tranquility at Lanercost Priory, Cumberland.

top right Sturdy northern proportions. St Michael's on Wyre, north Lancashire.

right The great 14th century east window, Carlisle Cathedral.

Pure and simple. A 'dale's chapel' at Mungrisdale in Cumberland.

left Strong and simple. St Agatha's church, Easby, north Yorkshire.

right Northern innovation, No. 2. The cast iron church of St Michael-in-the-Hamlet, Toxteth, Liverpool.

Bolton Castle, Wensleydale, north Yorkshire. Built in the late 14th century, it's almost a house but totally a castle too.

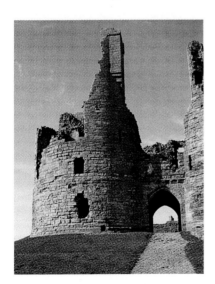 

left Dunstanburgh! The most dramatic of all the great coastal castles.

right Belsay Castle. 14th century. Rapunzel waz 'ere.

Halton Castle. 13th century house, 14th century solar tower.
All built of Roman stones.

left Lumley Castle, Chester-le-Street. Impressing the
neighbours, 14th century style.

right Dacre Castle, Cumberland. A 14th century towerhouse.

top Speke Hall, south Lancashire. Glorious romance
on the banks of the Mersey.

bottom Dalston Hall, Cumberland. Scottish influence
in the 17th century.

top left East Riddleston Hall. 17th century wildness
on the edge of the Pennines.

top right Baroque power. A gatepier at Ovingham
Vicarage, Northumberland.

bottom Bramham Park, west Yorkshire.
Early 18th century simplicity and dignity.

fortifications which had been invented in Italy, especially at Verona in the 1530s, but the Berwick walls have features which make them unique. Like Verona the walls have massive triangular bastions or forts which stick out in front of the wall to provide cannon fire along the lines of the walls so it is impossible for an enemy to approach the wall directly. What made Berwick unique though was that instead of relying on immensely thick walls for protection, Sir Richard Lee made his walls pretty thick and pretty high, but behind them he piled huge banks of earth, many times thicker than the walls themselves. The idea was that the earth was soft enough to absorb the shock of cannon balls.

So there you are – 500 years of castle development. Wonderful stuff, but what about the workers?

Smaller Castles

Of course, you might be relatively safe in the biggies, in the major castles, with the invading army fuming around you but unable to get in, but what about everybody else? How did they cope through this immense warlike period? Well, the poor coped very badly, needless to say. They got stuffed, but the rich and the fairly rich who didn't have full-scale castles had to make protection for themselves on a smaller scale and it is these smaller-scale castles which really make the greatest difference of all between northern castles and those further south. The north in fact is full of them. In older books they used to be called 'pele towers'. Nowadays we tend to call them 'towerhouses' but even this word isn't perfect because there are several different types of building.

1. Fortified Manor Houses.

Just a bit below the level of proper castles, these were built, usually, in relatively peaceful times and then given some rather panicky defences when the going got tough. Or indeed, when the tough got going. We happen to have two of the best examples in the country in the north – at Markenfield Hall near Ripon in North Yorkshire, and at Aydon

Castle near Corbridge in Tynedale. Two gorgeous buildings which date from the same time – Aydon got Licence to Crenellate (stick battlements on) in 1305, Markenfield in 1310. Aydon seems to have been orignally built a little earlier though, perhaps in the 1270s or 1280s (i.e. before the wars started). Its Great Hall was built on the first floor to give it a bit of protection but there don't seem to have been any other defences. The walls that surround it now were all added later. Markenfield also has a first-floor hall but it all seems to have been built at the same time – not as a proper castle, the defences aren't strong enough for that, though there is a moat, curtain walls and a gatehouse. It's a fortified manor house.

2. Solar Towers

Life in medieval big houses was a very public thing. As we've seen, it took place in a very communal way in the Great Hall but, as the Middle Ages progressed, rich chaps began to build solars. A solar was a room in a medieval house which the lord of the house could retreat to for a bit of privacy. It was usually as high up in the house as possible so that it could have nice big windows to let in sunlight (hence 'solar') without compromising security and it had a fireplace to make it as comfy as possible.

This is something that happened all over the country, but sometimes, and especially in the north, house owners built whole towers, big strong towers, at one end of the Great Hall – towers that they could retreat into if there was any sign of danger and pull the door shut safely behind them. Using strong iron doors, these solar towers could be cut off entirely from the rest of the house if the need arose. Some of the most exciting houses in the north have got solar towers. There seems to have been a fashion for building towards the end of the 14th century and they often look absolutely terrific. They're tall, beautifully built, they've got battlements, often nice Gothic windows high up. They've often got … and you'll be very excited by this … bartizans. Bartizans are higher corner turrets that stick out slightly from the face of the wall and give a deliciously romantic profile to the tower. There are lots of them all over North Yorkshire and Cumberland, but especially in Northumberland. Belsay Castle is a favourite of mine, and Chipchase. There's a smaller one, but an absolutely beautiful one called Halton Tower, just half a mile from Aydon Castle. It was built, like the others, in the late 14th century. They made it of Roman stones collected from the Roman fort on the same site. The original 13th-century hall is rather hidden behind it now and there's a beautiful, late 17th-century classical wing added onto one side, but it's the splendid tower that still dominates. So those are solar towers.

And then there are …

3. Towerhouses

Your basic medieval house had three sorts of rooms. There was a Hall in the middle with the private accommodation of the owner's family (the solar and great chamber and so on) at one end of it. At the other end of the Hall was the 'service end' – the working bit of the house, the kitchen and pantry and so on and the servants' quarters. In peaceful parts of the country these three different elements are laid out in rows or around a courtyard or something, dotted about. But in the warlike north you sometimes get a different arrangement where all of these rooms are scrunched together into one vertical block – one massive compact towerhouse – kitchens on the ground floor, hall up above, and private accomodation at the top. Essentially there tends to be one big room on each floor except that there are also four turrets, one in each corner, and so they provide four smaller rooms on each floor as bedrooms or toilets (garderobes) or chapels.

Some of these towerhouses can seem absolutely fearsome. Thirlwall Castle near Greenhead on the border between Northumberland and Cumberland must have been an awfully forbidding place. Dacre in Cumberland is more attractive because its corner turrets are quite splendid and stick out well beyond the rest of the tower walls. It seems to have had virtually no windows at all. But the best of the towerhouses, the biggest and most impressive, is Langley Castle near Haydon Bridge in Tynedale. One of its corner turrets was exclusively a toilet tower with, on each floor, a companionable little row of three or four stone toilet seats. Each floor also has a separate chute for the stuff to swoosh away down into a stream which was diverted under the corner of the building. It was a brilliant piece of construction to provide four separate chutes in the thickness of one turret wall – and an excellent way to keep the place clean. Not so nice for the neighbours downstream perhaps.

As time went by, stand-alone towerhouses in the Langley mould got commoner and smaller. They seem to have been a Scottish fashion first and imported from there. I think it's fair to say (and we are nothing if not fair, we Grundys) that none of the northern English examples are as splendid as their Scottish ancestors. There's nothing as romantic as Glamis Castle or Braemar or Ferniehirst, but there are lots of them, usually dating from the 16th century and usually found quite well north. Kirkandrews Tower near Longtown in Cumberland is typical of these later towers – very plain, no battlements but a solid parapet around the top which is corbelled out (i.e. it sticks out beyond the face of the wall) to make it nice and easy to drop loathsome substances down on the heads of attackers.

Inside all of them (and dozens exist) the ground floor is tunnel-vaulted and there is a stone spiral staircase in one corner. Often there is an extra room on the roof, behind the parapet, which might have been used for sentries, and probably all of them originally had at least some form of protective outer wall forming a courtyard around them. This was always known as a barmkin. This always sounds rather a sweet word to me, like a Yorkshire teacake or something but I don't suppose there was anything very sweet about these small, rough towers. One of them, Elsdon Tower in Northumberland, became the home of an 18th-century vicar who wrote about it in 1762:

'the vestibule of the castle is a low stable and above it is the kitchen, in which there are two little beds joining to each other. The curate and his wife lay in one and Margery the maid in the other. I lay in the parlour between two beds to keep me from being frozen to death, for as we keep open house, the winds enter from every quarter and are apt to creep into bed with one … I have lost the use of everything but my reason, though my head is entrenched in three nightcaps and my throat is fortified with a pair of stockings twisted in the form of a cravat … I wear two shirts at a time and for want of a wardrobe, hang my greatcoat upon my own back.'

Well, with such evidence of how bleak and uncomfortable life could be in the castles of the north, I think it's time to move on to a more civilised and hopefully warmer world. The world of ...

chapter four

Country Houses

There's an estate in Northumberland which now belongs to English Heritage and I can't think of a better one to sum up what makes the whole world of the country house so endlessly interesting.

Belsay Hall

At the top of a hill overlooking the grounds there is an iron-age hillfort, thousands of years old. Below it, at the foot of the hill, is Belsay Castle, one of the very finest of all the northern solar towers, a hugely romantic tower, oozing battlements and turrets and Rapunzel-type windows. This was the home of the Middleton family from the 13th century onwards until the wars with Scotland finally began to ease off, i.e. after the union of Scotland and England under one crown in 1603, at which point the Middletons added a nice uncastle-y house onto the side of their formidable tower. It has a classical porch inscribed to Thomas Middleton and Dorothy his Wife and the date, 1614, which makes it one of the earliest unfortified big houses in the Border area. Even in 1614 the Northumbrian countryside was still very insecure and it must have taken a big leap of faith to assume that the wars were over and it was safe to build a house without defences.

For Tommy and Dotty and their descendants, however, the gamble paid off and the Middletons were able to spend the next couple of hundred years consolidating their house and their estate. They built a nice set of stables in the early 18th century; they built a pretty Gothic-style farm in the earthworks of the hillfort; they added another wing to their house and a few years later laid out an attractive landscaped park in the approved manner with clumps of trees and pretty bridges over the stream.

But then, in 1799, the estate passed into the hands of a man who was presented with a bit of a problem – change your name, he was told, from Middleton to Sir Charles Monck as requested under the terms of your grandfather's will and thereby inherit all of his considerable dosh – or don't!

He did.

How to spend a honeymoon

In 1804 he got married and went on his honeymoon, not, as I did, for two nights to a pub in Bamburgh where I was confronted by a range of exciting new experiences – two eggs for breakfast, for example, that certainly made it memorable – but for almost two years. He honeymooned for two years on a Grand Tour of Europe where he did what every hot-blooded Englishman does on his honeymoon – he studied architecture.

The happy couple went first of all to Germany, to Berlin and Dresden, where they saw buildings like the Brandenburg Gate which had just been built in the Greek style. They went to Prague and Vienna, but then, instead of heading straight for Italy as most previous generations of Grand Tourists had done, they went to Greece. In 1804, Greece was still a much more unusual place to visit than Italy because it was still under Turkish rule and it was wilder and more dangerous, and the fashion for Greek things was only just beginning to grab Europe and had barely touched England at all.

But the Moncks went there, stayed a year in Athens, in fact they had their first baby there (inevitably called him Atticus), and they drew. Sir Charles sketched and studied the great monuments of antiquity and when he got home again (forced to leave by fears of the worsening war with France) he used his drawings to design himself the first country house in England to really try to capture the spirit of Ancient Greece.

The Greek Spirit

Belsay Hall is *very* Greek. It must be one of the most severe and unpretty houses in England but it is one of the most impressive and moving as well.

It's exactly 100 feet square (except at the back where there's a rather ugly sticky-outy service wing which breaks all of the symmetry, but you can't see that from anywhere else). Just like a Greek temple the house sits on a podium of three high steps. Even the entrance doesn't break the podium so you have to be able to leap like a young gazelle to even get into the house. I've seen smaller people and those with short legs arrive with crampons and climbing ropes to help them scale these steps. The entrance itself is wonderful – there is no porch or portico sticking out from the wall, instead two giant Greek Doric columns are *in antis*, as they say, which means that they are level with the walls on either side, and the porch instead goes backwards, into the house, so that the effect of the perfectly square exterior isn't spoilt. The windows have no decorations around them at all. They're just holes cut clean as a whistle through the wall. The roof isn't visible, a giant frieze and plain cornice hide it completely (which is perfect if you want to build a Greek temple but not so nice for the servants whose bedroom windows are hidden behind the cornice, blocking out any possible view). The design is like a stripped-down version of a Greek Doric temple, altered as little as possible to turn it into a house.

And finally, the stonework is superb. It is totally stonking good. Absolutely stunning. Smoother than the smoothest smooth in smoothland. Am I making myself clear? It is good. Sir Charles was looking for perfection and he got it. It is said that after he had trained up his masons at Belsay Hall, Northumbrian masons had a reputation for quality all over the country. Mind, they were working with good material. The stone for Belsay was quarried a couple of hundred yards from the house and it is one of the most beautiful building stones in a county of beautiful stone. It is a pale, buff-coloured sandstone flecked with tiny nodules of iron ore. Looks good enough to eat.

So, from outside the house is a marvellous intellectual experience – Sir Charles Monck's attempt to recreate the mood of ancient Greece. Inside, the house is almost as severe and almost as impressive. There's a terrific staircase hall which is the full height of the house – pure bare stone with two tiers of beautifully carved Greek columns all round the room. The other rooms are almost uniquely plain but ... I have a but here and it's a big but ... the huge and totally plain windows transform the severity inside into glorious richness because they put you into total contact with the beautiful garden outside.

The ultimate picturesque garden

You see, the Neo-classical period at the end of the 1700s and the start of the 1800s, which gave rise to Sir C.M.'s fascination with the far off past, was also the Romantic period when people didn't want to be separated from nature and so here, house and garden flow together. And what a garden it is. Hugely picturesque. There are terraces and lodges built like miniature temples. There are great banks of rhododendrons and azaleas, wonderful trees, sweeping views, but there is also another garden so special that I intend to start a new paragraph before even attempting to describe it.

In the quarries which provided the stone for the house, Sir Charles, followed later by his grandson who was called Sir Arthur Middleton, created the most picturesque garden that I have ever seen. Before English Heritage took over, the house was empty for over 30 years and the garden almost abandoned, but not quite. There was still a gardener who kept the wilderness at bay, and if you knew about him, and if you were brave enough, you could go and knock on his door and get permission to walk in his private domain. Not many knew, so it was always a solitary experience, like walking into a secret or imaginary garden. Deep in the quarries it's laid out in, protected by the high exquisitely coloured sandstone walls, among dripping green pools and dark clefts, among the twisted roots of trees growing down from the tops of the cliffs, the weather disappears, wind disappears, and once, alone on a late winter's day, I opened a mysterious door and found behind it a palm tree, and behind that I could see rhododendron flowers, shocking pink and weighted down with snow.

The arrogance of wealth?

There are still things I haven't mentioned about this place. For example, to create the landscape for his new house, Sir Charles swept away the previous landscape including the village and the chapel of old Belsay. He moved the main road and built a new village of Belsay along it, a curious row with arcades in front of all the houses like a town in Italy or southern France. Despite the fact that it seems so arrogant to replace a whole community in order to improve your own view, I have to admit, sadly, that in the event the new village looks really good. Nevertheless, it pleases me to tell you that he didn't get things all his own way. He wanted to create a lake between his new house and the new village. He had it dug out and built a boathouse on the edge of it but the villagers revolted (the villagers are revolting, my dear, I believe he said) because they thought it might flood their new homes, so the lake was never filled and he had to create another one instead on the opposite side of the garden. (Howay the lads. Power to the People.)

There are still other things I haven't told you about: the picturesque pigsties at the back of the house, the stables with a clock designed as a copy of the Temple of the Winds on the Acropolis, the heated garden walls, the new farms and well-ordered landscape throughout the surrounding estate ...

... I personally have lived my whole life in towns, in quite small terraced houses, I'm vaguely left wing. My family, like the Middletons, stretches back way into the mists of time, except that in my case I have no idea who any of them were – and yet I am fascinated by country houses like Belsay and by their owners. Their wealth and arrogance at times might move you to revolutionary fury (more like revolutionary irritation in my case, unfortunately, but I have always been a bit of a weed) but their money allowed them access to the newest ideas and allowed them to create beauty on a scale which we would never have had if they hadn't been rich and relatively idle. Just occasionally, in other chapters of this book, I'll be able to point out lovely things that have been done by public institutions like town councils and public committees, but not very often. It does hurt my little left-wing soul to say this, but most of the beautiful things in this country have been made by posh people with money.

Belsay – a truly northern experience?

So that's my justification for liking Belsay ...

... but is it not just an example of an English country house? Is it specifically northern? Well, yes it is – not obviously of course. There are ways in which it doesn't seem northern at all: the inspiration is Greek, houses and gardens of this scale and quality are to be found all over the country, Sir Charles Monck spent most of his formative years at his grandfather's house in Lincolnshire – and yet it is a northern experience in a number of ways.

It's *in* the north, first of all: proof, if proof were needed, that the north contains examples of the very best and could be as revolutionary and modern as anywhere else when it pulled its socks up. It's built of northern stone, cut by northern masons and, as we've already seen, that can't be beaten for beauty and solidity. It's set in a northern landscape, so all of this aristocratic elegance and European sophistication is surrounded by hills and crags and rolling emptiness. It's battered, more often than we want to tell southerners about, by northern weather.

But it's also a good example of a couple of key trends in Border architecture first of all and later on of northern architecture.

First of all, it illustrates very nicely what rich Borderers did when they no longer felt the need to hide in castles, and secondly it shows equally nicely what the north was capable of by the beginning of the 19th century when it had finally caught up entirely with the rest of the country.

Leaving the castles behind

At Belsay the move from castle to country house happened in two stages – in 1614, as I said before, whatever earlier buildings surrounded the tower were removed and replaced by a nice Renaissance house, and later on the castle was abandoned altogether and replaced by a brand new Neo-classical mansion. Elsewhere in the north, the extreme north, the same thing happened time and time again. Throughout Northumberland and Cumberland and to a lesser extent as far south as North Yorkshire and North Lancashire there are loads of houses with castle-y beginnings and later, more comfy and fashionable wings added to them. They are among the north's most characteristic and satisfying buildings.

Because Scotland and England didn't unite until the 17th century, the commonest thing to see is a medieval tower with a 17th-century wing attached to one side of it. In architecture, the 17th century was a period when builders were beginning to come to terms with the classical style. At the beginning of the century you still have the Elizabethan and then the Jacobean style; at the end of the century you have the Baroque style like I have already described at Castle Howard in Chapter one. Both of these styles are definitely classical but both of them are also playful and energetic, more concerned to make things lively than to do a perfect copy of the classical past. Only in London did court architects, like Inigo Jones, achieve a cool and properly classical style during the 17th century. In the north they certainly didn't. The effect is a lot of really entertaining buildings.

There's nowhere better to see this than at Hutton-in-the-Forest, near Penrith in Cumberland. The old bits of this house are shaped like an L. In the corner, at the junction between the two arms of the L, is the medieval tower with battlements and turrets and a spiral staircase inside it and a stone-vaulted ground floor just like it should have. The two arms (or wings) that spread out from it are like the perfect illustration of what the 17th century is supposed to look like. To the right is a wing dating from the 1640s, it has mullioned and transomed windows and a big bay window upstairs while downstairs it has an open colonnade of round-headed arches. To the left is a beautiful Baroque façade of about 1680 … 40 years later than the other wing and totally different in atmosphere. Chalk, you might say, and cheese. It's five bays wide and two-and-a-half-storeys high; the windows are big but they're all squashed too close together which makes it look exciting. There's lots of decoration – pediments over the windows, big bold surround for the door, pilasters and shields and bulgy bits, a line of big urns on the parapet. So this house, a typical northern house as I said, started in medieval times and was added to gradually in the course of the 17th century.

I could list you 50 like that …

… er, well … I've just been and counted, and in Northumberland and Cumberland and Westmorland I came up with 31 which is slightly less than I expected but enough to hang on to as a local type. The list includes some wonderful buildings:

In Northumberland, **Halton Castle**, where the high dramatic 14th-century tower built of small square stones stolen from the Roman Wall, towers over a beautiful wing added in 1696.

Chipchase Castle has one of the largest towers of all and still has a portcullis protecting the entrance. Its 17th-century wing was added in 1621 and is the finest Jacobean house in Northumberland.

West Bitchfield is almost a copy of Halton on a smaller scale.

Callaly Castle has a gloriously entertaining Baroque wing squashed between the remains of two towers.

Down south – in Westmorland – are two of the best of all; two superb Elizabethan houses alongside medieval towers in **Sizergh Castle** and **Levens Hall**.

In Cumberland, **Branthwaite Hall, Lorton Hall, Catterlen Hall, Hutton John, Moresby Hall** are all favourite examples of this touching mixture of the medieval and the 17th century but **Dalston Hall** just outside Carlisle is particularly fascinating. At Dalston, a medieval tower has 17th-century additions that don't look English at all. They look Scottish instead with the oddest windows surrounded by strange boxy sticky-outy window frames. The water spouts in the parapet are amazing too. They are elaborately carved to look like cannons – almost as a deliberate reminder of the warlike past, as if the builders were reluctant to let go.

I say 'touching' because you get the feeling, here in the far north, that the move towards peace was a very tentative affair, that owners took quite a while before dipping their toes into the waters of redevelopment. Hardly anywhere was anything built before 1600 and even afterwards it took decades for the pace of development to hot up. There's nothing this far north to resemble the great Elizabethan and Jacobean houses of the deep south ... .

Or Yorkshire and Lancashire as we border-dwellers call it.

Elizabethan and Jacobean houses in Yorks and Lancs

Yorkshire and Lancashire, protected from the full wrath of the naughty Scots by the stalwart strength of true northerners ... I'll re-phrase that ...

Both of these counties protected by their distance from the Border, are rich in late Medieval, Elizabethan and Jacobean houses. In the extreme south of the north there are some mansions of this period which, to be honest, hardly look northern at all, so splendidly Elizabethan and opulent are they. Burton Agnes Hall and Burton Constable are both in the East Riding between Hull and Bridlington. They've both been owned by the same families for hundreds of years and both are big, though Burton Constable isn't big, it's huge. Both are built of gloriously mellow brick of a type that no English person, even a far northerner, can resist.

Burton Constable is the most typically 'English'. From the outside it is a perfect Elizabethan house like something from the Home Counties, a civilised and restful grid of mullioned and transomed windows, quite flat and uneventful with just a couple of pretty turrets breaking the skyline. It'll remind you just a bit, if you happen to know it, of Hatfield House in Hertfordshire. Burton Agnes (really a Jacobean house since it wasn't completed until 1610) is a touch more restless, it has a front with three gables and a couple of turrets with richly carved parapets, but it too is really a most beautiful, and very English house.

So the East Riding towards the southern end of our region has a number of Elizabethan and Jacobean houses (Howsham Hall is another) which are beautiful but not specifically northern in feel. The rest of Yorkshire and most of Lancashire is quite different. Fountains Hall, near Ripon and overlooking the ruins of Fountains Abbey, is a good place to start. It was built in 1611, quite possibly by Robert Smythson who also designed Burton Agnes, but it is an even more restless building than its East Riding cousin. You come at it from below and you have to climb quite steeply towards it and this gives it a more dramatic, castle-like, almost cliffy, feel. It's much more in-and-out as well. Bits of it stick forward, other bits are boldly recessed so there's lots of light and shade. There are turrets and gables and bay windows and bow windows all squashed a touch too much together for comfort so instead of a restful and mellow feel it seems to be energetic instead.

And that is typical of the north at this period. There are two sorts of houses that give the feeling – the stone houses along the edges of the Pennines, and the timber houses of the Lancashire plain.

Not just northern pride but northern power

East Riddlesdon Hall near Keighley is one of the best examples of a Pennine house. It was built over a number of periods but the basic feeling is Jacobean – of a sort. There's a sort of mad gnomes quality about it. The rough gritstone walls are black. It's top heavy, especially the porch with its bizarre rose window above the door, and the windows are crushed together. There are huge rows of them but with small panes and thick stone mullions between them so that you feel that hardly any light could get through them. It's difficult to look at them without thinking of Heathcliff in *Wuthering Heights*, gnashing his teeth, smashing down the mullions and dashing innocent people to the flagstones as he searches desperately for the ghost of Cathy.

You think I'm exaggerating, don't you. Admit it. But I don't think I am. There are houses with this sort of intensity all over both slopes of the Pennines – in Calderdale (Wood Lane Hall for example) at Settle (the extraordinary house called The Folly of 1679 which has details like something out of *The Lord of the Rings*) and on the Lancashire side in the Forest of Bowland. Even the great Jacobean and Elizabethan mansions of eastern Lancashire, Astley Hall at Chorley, Gawthorpe, Hoghton Tower and Stonyhurst are excessive and exaggerated in their outlines, or the numbers of their windows, or the towers sticking out of the roofs like launch pads, or the sheer showy-offy excess of their sticky-outy bits (to use a technical phrase).

But even they pale into insignificance beside the great timber mansions of Lancashire.

I can't say 'gnome' again or 'Lord of the Rings' so I'm a bit stuck here, but there is something so intensely mythological about houses like Rufford Old Hall, Speke Hall, Salmesbury Hall, Hall i't Wood at Bolton. They are black and white, timber-framed, with a relish and an exuberance that has to be seen to be believed. They're like houses from the Black Forest going wild on holiday. There are millions of gables and overhanging eaves, scores of huge but irregular windows. They stick out and leap back again as if they can't contain themselves.

I know this isn't a very architectural description, but cool description doesn't do them justice. Normally when you think of timber framing, it's a bit like talking about Elizabethan houses, your first thought is of something mellow and southern. But there's nothing mellow about these houses; instead there's a startling and aggressive energy, a wild playfulness, which has to be experienced to be believed.

Some of them are almost as exuberant inside, in fact Rufford Old Hall is even more so. It's extraordinary, it's … I've run out of words. In terms of timber work there's nothing I can think of in England that's like it. The Great Hall is almost overpowering. It has an enormous hammer-beam roof with carved angels, all of the gaps between the main timbers of the walls are filled with traceried infills. There is a gigantic movable screen with some of the most barbaric carved figures in English art. It really is amazing. It's a room in which you can imagine giants throwing back buckets of foaming ale and thwacking their thighs noisily.

Where on earth they came from, these marvellous Lancashire wooden monsters, I don't know, but they are just the pinnacle of the pile. The north as a whole came out of the violence of medieval times later and with less certainty than further south and until the end of the 17th century there is an intensity about northern country houses which sets them apart from the common English run. There isn't exactly a northern style, just a northern feeling.

Which brings me rather hastily to the 18th century …

The Georgians

The 18th century started with an architectural bang in the north. Mighty Baroque masterpieces like Castle Howard and Seaton Delaval (mentioned in Chapter one) are only the tip of the iceberg and in the first 20 or 30 years of the century there were a whole heap of other houses built – not quite of the same quality but still pretty damn impressive. The best of them are in Yorkshire, especially West and North Yorkshire. Here's a list of them in alphabetical order:

Baldersby Park
Beninbrough
Bramham Park
Duncombe Park
Ebberston Hall
Fairfield Hall
Gilling Castle
Newby Hall
Wentworth Castle
Wentworth Woodhouse (the west side)

Of these, some are strong, silent and Baroque in a very noble sort of way – inspired by Vanbrugh perhaps, or even built by architects, like William Wakefield, who had worked with him at Castle Howard. Bramham Park's like this (wonderfully like this with an absolutely extraordinarily beautiful garden in a style which pre-dates the typical landscaped garden of Capability Brown and sticks instead to an earlier French style of long straight rides through woods). Gilling Castle and Duncombe Park are similar. Others are quite different. Wentworth Castle was built by a Frenchman living in Germany for an English client with big ideas. The result is a massive sumptuous palace which looks much more Central Europe than the English north. By contrast Ebberston Hall is a tiny pretty jewel of a house built as a love-nest by an MP called William Thompson, for his mistress, the dirty manbeast. Others (and Baldersby Park's the key example here) are ...

Do you know, I can't go on. I can't go on listing the Georgian Houses of the north and trying to talk about their features because there are hundreds of them and on the whole, for better or worse, they're much the same as posh Georgian Houses anywhere else in the country. You see, by the beginning of the 18th century, and by the 1730s definitely, the north had caught up entirely with the architectural tastes of the rest of the country. The earlier Baroque style faded into the Palladian style and then in the second half of the century it slithered sideways into the Neo-classical style, but to be honest only an expert can really tell the different periods apart and without oodles of illustrations it's pointless to try and draw the contrasts.

I love them in a way. I mean they're all very nice and beautiful and so on, but they've mainly lost the power to shock – classic English houses peacefully set down in classic English landscapes. But are they northern, eh? Is there any sign of a northern style among country houses? That's the question and the answer, I think, is no.

Local chaps

Some of them are built by local chaps of course. I'll re-phrase that ... the vast majority of them were built by local chaps. Right through the Georgian and early 19th-century period, a few nationally known and southern-based architects built things in the north. I've already mentioned Vanbrugh and Hawksmoor, I'm about to mention Henry Flitcroft and Robert Adam. Colen Campbell did a couple of important houses in the north. James Paine, he was the one most favoured up north and he pops up all over the place, but, as I say, it's local chaps who feature most heavily.

Another northern whinge

They're chaps, I might add, who barely get a mention in the nationwide text books. There's just one local son who tends to get recognised. He was called John Carr and he was born near York in 1723 and grew up to be the North Yorkshire Surveyor of bridges. He was responsible for dozens of beautiful 18th-century bridges, but he also built country houses which are as good as the best anywhere in the country. Do you know, it really irritates me, but the books always call him John Carr of York to separate him presumably from all the other John Carrs, none of whom has ever been an architect, but perhaps the writers are worried that you might confuse him with, say, John Carr, mastic asphalt spreader of Birmingham, or John Carr, sprocket turner of London. Nobody ever writes about Robert Adam of Kirkaldy or Sir John Vanbrugh of London. Call me paranoid, but I suspect he gets called Carr of York because people are surprised to find that so good an architect could come from so remote a place. Anyway, he worked all over our region and to prove it here's a very short list of very nice things by John Carr (of York):

Abbott Hall, Kendal (Cumbria)
Constable Burton (North Yorkshire)
Lytham Hall (Lancashire)
Raby Castle (County Durham)

Carr had a Yorkshire rival called Thomas Atkinson who was just as good and there were plenty of others all over the north – local chaps building fine big houses for the local aristocracy, rarely moving outside their immediate area and rarely getting a mention in any but local publications. I sense an opportunity for one final short list, a short list of the best local architects building country houses in the north between 1700 and about 1830:

Thomas Atkinson – Yorkshire
Ignatius Bonomi – County Durham
John Carr (of York) – York, I believe
John Dobson – Northumberland
William Etty – Yorkshire
Daniel Garrett – Yorkshire
Thomas Harrison (eek, a southerner – from Chester, slipped in
    without noticing but too good to miss)
William Newton – Newcastle

William Thornton – Yorkshire
William Wakefield – Yorkshire
George Webster – Westmorland

Wentworth Woodhouse – a big country house

The biggest Georgian House in the north, indeed the biggest in the whole country, was not built by a local architect, but by a Londoner called Henry Flitcroft. It's called Wentworth Woodhouse and it's between Wakefield and Sheffield. It was already pretty big in the 17th century and it was rebuilt even larger in the 1720s by Thomas Wentworth, Lord Malton, the 1st Earl of Strafford, but then, in the 1730s, the noble Lord seems to have had an attack of elephantiasis and got Flitcroft to build him another house. Actually it was just a new façade. All the other bits of the house are still standing round the back and Flitcroft just added a new east front – but quite a big one. In the interests of research I've tried to study my photograph of it and give you a few facts about it:

- I happen to know it's 606 feet long. That's 202 yards, roughly the same length as my terraced street which has 49 houses on each side – not to mention a cross street in the middle. A top Olympic sprinter could get from one end to the other in about 23 seconds but it would take me a little longer.
- 148 windows – that's how many I counted but there may be others I've missed
- 3 pediments
- 6 doors
- 2 nice glazed cupolas
- 2 towers
- 2 clocks
- Lots of statues on the roof
- and a whole heap of big stone balls

It's difficult to imagine, isn't it, actually living in a house like that? A former Duchess of Northumberland once told me in an interview that the worst thing about living in Alnwick Castle, which is a far smaller house than Wentworth Woodhouse, was that your hot milk got stone cold before you managed to get it from the kitchen to your bedroom. It's a hard life being rich.

Speaking of the Duchess of Northumberland reminds me to say that it's noticeable that up to the end of Georgian times, most of the really rich families, the really big aristocratic families in the north, tended to live as far south as they could. The Duke of Newcastle, for example, lived in Nottingham Castle and the Duchess's own family, the great Northumberland Percy family, though they live up north in Alnwick now, in those days mainly lived on estates near London or in Lincolnshire or in the southern parts of Yorkshire. In fact if the seriously aristocratic did want to live in the north at all it was Yorkshire they turned to and not too far north in it either. They seemed to be a bit wary of catching too much northern-ness so that's why it's no surprise that a family as big as the Wentworths chose to build right down in the southern part of the region.

Gangs of roaming Italians

None of the other country houses in the north are as big as Wentworth Woodhouse but a lot of them have incredibly rich interiors. Wentworth is awash with marble and there is fancy plasterwork in houses all over the place. It was often done by Italian fancy plasterers or *stuccatori*. There were gangs of these *stuccatori* roaming the north which makes them sound frightfully menacing somehow (the stuccatori nostra) but they did incredible work. In Northumberland there was a gang led by Pietro la Francini who settled in the nearby village of Cambo and did the gorgeous rooms at Wallington Hall in the 1740s and an even more fabulous job in the Drawing Room at Callaly Castle and another job, possibly even more fabulous still, in Lumley Castle in County Durham. In Yorkshire there was a rival gang led by Giuseppe Cortese (the Cortese mob, boss, they'll have you plastered if you don't watch out!). Lancashire had Francesco Vassalli – but there were locally bred chaps as well. Ingleby Arncliffe – that's not a local chap, it's a house which has plasterwork by a local chap whose name escapes me but it is among the most elaborate rococo plasterwork in the country – of quite fabulous richness.

Newby Hall – Adam perfection

I have a favourite among these gorgeous Georgian interiors. It's not the fanciest or the most elaborate, but I think it just happens to be among the most perfect.

It's at Newby Hall near Ripon in North Yorkshire which is a lovely early 18th-century house beside the River Ure, built in warm red brick with lots of stone details and lush gardens. It was built by the Blackett family who also owned Wallington Hall in Northumberland but in 1748 the Blacketts sold it to a man called William Weddell who went on the Grand Tour. He was what was known in the 18th century as a 'dilettante' – a lover of the arts, a collector of lovely things, and from his two-year hols in Italy he brought back the usual clobber – ancient statues by the ton of course and enough friezes to fill a case or two. He brought a gigantic marble sarcophagus (or possibly it's a bath) as well, which is … oh, I don't know, about five feet tall and about six or seven feet long with an equally gigantic marble lid. There was nothing unusual about this. All over the country young dilettanti were somehow managing to haul half the antiques in Italy back home with them. One of the most enthusiastic was a Lancastrian called Henry Blundell. At Ince Blundell just north of Liverpool he had to build himself a copy of the Roman Pantheon to fit in all of his holiday buys. His statues have all been sold now but they look extraordinary in old photographs – great gaggles of marble nudies and busts and nudie busts, dotted apparently at random under a vast vaulted ceiling.

Anyway, William Weddell's collection was similar and when he got home with it he had to decide where to put it. At my house we've just been having a similar problem trying to decide where to hang our nice little print that we brought back from Prague. It seemed irresistible at the time but where on earth do we put it? It helps of course if you have enough money to bring in Robert Adam, the country's finest and most fashionable architect to remodel the house and build a special gallery to house your mementoes.

A brief note about Robert Adam

Considering that he's the best known of all Georgian architects it won't surprise you to discover that Adam is just one more famous national name by whom there isn't a great deal of work in the north. He worked at Alnwick in Northumberland but most of his work there was pulled out in Victorian times. There's a house at Whitehaven which sank into the doldrums and eventually became a hospital before being turned into flats recently. There's some smashing work by him at Nostell Priory near Wakefield and a wonderful collection of interiors at Harewood House north of Leeds but that's all I can think of. There are plenty of other houses in something like his style, but by other architects, including Heaton Park in Manchester which was designed in 1772 by James Wyatt and which is one of the most beautiful houses of its period in the whole country – long and low, elegant and beautifully proportioned.

Nowadays, if you see an estate agent's blurb which says that 'the house benefits from a number of Adam-style fireplaces', your heart sinks. You can just picture them, twee and poncy, pretty in pink with white plaster bits, but when you get your teeth into some real Adam, like the stuff he did at Newby, it's a whole new experience. The best room by far, and it's one of the most beautiful rooms I've ever seen, is the sculpture gallery he built to hold William Weddell's collection. It is pink actually … and white … with pale green bits … but there the comparison with estate-agentese ends, because it is also a vision of arches and a complex room of constantly changing vistas. You enter from the library, which is another lovely Adam room, through an arch, into a square room with niches containing statues around the walls (he loved his niches, did Adam. Apparently his mother once said, I knew our Robert would find his niche) and from here you are constantly drawn forward to distant views through a series of new and unexpected shapes. You pass into a round room with a beautiful domed ceiling, and all the while, in the distance there is yet another arch giving promise of the final room to come, and framed in this final arch is the sarcophagus I was telling you about. Adam is famous for his desire to introduce 'movement' into architecture and there really isn't a better example of it than this extraordinarily shaped room which despite possessing all of the Georgian elegance you could possibly want, is still lively and entertaining. But there's another thing about Adam that makes this sculpture gallery even more interesting as well.

Robert Adam was another of those young men who set off to Italy on extended hols. He spent years there, studying and drawing the ancient ruins that littered the place and when he got home he revolutionised English architecture by designing buildings and interiors which took their inspirations *directly* from the stuff he'd seen. So this room is filled with a wonderful mixture. On the one hand you've got William Weddell's genuinely ancient statues, and on the other, Robert Adam's perfect copies of genuinely ancient ruins. A wonderful room then – sufficient proof, in fact, that what I said a few pages ago about Georgian architecture 'losing the power to shock', I was talking through my neck. Ignore me. At its best Georgian architecture can blow you away.

In the grounds at Newby there's a church built by a descendant of William Weddell in Victorian times which is worth a mention if only to act as a reminder to holiday-makers to take out adequate travel insurance, because it is yet another northern monument which owes its existence to rich people's desire to spend their holidays on the continent – except that in this case it was the holiday from hell!

It's built in memory of a man called Frederick Vyner whose mother lived at Newby Hall. Frederick was with a party of English ladies and gents who were on holiday in Greece in 1870 when they were captured by a band of brigands, which somehow paints pictures in my mind of eyepatches and filthy bandannas and villainous moustaches. This band of brigands was led by a famous Turkish baddy called Pakos who demanded a ransom of 1,000,000 drachmas – about £32,000 and a huge amount of money in those days. The Greek army tried to rescue the hostages but made a complete hash of the attempt and the brigands shot all of their captives.

Frederick's mother brought in William Burges, one of the oddest but one of the greatest of all Victorian architects, to build the memorial church which is dedicated, rather touchingly, to Christ the Consoler. It's a wonderful building, richly decorated, but solemn and moving, and I mention it now as the sort of cunning and creative link of the type that we TV people are so fond of, to take us from the Georgian elegance that Newby represents to a whole new unfolding world, the world of ...

The 19th-century country house in the north

I may be wrong but I think that the vast majority, if not all, of the country houses that I've mentioned so far were the homes of old landed families. I suppose there will have been some built by wealthy merchants and successful politicians but most of their owners started by having a name, a long line of well-heeled ancestors and a lot of land.

By the beginning of the 19th century, however, there were new forces at work. Money was being made in new ways and new sorts of people were making it and a lot of them spent it on new country houses. It's no secret that the north was the hotbed of the Industrial Revolution. The mining and heavy engineering industries of the North East, the wool industry in West Yorkshire and cotton in Lancashire made a lot of families rich so it really is no surprise that nowadays we are particularly rich in houses of this period.

Brass Castles

I have been reading a book called *Brass Castles* by George Sheeran which looks at the big houses built in the 19th century by just one relatively small group of industrialists – those in the West Riding of Yorkshire – and he records 97 surviving mansions – not all of them strictly country houses, I have to admit, since some of them were built close to the works that paid for them, but they're all big houses set in their own grounds. This is what the blurb on the back cover of his book says:

'The West Yorkshire families who grew rich through commerce and industry during the Industrial Revolution used their newly acquired wealth to build houses that were markedly different from those of older landed families.'

So, in West Yorkshire alone we have at least 97 houses, 'markedly different' and paid for by 'newly acquired wealth'. That's a remarkable collection and I'm sure, though I have no way of proving it, that the situation would be very similar in the industrial areas of Lancashire. Further north it's the same again. Around Carlisle, for example, which was an important cotton-making town, there's a whole ring of cotton manufacturers' houses and in the Lake District wealthy industrialists built a heap of beautiful rural retreats throughout the 19th century.

Coal Wealth

Some of the earliest and most impressive of these new houses were built of coal, if you see what I mean. They were built by families who had the good fortune to find that the land they'd owned for ages happened to have coal underneath it – the most obvious examples are the Lowthers in Cumberland and Westmorland and the Lambtons and the Londonderrys in County Durham.

These families had existed for ages but by the early 19th century the coalmines they owned started to bring in vast hods of dosh, as we Newcastle folk say in our picturesque way, and they ploughed some of that dosh into buildings. They wanted really posh buildings to make them look like members of the aristocracy so some of them chose to build castles – big Gothic castles awash with towers and battlements which would suggest that their families had been important for ages. Lowther Castle near Penrith and Lambton Castle near Chester-le-Street haven't got an ancient stone between them – but they're big, they're impressive and above all they're picturesque. They've both had a bad time with fires and things in the 20th century but they are both still thrilling to look at.

Other families chose the Classical style to suggest their status and respectability. The best example now is Wynyard Park near Hartlepool which was the home of the vastly coal-rich Tempest family who married into the ancient Vane family of Raby Castle to make the super-rich Vane-Tempests. I wonder how they decided whose name came first. I would have suspected that in those sexist old days it would have been man first, woman second but, in this case she was the Vane and he was the Tempest. Perhaps they played darts to decide, or had a mud-wrestling contest.

These two alternative choices of style – Gothic or Classical – were almost interchangeable in the early part of the century and architects were equally comfortable with both. The same architect, Ignatius Bonomi, was heavily involved at both Gothic Lambton and Classical Wynyard.

The Tastelessness of the Newly Rich?

I know what you're thinking. You can't hide it from me. You're thinking 'industrialists', you're thinking 'self-made men' and 'nouveau riche, I bet they built big, vulgar, tasteless houses full of pretentious show and flashiness'. Well, to be honest, on the whole, this was not the case. There were a number of reasons for this. First of all there weren't that many of the industrialists who were really 'rags-to-riches people' in the true nouveau-riche mode. There were a few of course. The Ickringills from Keighley started their working lives as mill workers and owned mills themselves before they died, but most factory-owning families rose gradually over a few generations. Anyway, the Ickringills who really were nouveau riche actually built themselves a very tasteful house called Laurel Mount in Keighley. Just because they were newly rich didn't mean that they had no taste. Of course, over the whole of the 19th century and over the whole north there obviously were some who tended to pull their socks up, roll their sleeves up and get stuck into something that would get them noticed. There was William Smith for example (also of Keighley) who called his first son Prince Smith ... and his second son Prince Smith II ... and his third son Prince Smith III which is where it stopped – until Prince Smith III changed his name to Prince Prince Smith. Now that is tasteless, and in architectural terms there were a few like the Prince Prince Smiths, who couldn't resist peeping over the parapet of good taste.

In particular there were those who liked to have a good tower or two, a nice showy-offy fancy profile. Some are splendid, beautiful even. Langham Tower in Sunderland, built in 1889 by the local architect William Milburn for a shipbuilder called William Adamson, is a highly picturesque house with a tremendously lofty tower and lots of

Arts and Crafts details, but others were not so tasteful. The profile of Cliffe Castle at Keighley, for example, which was built by Henry Isaac Butterfield, worsted manufacturer, in the middle of the century, had to be seen to be believed. Today most of its many towers have been demolished, which is sad, but could be a relief to the faint-hearted and the pure in mind, because it wasn't just that there were many towers, it was that they were absurdly high and unnervingly top heavy. At Haggerston Castle near Berwick, the house itself has mostly been demolished, but the 13-storey tower which combined the functions of water tower (to provide a good head of water for aristocratic ablutions), belvedere and heart attack inducer still stands like a giant … er … a giant … er … sticky-uppy thing in the sky. But my favourite tasteless tower is attached to quite a simple and attractive house at Wigton in Cumberland. The house had been built in 1810 and it really isn't very big as country houses go, but in 1887, the owner, Mr. William Banks, exporter of factory-made clothing, added a tower to it which is 136 feet high and exceedingly odd to look at. You could try to work out what style it's in but it would take you quite a while and half a library of architectural books – and you still wouldn't know.

So bad taste and pretentiousness are available, but on the whole the newly rich industrialists were not a flashy lot and built with some restraint and style. They were often practical men and wanted sensible rational houses with all of the latest technologies built in, but they were also traditionalists who wanted houses that would make them seem respectable. In the first half of the 19th century my local great country-house architect in the North East was a man called John Dobson and he pandered to both of these desires.

He didn't mind whether you asked him to build Gothic or Classical, he was equally happy with both, but in either case he could give you plenty of mod cons. By the 1820s, for example he was experimenting with damp-proof courses and with cavity-wall insulation because he'd watched a Roman example of it being excavated at one of the forts on Hadrian's Wall. He saw how the Romans used to attach hollow T-shaped tiles on the inside of bath-house walls and allow hot air from the furnaces to percolate up the walls, so he introduced a similar approach to his houses.

But he could also give you elegance and class. One of his houses –

my favourite actually – is called Longhirst Hall. He designed it in 1824 for an old Northumbrian land owning family called the Lawsons who had become newly rich through the nice kindly coal that lurked beneath their land near North Shields. He gave them a house which is really beautiful. Like Belsay, where I started this chapter, it's built of the most perfectly cut stone you could imagine and the design of the house manages to combine restraint and drama. The entrance portico is tall and very narrow with Corinthian columns and it leads into a small but perfectly formed (not unlike myself) entrance hall, all of it built in exposed natural stone of the most exquisite colour.

I realise, reading over what I've just written that I've rather over-done the superlatives: one beautiful, one exquisite and two perfects is like giving Olga Korbut a perfect 10 in gymnastics – it doesn't leave me anywhere else to go, so I'll ease off and just say that many, the majority possibly, of the early 19th-century houses built for the newly emerging industrialists are models of restraint and good taste.

But whether the same can be said of my favourite industrialist's mansion is a matter of opinion. Good taste – almost certainly, but restraint? I'm not so sure. I'm afraid you are going to accuse me of bias because this is yet another Northumbrian example. It's called Cragside and it was built for an industrialist who started his working life as plain William Armstrong but ended it as a Lord. He'd done a whole heap of things to achieve this lordshipitude.

What had he done? Well, he started off in life as a solicitor with an amateur interest in engineering and he became very good at hydraulics, in fact, in 1846, when he was 36 years old and still a solic-itor, he headed a project to convert Newcastle's quayside cranes to hydraulic power. It was a successful project and he gave up soliciting (does that sound right?) he gave up being a solicitor, and started a factory at Elswick upstream from Newcastle to make things hydraulic.

The factory was successful too but in 1855 he had an even better wheeze. Inspired or shocked by the poor performance of the British Army in the Crimean War he invented a new type of artillery gun with a rifled barrel. Apparently if you rifle, or groove, the inside of the barrel, the shell comes out spinning and can be fired much more accurately. This gun made him a fortune and was really one of the foundations upon which Tyneside's industrial power was based.

But then he had yet another wheeze, a cunning plan, in fact, which made him 'My Lord'. He handed over the patent to his gun to the government who, in gratitude, made him Lord Armstrong. After that he diversified into shipbuilding and made a huge success of that as well, an absolute fortune. Makes you sick.

Newcastle's full of reminders of Lord Armstrong. There's the regulation statue of him and a marvellous park called Jesmond Dene which used to be his garden and which he gave to the city. His house is a special school now and the successor to his vast factory complex still exists in the west end of the city, but the most visible reminder of him is the Swing Bridge over the Tyne which he designed and built in 1868. It's on the line of the original Roman bridge and its medieval successor and he designed it as a swing bridge, using hydraulically powered motors, to allow ships up river to his own factories. Since it first opened over half a million ships have passed through it, but there is said to have been a moment, early in its life, when the world's largest hydraulically operated bridge opened to allow the largest ship in the world up river to call at the world's largest factory to collect the world's largest hydraulic dock-side crane – and all of them were the work of Lord Armstrong.

Cragside – the talented Lord's rural retreat

So a talented chap, with a taste for the rural life. He bought an estate called Cragside in the Northumbrian hills near Rothbury. A measly 14,000 acres. There was a house on it, I think, but in 1864 he built another one in its place. It was fairly ordinary this house but then, in 1870 he started to rebuild and this time the result was anything but ordinary.

The architect he chose was Norman Shaw – Scottish background, London-based, massive national reputation but at least partly educated in Newcastle so we in the north do have a bit of a claim over him. He's said to have spent just one day coming up with his basic ideas for the house but it took 15 years to build (in three separate bursts).

I love this house, did I tell you that. I think it's a wonderful Victorian northern house. I would admit that there is a sense in which it doesn't seem at first glance all that northern because it is half-timbered which isn't really a tradition in the north. But even the half-timbering has a northern connection. Remember the extraordinary timber mansions of Lancashire, and the cities, Newcastle and York for example, were full of half-timbered houses and parts of the courtyard in the middle of Cragside are quite similar to some of the half-timbered buildings on Newcastle Quayside. But there are ways in which it is very northern indeed. It has a solid squat copy of a pele tower like so many border houses and its porch is vaulted in stone like the defensible porches of many northern churches.

Its main northern quality, however, is that it has a wild romance and a magnificently picturesque relationship with the landscape. It grows out of the rocks and climbs up the hillside, it seems to wander through the trees as if it was meant to be. There are millions of trees, incidentally, I seem to remember that Lord Armstrong planted seven million of them which must have cost a bob or two. We always feel pretty rash if we lash out on a berberis and a couple of primulas at the Garden Centre. We dither about, wondering whether we can afford an extra pot for the back yard, so what it must have cost him to plant millions of trees doesn't bear thinking about.

The inside of the house has quite a different quality to the outside. Of course being a great inventor and industrialist, Armstrong had to give it modern technologies. Water power from a series of artificial lakes in the estate operated hydraulic lifts and spits in the kitchen. The same lakes provided the world's first domestic use of hydro-electric power. But beyond these revolutionary developments its atmosphere is lovable rather than romantic. Wouldn't it be nice to be able to combine both of those qualities yourself – romantic on the outside, lovable on the inside; the opposite sex would worship you. That's what the house is like though. The rooms are big by comparison to my house, of course, but they're eminently liveable in, cosy rather than grand. In the dining room there's a charming inglenook fireplace whose lintel is carved with the phrase 'East West Hames Best' which I take to be a quaint Scottish way of saying you can travel where you want but it's nicest of all to snuggle up beside your own fire in your own little home ... the domestic dream of a great northern self-made man.

chapter | **five**

The Countryside

The north is beautiful – official!

When my mum was a girl she went to Keswick school. Because she lived in a village a few miles outside the town she was a weekly boarder which meant that she stayed at school during the week. In the sixth form her dormitory was in the old house called Greta Hall which was part of the school and her room had been, from the 24th July 1800 and for many years after, the study belonging to the poet Samuel Taylor Coleridge.

That's one of my claims to fame.

Until early 1800 Coleridge had been living down south but the previous year he'd come with his friend William Wordsworth, for what he called a 'pikteresk toor' of the Lake District. They walked miles. Miles, miles and miles and despite the fact that it was November and the weather as wild as it can be in the north at that time of year, Coleridge was blown away by it (metaphorically of course) and determined to move up north at the earliest opportunity ...

I'm just going to write that again ... Coleridge was blown away by it and determined to move up north at the earliest opportunity ...

I've spent so long up to now on the defensive, attacking people for ignoring our region or lambasting them for criticising it that it's a relief to finally hit on something about the north that I believe gives universal satisfaction – our glorious countryside. It certainly tickled Coleridge. Shortly after moving in to Greta Hall he wrote to a friend

that even the mundane business of shaving had taken on a new significance because his shaving mirror was opposite the window ...

'I seldom shave without cutting myself. Some mountain or peak is
rising out of the mist, or some slanting column of misty sunlight is
sailing across me so that I offer up soap and blood daily as an Eye-
servant of the goddess Nature.'

Within a month of arriving in Keswick, Coleridge was leaping over
the hills ('Lowping' my mother would have said), bounding up
Blencathra, flashing over Helvellyn in the moonlight, generally doing
what the rest of us have been doing ever since – fellwalking, appreci-
ating the beauty of the northern landscape.

In Northumberland a few years earlier, another of the great
writers of the Romantic period was doing much the same thing. In
1791, Sir Walter Scott went on holiday with his uncle and stayed at a
farm called Langleeford deep in the Cheviot Hills from where he
wrote a letter home. It goes:

'I am very snugly settled in a farmer's house ... in the very centre
of the Cheviot Hills, in one of the wildest and most romantic situations ... we are amidst places renowned by the feats of former days;
each hill is crowned with a tower or camp or cairn, and in no situation can you be nearer more sites of battle ... My uncle drinks the
goats whey here, as I do ever since I understood it was brought to
his bedside every moning at six by a very pretty dairy maid.

All day we shoot, fish, walk and ride; dine and sup on fish strug-
gling from the stream, and the most delicious heath-fed mutton,
barn-door fowl, pies, milk-cheese etc all in perfection; and so much
simplicity resides among these hills that a pen ... was not to be
found about the house, even though it belongs to a considerable
farmer, until I shot the crow with whose quill I write this letter.'

He sounds a nice appreciative guest, doesn't he, and this could be one
of the most favourable accounts of dinner, bed and breakfast in a
northern B & B ever written. It sounds better than anywhere I've

ever stayed and though I have searched high and indeed low, I've never had my goat's whey brought to my bedroom by any sort of dairy maid, pretty or not. It just doesn't seem fair.

There are still a few bits and pieces here of the sorts of attitudes I was writing about in the first chapter. It's a bit patronising maybe – there's lots of 'wild' and 'simplicity' and so on, as if the north was populated by some strange alternative tribe; the trouble with Walter is the same as the rest of us who spend our brief hols in the country-side, he saw it as a lovely spot full of simple chaps – but there's also something new and refreshing in Scott and in Coleridge – a love of the northern landscape, a delight in its history, and an appreciation of its hospitality (the very things that have been bringing people back ever since).

And finally there's something else. There's an interest in country fare, country life, country farmhouses and the simple buildings of the countryside … in vernacular architecture.

Vernacular Buildings

Vernacular buildings are not posh buildings. They are more ordi-nary buildings built of local materials by local chaps for local purposes in a local style, and before you ask, no there isn't; there isn't one single typical northern style of vernacular building. And don't ask me why either because the reasons are obvious. There are lots of different local building materials. A local chap in the Yorkshire Wolds, to take an example, can't possibly be local in Cumberland. And you can't have a local purpose either when sheep farming is the most important thing in one area and wheat growing in another. So there.

So there. There isn't one particular northern style of rural vernac-ular buildings because each part of the north has developed its own intimate traditions. And what traditions they are. We have some of the most distinctive farming buildings and farming landscapes in the country.

Not many of them are very old. They always look old and we have a tendency, because they're in the countryside, to assume that they are old, but really old bits are few and far between.

The oldest landscapes

What is there that's old? Well, there are quite a lot of old fields – really old fields – in some parts of our area. They're called 'lynchets' and they're sort of terraces or strips on hillsides. They're almost always in hilly places and they're there because way back, when they were made, the valley bottoms were either too wet to farm or too wooded, or both, so the slopes had to be shaped to make them suitable for farming. There are lots of lynchets in Wharfedale, for example and up around Malham but there are also lots in the Cheviots and especially in the Ingram Valley. Often they're marked on OS maps as 'celtic field systems' but one group in the Eden Valley has the most picturesque name of 'The Hanging Gardens of Mark Antony' – for no reason that I know of. These hillside lynchets are notoriously difficult to date but it's pretty safe to assume that they are prehistoric and they were created by farmers in a bid to create some usable land.

By the early Middle Ages farmers had gradually begun to clear the valley bottoms – which is easy for me to say but not so easy for them to do.

A really good example of how much effort was needed to create our modern countryside is to be found in one of the most distinctive and beautiful farming landscapes in Britain, the upper reaches of Swaledale and Wensleydale in North Yorkshire. The earliest parts of the dales to get used were the valley sides. Farms and villages were built there in Anglo-Saxon times for two reasons – to take advantage of springs of fresh water on the hillside, and to be above the mire, mud and fog of the valley bottoms. When the villages were first settled the valley bottoms were a wilderness of peat bog and rough open woodland. But look at them now.

The green, green grass of Yorkshire

Nowadays the grass in the valley bottoms in the two most northerly Dales is the most glorious green of any fields you have ever seen. Except in spring when the green is temporarily obliterated by the brilliance of the buttercups, the fields are really startlingly green. The fields are smooth and surrounded by neat dry stone walls as well, and virtually every field has a sweet little farm building called a field barn in it. It's a marvellous sight but it isn't a natural one. It's an artificially created landscape and the effort required to make it like that was immense. First of all, the stones that had been washed down by rivers and scraped down by glaciers and rolled down from the hillside because of gravity had to be cleared away – an extraordinary effort, and all done by hand. The walls that surround the fields give some sort of indication of how much stone needed to be shifted. But when the stones had gone the fields still weren't ready. The sodden, acid, marshy earth had to be turned into usable soil and that took generations. There was a continuous process of scraping up the soil and burning it, mixing it with wood ash, burning it again to clear out the unwanted vegetation, adding crushed lime from the surrounding hills to enrich it. It's a process that went on hundreds of years ago but even now, because so much preparation was done, the grass in Swaledale and Wensleydale is indeed greener than any other grass. I know this because I have tested it with my grassometer.

Field barns

The field barns of Wensleydale and Swaledale ... I seem to remember that they're actually called field houses ... are the other most distinctive feature of the landscape – because there are so many of them and because they're so well built. They are really combined byres and hay barns. On the ground floor there are a few cattle stalls with a hay loft above which is a common enough arrangement on farms elsewhere but only in these northern Dales do you find them in vast numbers scattered about the fields of the valley bottom like confetti.

But they aren't very old. The oldest known surviving field house is dated 1687 – so is there any evidence that shows how our earlier ancestors farmed and lived in the countryside? Not much, at least not very much still standing. Virtually all visible traces of the houses and farms of ordinary people in medieval times have disappeared because they were built in sensible places and later generations have knocked them down and built bigger and better on top. The only places you can get a glimpse of what they might have been like is to look in the high places, the most remote places.

Sheilings and saeters, scales and ergs

The high moors above valleys in lots of parts of the north were only gradually brought into use – at first not as permanent settlements but as summer pastures for cattle brought up from the surrounding lowlands. In geography books it's called transhumance and I'm sure that at school I was given the impression that it only ever happened in Switzerland but in fact, until the Middle Ages, it happened all over the north of England as well. Gradually though, the practice died out in most places until by the 16th century it was restricted to a few areas.

In 1599 a writer called Camden talked about, '... ancient nomads, a martiall kind of men, who from the month of Aprill into August lye about scattering and summering (as they term it) with their cattle in little cottages here and there which they call sheals or shealings.'

Camden was talking about the Borders, about Northumberland and the border area of Cumberland but I think it's almost certain that this sort of seasonal farming still went on in a few other upland areas of the north. It certainly happened in the Lake District. In 1698 the traveller Celia Fiennes kept a diary of her travels in the north. Travelling over the moors south of Penrith she described seeing settlements of the same type that Camden had described a hundred years earlier:

'... little huts made up of drye walls, only stones piled together and the roofs of same slatt (slate?), there seemed to be little or noe tunnells for their chimneys and have no mortar or plaister within or without ...'

If you look at an Ordnance Survey map of the northern north you'll see plenty of evidence that transhumance existed. It had been going on in the Lake District since at least Viking times. There were three Viking words which referred to summer pastures – there was *scale, erg,* and *saeter* – and all of these are common in modern Cumbrian place names. Seascale and Portinscale, for example, are obvious scale names. Sizergh Castle actually has an erg as part of its name but there are lots of other places that just end in er (Mosser, Birker, Whinlatter) and they were ergs as well. Saeters are common too; at the head of Borrowdale there are two of them side by side.

Seatoller was the saeter among the alder trees while Seathwaite was the saeter in the clearing. In Northumberland, as Camden said, the word was *shiel* or *shieling* and there are scores of place names ending with the word 'shield' – Carrshield, Ridley Shield, Whitshield, Lowshield Green.

Lots of these temporary summer farms were eventually colonised as full time farms and villages and lots must have disappeared entirely but lots survive in ruined form in the wildest parts of the region. There are sufficient remains on the moors round Bewcastle in Cumberland to show what they were like. Rough. That's what they were like, very rough, not at all bijoux. There's one by the Kingwater on Tinkler Crags, for example, which seems to be fairly complete though it has been partly reconstructed as an animal shelter, but it's only about 13 feet long by eight wide with a door, or at least a hole in the wall, no windows and a turf roof. That's rough. Another, on Whitelyne Common, is bigger (about 27ft by 13ft) and it does have one small window but in other respects it's just as rough. The side walls were only about six feet high, the gable end about nine feet so it must have felt incredibly low and dark inside. There was no fireplace so presumably there was just a hearth in the middle of the floor and the smoke drifted out through the roof. Some of these shielings only had one room and at the most there were only two rooms – and yet these pretty miserable little hovels weren't just meant to keep the odd solitary shepherd dry – whole families, whole communities decamped up to the summer pastures for months on end. Elsdon in Northumberland, for example, was really two separate villages. There was Ellesdon Wintersteads (which I presume is the present village) and Ellesdon Sheylding Grounds where the whole village spent the summer.

I'm not suggesting ... I don't think I'm suggesting that the permanent houses of early farmers were as rough as this but I don't suppose they were that much better. Certainly later generations didn't think highly enough of the permanent houses to keep them because they've all disappeared, but the evidence from excavations (at Wharram Percy in the Yorkshire Wolds, for example, and at West Whelpington in Northumberland) suggests that they were all ...

Long-houses.

A long-house is a farm building which has room for the people at one end and accommodation for the animals at the other. Both groups share the same outer door which opens into a passage with doors off it into the house and the byre.

The earliest farm buildings in the upland areas of Britain were probably all long-houses of this type but nowadays, as far as I know, there are no unaltered examples of them in the north though there's a smashing reconstruction of one in the Ryedale Folk Museum at Hutton-le-Hole in the North York Moors, but the spirit of them lives on in lots and lots of later farms where the same range of buildings houses people and animals – only nowadays the two different groups each have their own separate doorways. They're called linear farms. In Yorkshire they're called laithes and in the hilly areas they're the commonest type of farmstead. They always lie along the hillside, long and low and oh, oh so satisfying … I love them so much.

A naughty fantasy

I've got this fantasy, in fact, which I've never told my wife about because I don't think she would understand. She has fantasies of her own of course, but I think that mine is at variance with hers and it might easily give rise to conflict if I was to share it with her.

Mine's a lottery fantasy (what were you thinking about?) and it involves me winning a lot of money. I think her's is rather similar but the problem arises when the virtual money gets spent on virtual goodies because she, I suspect, imagines us buying a nice little place in the sun, somewhere she can grow ratatouille and eat it on a terrace, shaded by vines to protect her from the pitiless heat of the noonday sun.

I, on the other hand, want to buy a Lake District farmhouse and go for walks in the rain. It's a problem. A virtual problem.

I know exactly what my farmhouse looks like, though I've never seen it and it's possible it doesn't exist in exactly this form. I know where it is roughly. It's deep in one of the dales, on the hillside a little above the valley bottom. There are oak woods to one side of it. Below it there are small irregular fields surrounded by dry stone walls; sheep needless to say, are chomping the grass in a sheepy sort of way; behind it is the fellside with long straight walls climbing impossibly up the steep slopes. And beyond the last wall, the glorious wastes of the high fells. The view from the front door is unparalleled in England, though of course you had realised that already.

Obviously, it is a linear farm. The house itself is two storeys high with quite irregular windows and a roof of lovely old Honister slates, quarried just a mile or two away in the heart of the hills – you could call them green if you wanted, but that would be to ignore the way the moss and lichen have added splashes of grey and yellow to them. The house walls are limewashed, though attached to one side of it is a barn (or a byre, I don't really mind which because I'm very open-minded about my fantasies) which hasn't been painted and its walls are the natural grey-green of Lake District slate. The two look so lovely together, the white of the house, the natural stonework of the barn.

I've got a porch, of course, which protects my lovely old iron-studded door of ancient oak planks, and the door opens into my favourite room in the house, the only one about which I really have strong feelings because it is, in fact, just the way it should be (or juste le job as they say in France), just the way Lake District farmhouse rooms have been for centuries.

My favourite room is the main room of the house and it's quite big – about 20 feet by 30 feet and it's called 'the Firehouse'. In other parts of the north it might have a different name. Sometimes it's called merely 'the house' or sometimes 'the house place', in the North York Moors it's called 'the forehouse', in parts of the West Riding 'the house-body' but here in the Lake District it has always been called the firehouse because originally it was the only room in the building to have had a fire – of course even my fantasies require a certain degree of comfort so over the centuries changes have been made and the place is awash with extra fireplaces now – but originally the firehouse had the only one. It's a nice one though. It's what you might call an inglenook in other parts of the country but it's just the fireplace up here. It's big enough to sit in – about ten feet wide and perhaps six feet deep and above it is a big square chimney hood for the smoke to go up. To one side is a little window, the 'fire window' which gives a bit of light as I sit there. On the other side there's a very simple but very lovely old oak screen which I, in my knowledgeable little Lake District way call '*the heck*'. It has a high-backed settle leaning against it and the heck's there to protect me from the draughts which might come from the door which leads off to the back of the house.

My fireplace, my cosy fantasy fireplace, used to be just a few stone slabs on the floor big enough to hold a fire of peat cut from the hills above the house, and stored in a little '*peat house*' built low into the hillside behind the house, but at some time in the 18th century one of my predecessors fitted a proper little hearth and fire surround into the chimney so that I could burn coal and wood, which is what I am doing now ... in my dreams.

All of this is nice, of course, but it is as nought by comparison to what greets my mind's eye when I turn around, because the rest of my fantasy firehouse is a beautiful room, far more beautiful than most people would expect if they looked at my house from outside. From outside they would expect rustic simplicity, which my house has of course, but it has more as well. It has oak! Loads and loads of oak. It has a ceiling of huge rough oak beams. The lower parts of the side walls are oak-panelled and the staircase on the back wall is oak too with nicely turned balusters. But the pièce de resistance (or the piece of resistance as we say in England) is the far wall which is of simple oak panelling with an oak door at each end and between them, reaching from floor to ceiling, is a richly polished oak cupboard of absolutely stunning elaboration.

I'm very particular about this part of my fantasy. Some people would be satisfied just to have any old nice Lake District oak cupboard but I accept no substitutes and demand a perfect Lake District cupboard of the finest type and period with all of the proper decoration. So mine is carved with the date 1684 and every bit of it is a riot of intricate decoration. I've seen others where the decoration is made up of geometric shapes or sometimes there are flower patterns but mine is of another type, more unusual anywhere else in the country but typical of the central Lake District farmhouses. It has carved interlaced patterns and scrolls along all of the edges except where it's carved with the date and the initials of its original owners. The cupboard doors also have interlaced patterns which end in stylised heads like dragons' heads ...

The Viking Legacy

Wherever in the country you look at 17th-century furniture you will find it enriched with carved decoration but some of the patterns used in these built-in Lake District cupboards, and especially the sort of interlace and scrolly patterns I have been describing, aren't found anywhere else – not in the 17th century anyway. On the other hand they are found hundreds of years earlier on the carved crosses and gravestones put up by the Vikings which can still be seen in churches and churchyards all over and all around the Lakeland fells. Viking art itself was influenced by the Anglo-Saxon and the Celtic art that preceded it. All three of these races used the same sort of intricate patterns which are found on the farmhouse cupboards. I'm not the first to suggest this, other people have wondered about the connection, but it is difficult to look at the cupboards without wondering whether they were part of a tradition which went back hundreds of years. It wouldn't be so surprising if that were the case because there are loads of other ways in which the Lake District and its farms have been influenced by the Vikings.

Sheep for example. Lake District farmers breed 'Herdwick' sheep. I was once attacked by some Herdwick sheep and ran away from them in a craven manner so I have the healthiest regard for them. I also think they're really beautiful (and any unsuitable mirth about my Cumbrian tastes will be met with a fierce and disdainful stare). They are lean and mean and their wool is unusually grey. It is also – and you'll be impressed by this – *heterotypical* which means that it changes from season to season. It's coarse in summer and fine in the winter which makes it denser and more protective when the weather is colder. This is a feature which is very rare among sheep and is only shared by a number of breeds found in Scandinavia such as the Goth sheep (the ones with black lipstick on).

So that's one Viking connection with the more recent landscape. Another is the language of the fells. I've already talked about saeters and ergs but *fells*, for example, that's a Viking word and *beck* and *thwaite* and *dale* and *how* and *bracken* and *force* and *tarn*. You look at a map of the Lake District in the most casual way and Viking words leap out and hit you. Literally. But at a level below the place names the Viking language remains, especially when applied to activities that have gone on for a long time – like farming activities. The old sheep counting numbers for Lake District shepherds (*yan, tan, tetheran, metheran* etc) are well known. I couldn't personally guarantee that I've ever heard them used, though I do remember climbing on St Sunday Crag near Ullswater when I was young and hearing a shepherd calling his dogs in a language I didn't understand. He may, of course, have merely been swearing at them and I, well-bred and nicely brought up as I was, failed to recognise the words, but I don't think so and he would certainly have used a load of other Viking words in his conversation about them. He would have talked about *hoggs* – he would probably have had a building on the farm called a *hogg house* which had nothing to do with pigs but referred to the Viking word for a lamb. New-born lambs are always weaned on their own particular piece of fellside. It's called being *heafed* and it's done because sheep are territorial and they'll always return to their own *heaf* when they're threatened so it's easier to keep control of them.

So there's plenty of evidence that Viking influences continued to have an effect in the Lakes for hundreds of years and I don't think it's too unlikely that their artistic style continued to be remembered as well. It's certainly true that the carved cupboards that are still found in dozens and dozens of farmhouses in the area have a raw power which makes you think of a long-standing and traditional folk art.

Lake District farms – the great re-building

The vast majority of the farms in the area (including my fantasy one) were built between about 1630 and 1750 by a population of yeoman farmers who are often called 'statesmen'. It is possible that the Vikings introduced the long-houses that existed before the present farms were built, but no one really knows.

What we do know is this. After the Norman conquest, all of the land in the upland areas of the north was granted to great Norman Baronies. The big Norman barons themselves didn't want to live in the wild recesses of the hills, so they allowed some of the deep valleys to be colonised by farmers, and over the centuries the farmers won privileges which were at least partly based on the fact that they were farming land that nobody else wanted. They were able to hold onto their property in ways which made them almost as secure as freeholders. They could sell land sometimes and when they died they could leave land to their next of kin, both of which are really rare privileges for tenant farmers. Of course you don't get privileges like that for nothing. They had to pay rents and provide labour to the landlord and cut peat for him – stuff like that – but up here in the northern hills they also had to promise to turn out to fight the Scots if the need arose – which it often did, so over the years they really earned their extra freedoms.

Eventually of course, we who have read this book know that the need to fight the Scots faded away. After 1603, when the two countries were united, the threat of war gradually disappeared and you might have expected the old privileges to fade as well but they didn't. They'd lasted so long and the farmers held onto them with such tenacity that as the 17th century progressed the Lake District farmers became a most unusually independent bunch – virtually owning their own farms, passing them down through the generations and having enough confidence in the future to build themselves sturdy farmhouses and decorate them in the way I've described, enough pride to carve their names on the furniture and enough energy to transform the harsh Lake District landscape into the wonderful blend of wildness and human history that it has become.

The great re-building further south

Almost all over the country there was a process of rebuilding old farmhouses. It happened in different parts of the country at different times. In Kent, for example, safe from war and nicely rich, farmers started to rebuild their ancient farmhouses way back in the 15th century, from about 1450, so that county is filled with a wealth of late medieval timber-framed farmhouses. Up north the process started later because of the old Border syndrome, but by the end of the 1500s as the Border effect began to lessen, in the more southerly parts of our region, farmhouses along the edges of the Pennines in Yorkshire and Lancashire were being rebuilt and by the early 1600s they were appearing in large numbers. Most of them were built for yeoman farmers – yeoman farmers who, because of the marginal nature of the land they were trying to farm, improved their incomes by becoming clothmakers as well – improved their incomes very substantially I may add if their houses are anything to go by.

They're fab. Let me say that straight away. I don't lust after them personally in the way that I do after my Lake District fantasy but that's merely because of the accident of my Cumbrian birth. Like the Cumbrian farmhouses, they are always built of stone but they don't get whitewashed. Instead they're left in their bare millstone grit which blackens in the weather and gives them a dark and forbidding look. Their roofs are covered with sandstone flags so solid and heavy that they look like real rock. They tend to be built on hillsides too, often nestled into the edge of the hill and with their low walls and shallow-pitched roofs they can almost seem to be part of the natural landscape, as a better writer than me once put it ...

'... the architect had the foresight to build it strong, the narrow windows are deeply set in the wall, and the corners defended with large jutting stones.'

That was Emily Brontë talking about Wuthering Heights and she goes on to describe a room not unlike my fantasy firehouse in the Lake District: 'One step brought me into the family sitting room, without any introductory lobby or passage: they call it here "the house"' ... She mentions the 'huge fireplace' and then says: 'One end, indeed reflected splendidly both light and heat from ranks of immense pewter dishes, interspersed with silver jugs and tankards, towering row after row, in a vast oak dresser to the very roof.'

I couldn't have put it better myself. No, actually that's true, I couldn't have put it better myself. Architecturally (I have to admit) the Pennine farmhouses themselves are more impressive than my Lake District beauties. They have posher porches and the windows to the housebody (the firehouse) are often tremendously impressive, divided up with rows and rows of stone mullions and transoms. At each end they often have projecting wings with even more mullioned and transomed windows, so that the front of the house, including the porch, makes an E-shape. To a far northerner, used to something a little less fancy, they look more like the houses of minor gentry than yeoman farmers and I suppose that that's how some of them started off. But in the main they are posher because of the wealth of the farmer/clothiers who built them and the long period of stability they experienced.

Unlike the Lake District farms, the Pennine farms don't usually have farm buildings attached to one side. They do sometimes of course but more typically they have a separate farm building, usually a barn or cowhouse, or both combined. The oldest of these barns are *aisled* – that means they've got a main room with an open timber roof, but separated off at one side by a line of timber posts is an aisle, just like in a church. Often the aisle was divided up into stalls for cows while the main part of the barn would be used for storage and for threshing. I've only been in a couple of unaltered examples of these barns but they were both fantastic structures. You see pictures in architectural guide books of the great aisled barns and tithe barns of southern England – Great Coxwell in Essex is the example that everyone talks about. It's amazing. Medieval, with beautiful wood-work and a steeply-pitched and soaring timber roof – but the Pennine barns are nothing like that. Their woodwork is much thicker and coarser and their stone roofs are much more massive and lower-pitched so the interiors are less uplifting but heavy, primitive and extremely impressive – in their own northern way.

Crucks

I said before, at the beginning of this chapter, that there wasn't one single northern style of farmhouse, that each separate bit of it has produced its own special style. East of the Pennines, in the North York Moors another sort of farmhouse was being built during the great farm rebuilding of the 17th century. The Royal Commision on Historic Monuments has recorded at least 220 farmhouses with *cruck* construction.

Ah! Another of those 'what do I tell?' moments. Hmm ... A cruck, well, a pair of crucks is a pair of big curved oak beams – two halves of a big curved tree trunk in fact, split in two and then leaned against each other so that they form a shape like an upturned boat. The two crucks then get joined to each other at the top by cunning carpentry, and strengthened just above the middle with a cross beam called a *tie beam*. This makes them look like a big capital A, and then several of these pairs of crucks are placed in a row, joined together by a wooden ridge beam along the top of them. What you have then is like a big wooden tent frame with no cover and that forms the basic structure of the house. The crucks hold the roof up which means technically that the outside walls of the house have no work to do so they could be made of anything – mud, wattle and daub, whatever, though in the North York Moors all of the outside walls are made of stone.

I filmed in one of these houses recently, a beautiful cottage called Delves Cottage at Egton in the utterly glorious middle of the Moors. It has a thatched roof which makes it look picturesque but from outside there aren't many signs that it is old. It does have a little fire window which suggests that there might be an inglenook type fireplace lurking inside but the stone walls give nothing away about how it's constructed. Inside however … a different story. Three pairs of beautifully cut crucks rise right from the ground and sweep up to the apex of the roof. In the main room there's a fireplace like my fantasy fireplace except that this one has, to one side of it, a curiously carved wooden post called a witch post, designed, they do say around these'ere parts, to keep they witches away. There are only 20 known witch posts in the country – 19 in north Yorkshire and one in Lancashire. I felt really tickled pink to see one of them in the flesh, or at least in the wood.

Cruck-built houses feel really ancient, but in actual fact they aren't. Like the Lake District and Pennine farmhouses they're another of the different styles that emerged at the great farm rebuilding. They were built in the 17th century and even as late as the 18th century. It is unexpected to find them in the North York Moors though, because crucks are really rare on the eastern side of the country and there are none at all south of here. Further north though there are plenty of them.

I have a favourite example near Bardon Mill in the Tyne Valley. It's a barn at a farm called High Meadows. It's quite long and low and it has a steeply-pitched roof thatched with heather. Heather thatch used to be common in the North East but High Meadows is one of only five buildings I can think of that still has it and this extraordinarily rare and exceedingly shaggy survival suggests a wild antiquity. Inside the wildness is even more evident. It turns out to be a cruck barn, but these crucks are not any old crucks … oh no, no, no!

111

When I was at school I had a woodwork teacher who once threw my carefully made dovetail joint through an open window and said, 'There it is, Grundy, if you think it's worth looking for go and find it.' He wasn't a nice man. Well, the crucks in this barn are about my sort of standard of carpentry. Rough, primitive, not a joint in sight. The rafters are just untrimmed branches, wiggling all over the place and the heather thatch is laid straight on top of them; it's all tremendously primitive and yet this barn's neatly made stone walls reveal that it can't have been built any earlier than the middle of the 18th century.

Clay Daubins

Further west, around Carlisle on the Solway Plain, lots of the cruck buildings have an extra layer of interest that people don't usually associate with the north. Mud walls. Clay walls, I should say really. On the Solway Plain stone is scarce but clay isn't, and it seems likely that people built clay houses and farm buildings since time immemorial. The Cumbrian name for them was 'clay daubins'. They were built, it seems, by community effort and in the course of one day. When the site for a new house had been selected, the neighbours were invited to come and build it with a promise of revelry to follow. Everybody was given a job. Some dug the clay. Robert Anderson, a Carlisle dialect poet of the early 19th century said that it was the job of 'the rustic girls (a good many of whom attend on this occasion)' to fetch the water from neighbouring ditches. Others mixed the clay and water together, some rolled it into sausage shapes and laid it on the rising walls, some smoothed out the walls. And then, when it was all done, Anderson says

> *'The waws were aw finished ere darknin'*
> *Now grypes, showls and barrows thrown by'*

and the party began in earnest, 'the company have plenty to eat and drink; after which the lads and lasses, with faces incrusted with clay and dirt, take a dance upon the clay floor of the newly erected cottage'

'... ... *a rare caper we had*
Wi' eating and drinking and dancing
And roaring and singing like mad'

You would think, wouldn't you, that clay houses would wash away in the rain that is so prevalent on the west coast of England. But they don't. The clay was protected from horizontal rain (of which there is lots) by a layer of limewash, and from vertical rain (of which there is more) by the deeply overhanging eaves of thatch. You do see some eroded clay walls, particularly of old farm buildings, but many of these earth walls must be approaching 250 years old now and still going strong. Will we be able to say the same for the little brick houses we build today? he asked, controversially.

The Northumberland super-farms

Cast your mind back a few pages to the stalwart and independent yeoman farmers of the Lake District. Imagine one of them in about the year 1650. Let's call him Will Atkinson for no reason other than it's a good local name. For the past 150 years, his family has virtually owned the farm on which he lives. He pays rent, but not too much, to a distant landowner who doesn't bother him often and it's more than 50 years since any member of his family had to go to war in the service of his lord. Is it any wonder he has the confidence to build himself a fine new farmhouse and fill it with polished oak furniture?

Now, leap sideways into Northumberland about the same year and you find a very different picture. For much of the 17th century parts of Northumberland were still very dangerous and insecure. The wife of one of the Ridley family from Willimoteswick in the Tyne Valley successfully sued for divorce in the 1650s because she felt threatened by the number of armed men in her husband's house and there were still the occasional border raids as late as 1685. It took Northumberland far, far longer than any other part of the north to settle down and start to build the new farmhouses that had already appeared everywhere else in the country. In the Pennines, if you remember, they began to rebuild farms in the late 1500s, in the Lake District and the North York Moors it was the mid-1600s but in large parts of Northumberland a farmhouse older than 1750 is a real rarity. That's how long it took. Before about 1750 the vast majority of ordinary people in the countryside were still living in buildings which were far too mean to have survived down to the present day. In Northumberland the great farm rebuilding took place from about 1750 to 1850 and when it finally happened it produced buildings and landscapes which are very different from any of the others in the region.

In the 1980s I worked for the Historic Buildings and Monuments Commission. My job was to help choose the Listed Buildings in Northumberland. Those nice people from London paid me to set off into the countryside in my little car each morning and visit every single building, every single man-made structure in a given area in order to decide whether it was interesting enough to become a listed building. It was hell, I tell you, hell.

Obviously I already knew a fair amount about the old buildings of the county – they wouldn't have given me the job if I hadn't – and I had looked at the landscape in a generally appreciative way, but I have to admit I had never really looked at its vernacular buildings properly, or the effect that farming had had on the landscape. When I did, it came as a bit of a shock.

I remember my very first morning on the job. I drove north from Newcastle towards the parish where I was going to start my detailed survey. It was a beautiful May morning but I'm a little embarassed to have to reveal that I was less interested in the weather than in the fact that for the first time in my life I was receiving a car mileage allowance and as I drove north, I gleefully totted up my winnings mile by mile ... 36p ... .72p ... 108p ... 141p (I was never great at maths).

Eventually, 48 miles and £17 and 28p later, I arrived at the first village I had selected to look at – or what I thought was a village – two or three miles north-east of Wooler. Imagine my surprise when I discovered that it wasn't a village at all. It looked villagy shaped on my map, nestled around the junction of three roads and there seemed to be indications of sufficient buildings to justify the description of village, but when I got there I discovered that it was just two farms side by side ...

... but what farms! Big farms. Along one side of the road there was a long row of single-storey farm-workers' cottages – I've forgotten how many now but lots of them – maybe nine or ten separate cottages attached to each farm. On the other side of the road were the farm-houses, big enough and posh enough to be manor houses. On that first morning they really scared me. They looked far too posh for me to ring the bell. And behind those – vast farm buildings, I mean really vast. There were great long buildings with rows of arches along the front; equally long buildings without arches. There were tall chimneys like factory chimneys. There were buildings on buildings on buildings. I must have driven past hundreds of others like them but I realised that I hadn't a clue what any of them were for or why they were so big.

I had to learn. Northumberland is full of big farms. They call them 'farm steadings' up here and to a considerable extent they really do take the place of villages. They are planned farm buildings, products of the Agricultural Revolution.

Usually they're arranged with all of the farm buildings forming a regular shape – sometimes they form a U-shape, sometimes it's more like an E, sometimes they form four ranges round a big courtyard in the middle. Every one of the buildings and every bit of the space in the group has its own specialist purpose. I'll give you a list of all the specialist buildings you can expect to find on a planned Northumberland farm:

- **Fold Yards**. In the middle there will be walled enclosures for cows to wallow around in their own doo dah. Some of the even more advanced farms of the middle 19th century have these fold yards covered over with roofs.
- **Hemels** – or shelter sheds for cows. These are usually along the back of the farmyard and on the ground floor they are open-fronted with rows of arches. On the first floor above them there are granaries and often in a particularly cunning wheeze there are holes in the floor of the granaries so that food can be dropped straight down into the cows' feeding stalls (cunning or what!)
- **Byres**. Down one side of the fold yards a row of byres, one of them will be specifically for calves. You'll be able to tell they are byres because there will be doors but no windows – only ventilation slits. The amazing thing ... it's a thing I've never understood ... is that cows were always kept in the dark.

- **Stables**. Down the other side of the fold yard, a row of stables. Apparently horses need light so the stables have windows – I think I'd rather be a horse than a cow if I had to choose, which I don't suppose I ever will.
- **Cart shed**. This too will have rows of arches so that loaded carts can be conveniently backed into it.
- **Blacksmith's shop**. These farms were so big they needed their own blacksmith.
- **Tack room** and workshop.
- **Pigsties** ... or poultiggeries. The pigs each have a little individual yard in front of their sty and often there's a hen house upstairs so that the hens are kept warm (and perhaps a little safer from the fox) by the pigs downstairs.
- **Dovecote** or pigeon house.
- **Netties**
- **Bull house**. This is often at the back, a long way from the cows, poor bu ... beast.
- **Threshing barn** and threshing machine. This is also at the back, behind the hemels and granaries so the threshed corn can be immediately stored in the granary. If there's a big tall factory chimney beside it, it means that the threshing machine was driven by a steam engine. If there's a water wheel it means that it w ... well that's obvious. If there's a low circular building with a conical roof, it's called a **gingang** and it was a horse engine shed. In it a horse or pair of horses were attached to a yoke and walked endlessly round and round driving the thresher. An interesting job. I have heard it suggested that it was not unlike being a teacher nowadays – that same sense of going round in circles – only teachers aren't allowed to thrash things any more.
- **Turnip house**.

The sort of farming I'm describing here needed massive outlay of cash, lerds of dosh, and that was only available because land in Northumberland, unlike the Lakes and most of Yorkshire, was still absolutely in the control of the big powerful families.

A small note on the importance of turnips

A farmer in North Northumberland told me that he had heard about a turnip that was grown on a farm near Bamburgh which weighed 60 lbs! 60 lbs of nosh grown on one square yard of ground! Can you imagine that ... a fantastically efficient way of turning ground into goodies. Farmers in Britain began to discover in the 17th and 18th centuries that turnips were a brilliant way of providing winter feed for animals. In Northumberland a farmer called John Proctor was growing turnips at Rock near Bamburgh in 1727 and he was one of a whole heap of adventurous farmers who made enormous changes to agriculture in the course of the 18th century.

Probably the best known in our area were two brothers called George and Matthew Culley who were born near Darlington in 1735. They farmed near their home first of all and then, in 1767, they moved to Fenton farm which is near Wooler in Northumberland, in an area of flat and very fertile farmland called Glendale. There they began to revolutionise Northumbrian agriculture. One of their neighbours was an equally adventurous farmer called John Bailey and there were others all around and together they experimented with turnips, with field drains to improve the land, with new forms of irrigation. They worked on improving the breeding of animals – shorthorn cows for example – and especially sheep. Their new cross-bred sheep, the Border Leicester, revolutionised sheep farming in the north. Apparently it was very fatty meat ... but cheap and therefore very desirable. All of these changes were important, of course, but from my narrow-minded little architectural point of view the most important thing they did was to develop the new farm buildings I have been describing.

What had happened was this. Because the Border wars were so much worse in Northumberland, ordinary farmers were much, much poorer and fewer and further between as well. The rich, on the other hand were super powerful up here because for hundreds of years they had been desperately needed by the government to control the Border – so when the wars ended, more than anywhere else in the country, the rich found it easy to hold onto the land and it paid them to introduce the most up-to-date agriculture possible. John Bailey was land agent to the Earl of Tankerville at Chillingham Castle and the Culleys were their tenants as well so that estate played a big part in the revolution. The Percy family in Alnwick Castle did too, and especially the 2nd Duke of Northumberland who gets loads of praise from contemporary writers for making improvements – for building whazzo farms and introducing long-term tenancies so that farmers had a chance to commit themselves to their land, and not least for building new and improved cottages for farm labourers – usually with a third to half an acre of land attached as a garden (and the right to be given a pig a year for friendship and added bacon).

Lots of other estates followed suit and the result is that Northumberland has far fewer old farm buildings than other counties in the north, but what there is instead is often superb. There are the splendid farm buildings of course but there are also thousands of solidly built estate cottages from the first half of the 19th century. They're almost always built of stone with slate roofs, plain, but pretty with it, if that isn't too silly a thing to say. The farmhouses themselves are terrific. They tend to be four-square and totally undecorated. They have none of the blissful beauties or quaint picturequeness to be found among farmhouses elsewhere, but they have beautiful proportions, beautiful simplicity and they are, almost to a man, built of beautiful stone.

The Seaside

Part One: all the fun of the fair ...

Oh! I do love to be beside the seaside. I do love to be bes ... I really do, you know. I love the buildings by the seaside, the funfairs and the boarding houses, the beach huts and the ice cream stalls – all of the delicious froth of seaside architecture that makes up resorts like Blackpool and Scarborough, Whitley Bay and Bridlington.

But then I love the peace as well; the beautiful, tranquil and unspoilt beaches of Northumberland, the salt marshes of the Solway Firth, the vast skies and empty sands of Morecambe Bay. But, to be honest, I sometimes wonder why I do love it so much because it isn't all that comfortable, especially up here in the north. The water's cold, the sand gets in your er ... erm ... er ... your Marmite sandwiches. The moment you arrive to have a picnic it's just about to start raining, the fog's rolled in or there's a brisk and biting breeze.

I took a party of visiting German students for a walk along the Northumberland shore to Dunstanburgh one June day and, by the time we arrived, there was snow hitting them horizontally. It wasn't even falling on their heads; it was hitting them horizontally, driven by a fierce easterly gale. Did I mention that this was June? I wondered why on earth we'd come but for some bizarre reason my overseas visitors loved it. Why? Why do any of us brave such elements to visit the northern coast? When did people start coming to the northern seaside and have people always liked it?

Well, there is evidence that people have been coming pretty well as long as there have been northerners. Recently (2003) the remains of the country's oldest known house – built 10,000 years ago – has been discovered on the Northumbrian coast at Howick. In the Stone Age, hunter-gatherers are known to have had settlements along the Cumbrian coast at places like Eskmeals and Drigg and later, in the Iron Age, there were fortresses – certainly on the rock that now houses Bamburgh Castle and probably on most of the other great headland outcrops as well. The Romans came too and built signal stations at places like Scarborough and forts – Ravenglass, for example. All of these people lived by the seaside, had to be there, but the first people I want to talk about in our area who actually made a decision to go to the seaside, out of choice, were the monks who founded the monastery on Lindisfarne in 635.

A Saxon dip

The most famous of the Lindisfarne monks was Cuthbert and there's a story about him, written by the Venerable Bede, which is very revealing about what the coast meant to our ancestors. Apparently Cuthbert used to sneak off in the middle of the night and the other monks, puzzled as to what he was doing, followed him. They found that he was immersing himself in the North Sea all night up to his neck! What he was doing, of course, was mortifying his flesh, making sure that he had no naughty thoughts, keeping himself pure. Now even today most of us know that there are few things better at morti-fying the flesh than a dip in the North Sea. Bits of me, I have to admit, have been so well mortified in the North Sea as to be rendered almost useless, so you can see that Cuthbert wasn't exactly going to the seaside for fun.

Cuthbert spent a number of years as a hermit on the Farne Islands off the Northumberland coast. This is what the Venerable Bede says about the Farnes:

'No-one before the Lord's servant Cuthbert had been able to live alone on this island without trouble because it was haunted by evil spirits; but when the soldier of Christ entered there, armed with the helmet of salvation ... the wicked foe himself ... was driven far away.'

So, the implication is clear. Monks like Cuthbert didn't come to the seaside because it was nice but to pit themselves against it – to fight against the devil who lived there and to prove themselves as holy as possible.

And yet ... and yet ... .

Bede finishes the story about Cuthbert's sea bathing exploits by telling how when the well-mortified flesh emerged from the water the following morning two sea otters rose out of the sea and rubbed him with their fur and warmed him with their breath before disappearing back beneath the waves. Another writer of the same period, a monk called Eddius, wrote about Cuthbert's relationships with eider ducks which are still common on the Farnes and which today are still called Cuddy's Ducks in his honour. Apparently they 'were so tame that they would allow themselves to be stroked and petted, would come running when he called and would build their nests under his bed'.

Stories like these reveal that the Anglo-Saxon monks, whatever they thought about devils and the wild seashore, must also have been aware of its natural beauty. Apart from anything else they chose the most glorious and fantastic places as their homes. Holy Island, Beadnell, Newbiggin, the cliffs of Tynemouth, the Headland at Hartlepool and of course the even more dramatic headland at Whitby. There must have been bad days at such places, but there must have been wonderful ones as well.

When did the seaside become popular?

So the earliest visitors to the seaside were a bit hitty missy about the place. It seems that they feared it but liked it. How long was it then before anybody chose to go to the seaside for pleasure alone?

A long time.

I'll give you an example. In Chapter one I wrote about Sir John Vanbrugh and his two houses, Castle Howard and Seaton Delaval, which were built in the early 1700s. Castle Howard is inland, in the beautiful rolling country of the Vale of York and the house he built there was sited so as to take full advantage of the view. The countryside was obviously important in the planning.

Seaton Delaval, on the other hand, is close to the sea, half a mile from the sea, and yet it totally ignores the sea. The house faces north and south while the sea is off to the east. A projecting wing, high walls and a plantation prevent any view of the sea at all. As late as 1718 when this house was built no one was interested in the sea as a source of beauty or romance. They were beginning to be interested in nature and the countryside, but the sea was still too wild to attract anyone for pleasure.

Changing Attitudes – a tale of two towns

One: Scarborough

The situation was beginning to change though, and to be honest, the place where it first began to change, not just for us in the north, but for the whole country, was Scarborough.

In 1626 a woman called Mrs Farrow noticed a mineral spring on the beach at Scarborough. Mineral springs (spas) were just beginning to get fashionable so she advertised it and pretty soon 'people of good quality' were coming to Scarborough to 'take the waters'.

A few years later a chap called Dr Wittie from Hull bought the spa and he had this really good witty wheeze. He realised that the sea was right beside his spa and that sea water and spa water have a number of things in common ... they're both wet, unbelievably cold and they both taste repulsive, so he started to advertise the sea as well as his spa.

Smart stools

Now, there's two things you can do with sea water. First of all, you can drink it, though it does taste repulsive and it does make you go to the toilet. In fact this was sold as one of its virtues because it gave you a good cleaning out. One 18th-century quack said that 'A pint of sea water will commonly produce two or three smart stools,' which is something to look forward to, I'm sure we will all agree.

Georgian skinny-dipping

But the other thing you can do with sea water is bathe in it and Scarborough was quite possibly the first place in the country where organised sea bathing went on. Dr Wittie advertised this too and by the end of the 1600s bathing was happening on a pretty large scale. The interesting thing was that for the first 100 years or so, through the 18th century, it seems to have gone on in the nude.

When I was telling this story once on TV, in the interests of verisimilitude, I stripped off my clothes on Scarborough Beach and ran into the sea wearing nothing but a flesh-coloured and deeply uncomfortable thong. I still see clearly in my mind's eye the looks of startled pity in the faces of children as I ran past them.

There's a picture, by an artist called Settingham, painted at Scarborough in 1735 and there do seem to be naked people on the beach and in the sea. I've also seen a print by the artist Thomas Rowlandson which shows gaggles of lascivious old men on a cliff, I think it's in Worthing, peering at the naked beauties through their telescopes.

I'm only telling you this stuff about nudiness to stir your imaginations, the real point I want to get across is that, by the first half of the 18th century, the seaside was becoming fashionable as a 'place of resort' for the gentle classes. There's nowhere better to see the sort of place they liked to come to than South Bay in Scarborough, on the cliff above the site where Mrs Farrow found her spa.

Regency elegance ...

The first great building period in Scarborough was the early 1800s and the south end of the town now is still filled with elegant terraces of Regency houses, light-heartedly decorated with painted stucco walls, ornate ironwork and the delicate rhythm of repeated bay windows where visitors could sit and watch polite society strolling by. Because that was the idea – for posh people to go to the seaside and indulge in genteel holidays with other posh people.

Most of the early visitors stayed in these terraced houses but gradually there grew up a new breed of accommodation – the resort or holiday hotel. The first resort hotel seems to have been built in Weymouth in the 1770s but Scarborough has one of the earliest in the country. It's the Crown Hotel and it was built in the early 1800s. These were the first hotels in the country which were built to provide fun rather than as a stopover on a journey. The Crown Hotel is on a street called the Esplanade which I think is one of the most beautiful streets in the north. It rises in a gentle curve along the top of the South Cliff. There are only houses on the landward side of the road and they form an informal terrace of big Regency-style houses, painted in lively colours. The other side of the street is open. There are gardens and there's the sea and a glorious view of the cliffs striding away along the Yorkshire coast.

Victorian inelegance

Stand facing the sea and glance off to the left, however, and an extraordinary object hits you in the eye. It too is a resort hotel, a resort hotel of a different generation; it's called the Grand Hotel and if you translate the word 'grand' as huge then it's well named. It rises from the sea shore and climbs up the side of the cliff and then just keeps going until it towers above the rest of the town. On the seaward side there are 13 storeys, on the other side a few less but still loads. Its roof is amazing. It has sort of giant upturned eggcups on the roof and the whole thing is built of yellow brick with bands of bright red terracotta decoration.

Does it sound revolting?

It isn't! It is amazing. It stands right in the middle of Scarborough. To the south of it is the exquisite Regency resort I've been describing to you, to the north the medieval town complete with castle and parish church and in the middle this remarkable pepper pot. It ought to be awful. It wouldn't stand a chance of getting planning permission these days and yet it is a great building by a remarkably talented northern architect called Cuthbert Broderick (from Leeds) who has managed, somehow, to make his vast hotel the centre of the town, the hub of the wheel.

He built it in 1863 and it has huge public rooms and a vast staircase rising to about 4,000,000 bedrooms which were needed because, by the time it was built, seaside tourism had been changed by the coming of the railways. By mid-Victorian times millions of people were pouring to the seaside – and not just the posh who had started the trend but the lower middle classes as well and even … and I don't like to mention this to my gentle readers … even the working classes. Shocking.

Class was a problem. It was a problem for hotels like the Grand because if you built something this posh you wanted, on the whole, a nice class of people to fill it with – you certainly wanted people with enough money to pay for its very expensive upkeep, but in an age of mass tourism such people weren't all that easy to find. Surrounded by … working-class people … the posh tended to dicky off to the continent leaving places like the Grand high and dry. One of the solutions to that problem, one of the ways that so many hotels keep going, was first advertised in 1881 – the weekend break.

So Scarborough started posh and then had to find ways of coping with the influx of working-class holiday makers. That's its glory nowadays. At Scarborough you can stroll like Beau Brummel among the Regency terraces, you can sweep like Lord and Lady Brass down the great staircase of the Grand, or you can eat fish and chips and whelks, you can wallow in the tawdry tutti frutti land down along the shore. Or you can still do none of those things and instead walk along the beautiful beach, under the beautiful cliffs and feel the wind in your face. To my mind it's got everything an English seaside resort should have.

So where does that leave its neighbour on the opposite coast? Where does it leave …

Two: Blackpool

Blackpool's a golden memory to me. I've only stayed there once, on a schools' rugby tour when I was a boy. It was the week after Easter and the amusement arcades and the entertainment centres were still open but the crowds had gone home. We wandered through the empty but noisy fairs, took up all of the seats at bingo stalls so that one of us was bound to win (guess who didn't), we travelled on the Big Dipper (guess who was sick and has never been on one since), we found a coffee bar with Bruce Chanell's 'Hey Babe' on the Juke Box and played it endlessly (guess who loves it still), and we walked along the Golden Mile at night, along the whole tawdry glitter of it and ate chips and ice creams and toffee apples (just guess). We loved it in fact. And we beat Lancashire 8-3.

Blackpool's quite different from Scarborough. Its history's quite different. In the middle of the 19th century it was still a village with about 3 point 4 people in it. And a donkey. It just happened to be a village parked beside seven miles of pristine sand a few miles from the densely packed and rich towns of the Lancashire cotton industry. Those sands were clearly going to be a draw, and they soon were. The railway arrived in 1845. The first pier was built in 1863 (£11,500, 1410 feet long, admission 1d). The Winter Garden was added in 1875 and the rest, as they say, is history. The town's website claims that seven million people still visit the town each year which, if it's true, means that all of them had decided to turn up together on the one day I went last summer. I know nothing about economics and anyone reading this book will be struck by a suspicion that I sometimes make statistics up, but I was surprised, after reading for so long about the demise of the English holiday resort, that I could barely move on the Golden Mile. It seethed as tawdrily, but also as excitingly, as ever it did when I went on my rugby tour in the 1960s.

There is a series of books that I use when I'm writing about architecture. It's called *The Buildings of England* by Nikolaus Pevsner. There's at least one volume on every county in England and as a set these volumes are my Bible. I've been using them incessantly while writing this book. I love them. I was actually involved in the re-writing of one of them. So imagine my distress when I turned to the volume that included Blackpool (North Lancashire) and discovered that the place barely gets a mention. The town's 12 churches are mentioned, the Town Hall, the Library and the Technical College and then there's less than half a page on all the rest of the entertainment buildings, on the Winter Gardens, the Tower, the Piers, the Golden Mile, the Trams. About the tower the book says this:

'1891 by Maxwell and Tuke. What a pity the base is wrapped up in a big brick building! Just imagine how beautiful are the ascending curves and arches of the Eiffel Tower of 1889, Blackpool's admitted model.'

What a mealy-mouthed description. This 'big brick building' contains the finest circus in Britain. Those 'ascending arches and curves' which Pevsner so bemoans are the corners of the splendid space which holds the circus, and the brick building also contains the Palace Ballroom which is quite possibly the most elaborately decorated room in the whole of Britain. It was designed in 1899 by the most famous of all Victorian and Edwardian theatre and entertainment-spot designers, Frank Matcham, and it is of a quite fabulous richness. It oozes brilliantly coloured and deeply moulded plasterwork from floor to ceiling. It's like being in some Viennese palace or fabulous central European opera house – except that this was built, not for the crowned heads of Europe but for Lancashire mill workers on their annual week's hols.

I've just been looking at my notes and I find that I thought the Grand Theatre which Matcham also designed (1891 this time) was even richer. Unbelievable. And I haven't mentioned the Empress Ballroom. Blackpool is, and has been since it was invented, an extraordinary place – a gigantic people's palace. You can't judge it really by normal standards. Especially not its architecture. To love it you've got to love the brashness as much as the plasterwork, the chip shops as much as the churches. You have to recognise that there's beauty too, beyond the slot machines. The trams or trolley buses are beautiful and so is the beach. The Big Dipper that removed my lunch has long gone and been replaced by objects called 'Valhalla' and (more embarrassingly) Pepsi Max Big One, which are infinitely more terrifying but in their modern way they are just as thrilling to look at as the Victorian Tower … marvels of modern amusement engineering.

… and if you're tired of all that you can always take time off to visit the Grundy Art Gallery which is very good I'm assured – though I haven't been there.

Any more seaside resorts?

Well, of course there are, there are dozens and dozens. Some have given up the attempt to stay traditional resorts altogether and have slipped back to being nice places by the seaside, others have become dormitory suburbs. Some of them are vibrant still, others have a slightly faded charm, and a few are utterly dire. But that's not just the north. That's 21st-century Britain as a whole.

Part Two: down to the sea in ships. The working shore.

Shielings again ... and fishermen

Just south of Berwick, among the sand dunes at Cheswick on the Northumbrian coast there's a little one-roomed cottage, quite picturesque with its white walls and red pantiled roof. The ground around it is littered with fishy things, nets and what not and though you can't see it, you can always hear the sea, 40 or 50 yards away beyond the dunes.

It's called Cheswick Shield, this cottage, which is interesting because a shield (as we've seen in Chapter five) is an old word that was used for a seasonal dwelling, usually a summer dwelling used by shepherds who accompanied their flocks up into the summer pastures. The Northumberland uplands are littered with 'shield' names but there must have been lots of coastal shields as well. Some survive just inland from Berwick, along the banks of the Tweed, and North Shields and South Shields, for example, though they have turned into major towns now, started their lives, in the 13th century, as groups of huts or shields, seasonal fishing camps.

But Cheswick Shield is still a proper fishing shield, possibly the last one on the coast to be used in the old way – as a seasonal shelter for fishermen attracted to the summer fishing. The fishing on the coast was for salmon and the nets were run out from the shore by teams of men wading out into the surf. I've never seen it done, though I have seen old photos, and the effect is incredibly dramatic and looks ancient and primitive and remarkably frightening.

I *have* seen fisherman – solitary fishermen this time – behaving in a similar way on the Solway Firth in Cumberland – striding out into the rushing tide in their long waders with their odd nets called haaf nets strung from a T-shaped wooden frame, standing there with the down stroke of the T stuck in the sand and the nets across the current to catch the running salmon. It's a process that must have gone on since Viking days and once again it looks very frightening to a pitiful little towny like myself.

Those in peril on the sea ...

It's easy to think of the seaside as a romantic place and the coast as a source of fun and frolics as I was doing in the first part of this chapter, but places like Cheswick Shield and fishermen like the Solway haaf-netters are a useful reminder that the sea has never just been a source of fun. One of my favourite hymns is that one about those in peril on the sea and long before people started coming down to the shore for pleasure, the seaside was a place to live, to work, and to die ...

Bamburgh is one of the best places to visit if you want to be introduced to the dangers of sea travel but also to the measures we have taken to improve the situation. Its churchyard is rich in reminders of the dangers, none more affecting in my opinion, than the monument to the Reverend John Morell Mackenzie, a professor of Biblical Criticism who died when the steamship *Pegasus* ran into the Goldstone Rock among the Farne Islands on the morning of 20th July 1843.

His gravestone is a striking object, a broken column which symbolises, presumably, the temporary nature of human concerns. The inscription on it starts off in the usual way by telling us what a lovely chap he was, and then it says:

'Amid circumstances of a peculiarly appalling character he offered a striking example of the power of that religion which he professed ...'

What happened was that as the survivors of the wreck huddled on the rocks and as the rescuers attempted to reach them but failed, driven back by the force of the storm, they could hear the Reverend Mackenzie leading his fellow travellers in prayer and hymn singing as the waves picked them off one by one.

Lovely, if tragic stuff, but right beside that grave there's another which is part of a better known story. It's in memory of another Scottish minister, the Reverend John Robb, who died five years earlier, in 1838, in the wreck of the *Forfarshire*. The *Forfarshire* was the wreck in which Grace Darling was involved.

An especially northern heroine

Grace Darling is buried in the churchyard and there is a monument to her, put up a number of years after her death. It's a very Victorian monument. She lies dead in a little stone four-poster bed – little but very elaborate, the canopy over the bed is richly Gothic. The situation is fantastic. The graveyard slopes upwards away from the church so she is looking down over the church (which is beautiful) and over to the castle (which is extraordinary) and beyond to the wild, wild sea and the Farne Islands which made her famous.

In a nutshell this is what happened. She was the lighthouse keeper's daughter in the Longstone light on the Farne Islands and she spotted the wreck from her bedroom (which still exists incidentally, empty but little altered with faded colour-washed walls). With her father she rowed to the rescue of the survivors – across a mile of rough seas in an open coble, 21 feet long and six feet wide. Her father with some of the rescued seamen repeated the trip until the survivors had all been rescued, but it was Grace's trip that caught the public imagination. She was only 23 and a local lass and that was an irresistible combination for popular heroism. In the Grace Darling Museum beside the church, alongside the famous rowing boat there are scores of contemporary bits of evidence of the media frenzy and the virtual cult that arose around her. The manager of the Adelphi Theatre in London, for example, offered her £10 a week to appear on his stage.

But she didn't. She died instead. Four years later, of TB. The cottage where she was born is right opposite the church and not marked, the one where she died is by the village green and is marked with a little copper plaque. The nice thing about her presence in Bamburgh now, is that everything is still there – the cottages still lived in, the tomb and monument visited but not commercialised, the museum, little, overstuffed and fascinating, the lighthouse still lighting and the seas still raging around the rocks that made her famous.

But that's not all …

Bamburgh Castle has already featured pretty large in this book so far, as a castle and in terms of medieval warfare, but in the annals of safety at sea, Bamburgh has another claim to fame. In the early 18th century, the castle was owned by a Bishop of Durham called Lord Crewe and when he died without any direct heirs, he left the castle and the estate to the care of a charitable trust called the Lord Crewe Trust. One of the trustees was a man called Dr John Sharp and he took the charitable nature of the bequest seriously and started a series of remarkable charitable activities. He started boys' and girls' schools. He opened a lending library which was free to neighbouring house-holders. There was a windmill built at the north end of the castle (it's still there) which provided corn for the poor at fair and intervention prices when there were shortages. These were all very impressive innovations but he also interested himself in the thorny question of safety at sea. The castle included a hostel for shipwrecked mariners and the trust devised a rescue system of flags and beacons for calling out rescuers to different parts of the coast. In the keep you can see the gigantic chains that were used to haul wrecked ships up on to the beach. In 1785 the Trust even commisioned a Londoner called Lionel Lukin to design what was probably the world's first purpose-built lifeboat, or would have been if it had been truly effective.

Which it wasn't, so to trace the next stage of the development of safety at sea you need instead to travel 40 miles south to the mouth of the River Tyne.

Safety on the Tyne

The mouth of the Tyne was always, in the past, an extraordinarily dangerous place. I've already quoted the letter from that monk, the one from St Albans who came north to build Tynemouth Priory, the one who wrote about the 'frequent shipwrecks' and the seabirds 'greedily feeding on the bodies of the drowned'. What made the mouth of the Tyne so dangerous was a series of shifting sands but especially a reef of rocks called the Black Middens which was always covered but lethal at high tide and for hundreds of years a readily available source of death.

One of the worst accidents occurred in 1789 when a ship called *The Adventurer* broke up on a sandbank called Herd Sands in broad daylight. People on the shore could see it happen and though they were able to watch people drown they were unable to do anything about it ... except build a lifeboat. Appalled by the tragedy, South Shields people set up The Tyne Lifeboat Society – the first in the world – and they announced a competition to design a lifeboat. It was won by the local parish clerk, William Wouldhave, who had no seafaring experience at all, and it was built (and improved a bit) by a local boatbuilder called Henry Greathead – the world's first purpose-built and practical lifeboat. An 1833 version of the same design which is said, on its own, to have saved 1000 lives, can be seen under a pretty iron canopy on Ocean Road in South Shields.

But if South Shields wins the prize for world-changing, seaside-safety innovation, North Shields wins it in the best-seaside-building-with-a-safety-connection category. On the headland, above the Black Midden Rocks is a brightly painted wooden building which is the HQ of The Tynemouth Volunteer Life Brigade, an organisation founded in 1864 in response to yet another distressing tragedy in the river below. In that year, on the 24th October, two ships struck the Black Middens and no one could do a thing about it. Watchers on the shore could hear the cries of the drowning but could do nothing to reach them so the town started this Life Brigade (yet another world's first, incidentally) and a few years later, in 1887, they built themselves a watch house.

It is glorious! Well, from the outside it's OK – appropriately seasidey and quite pretty, but inside it's *really* glorious. It remains a working watch house and the Brigade still exists and is still involved in sea safety, but the men who run it have turned out to be an interesting set of chaps. Messy, you might say. Hoarders. Over the years they've been involved in hundreds of rescues and anything they've used and anything they've found, they've kept and hung up in their watch house, stuck on the walls. Big-bosomed figureheads abound. I had to close my eyes. The decoration from the stern of the good ship *Bristol* (sic) made me blush prettily. There are ropes, ships' bells, clocks, photographs, breeches buoys. There is a collection of barrels which the crew of a sinking Russian ship lashed themselves to in an (unsuccessful) attempt to keep afloat. There's another barrel which the captain of a Dutch boat lashed his five-year-old daughter to before throwing her overboard. She survived, though he didn't and neither did her mother. It is a room of the deepest atmosphere and a perfect reminder of how fragile is our relationship with the sea.

From the window of the Brigade House you look down on the Tyne piers which are one of the wonders of the Victorian age. Before they were built, not only were the Black Midden Rocks even more dangerous than they remain today but there was a shallow bar across the mouth of the Tyne between North and South Shields. It was apparently shallow enough at low water for people to risk wading across but it was also shallow enough to keep ships stranded in the Tyne for weeks on end. And that mattered, cos the Tyne was a major port and certainly couldn't afford any slowing down of trade. So, in 1852 they made the decision to build piers. Designs were prepared by James Walker, the President of the Institution of Civil Engineers, and in 1854 the work started.

Now, I don't know about you, but even today piers seem to me to be almost impossible things to build. The sea is so nasty and cold and rough, the sea bed so unpredictable, the currents so dangerous that it doesn't surprise me one jot that it took 50 years before these particular piers were completed. They were nearly finished loads of times but the sea fought back and washed substantial chunks of them away; but the builders kept on going. Men kept on going down in diving bells (for a generous extra 2/6d a day). As the century progressed they moved from limestone to concrete for the core of the pier. And they kept on moving out – 2,900 feet for the north pier, a massive 5,400 feet for the south pier which has no headland to start from and which snakes out to sea in a series of elegant serpentine curves.

At the end of the north pier there's a beautifully built lighthouse with a perfectly preserved Victorian interior. I filmed there once and signed my name in the visitors' book which also recorded visits by kings and prime ministers, home secretaries and ministers for war who all came to these piers because they are, as I said, one of the marvels of the age.

Lighthouses (and Trinity House)

I've now mentioned two lighthouses that I have visited (Tyne North Pier and Longstone) which makes approximately ... nay exactly 50% of the ones I have visited in total – because I have also visited Souter Point Lighthouse at Marsden near South Shields, the first lighthouse in the world to be powered by alternating electric current, and I have climbed to the top of St Mary's Island Lighthouse in Whitley Bay which was built in the 1890s and required over 750,000 bricks to achieve its 126 feet height.

If you were paying attention to that last paragraph you will have noticed that I emphasised that I had *climbed to the top* of St Mary's, instead of merely mentioning visiting it. I put it like that because the climb involves using the entirely cantilevered spiral stair which hugs the inside walls of the hollow tower and allows you to gaze down into the terrifyingly empty centre. All 126 feet of it. I thought it was the most frightening staircase I had ever climbed (except the 12-ladder horror in the Goole Harbour Water Tower ... but I never made it to the top of that one. It was a moment of ignominious Grundy failure, so that doesn't count) so I was very proud of myself and thought it was worth the terror to see, close up, the glorious and romantic gleamy-gleamy light at the top just like the Famous Five always seemed to do.

There's only one major lighthouse (St Bees) on the North West coast but 13 on the North East coast which reflects (a) the volume of traffic using the East coast sea lanes and of course (b) the treacherous nature of the coast. They're all beautiful these lights – elegant and isolated, practical and strong. Most of them have no architectural pretensions, they gain their effect from the simplicity of their form, which is, of course, just the way it should be. Only one, the lighthouse on the west pier at Whitby, is posher. It was built in 1831 and it is in the form of a stone Greek Doric column, 71 feet high and accurately fluted; just the right degree of entasis (or swelling in the middle) to be a truly accurate Greek Doric column, and at the top a proper squashy Greek Doric capital with a plain square abacus on top of that, all just as it should be. The light sits prettily on top of the abacus and has a nice little lead roof.

The history of lighthouses is interesting. They've existed at least since Roman times and the Roman lighthouse at Dover is still standing and there could well have been lighthouses associated with Roman signal stations on our northern coasts at places like Scarborough and Bamburgh. There were a few built in medieval times, often by the church as an act of charity. Sometimes they would be beacons lit in church towers but by the end of the middle of the Middle Ages, though, most lighthouses were built as commercial concerns, by landowners who collected tolls from passing ships. I have to admit that I have a very hazy understanding of how they organised this. You'd think that unscrupulous captains would say they hadn't looked so it hadn't helped them (I never saw it, I'm not paying) or that they would just sail away, but apparently it could be a very profitable business. In fact when the last of the private lighthouses (on the Skerries protecting the approaches to Liverpool) was sold to Trinity House in 1841, it cost nearly £450,000.

Trinity House is responsible for all of the lights around the English coast nowadays. They've been totally responsible since 1836, but that is an arrangement that started to happen in the north of England, in Newcastle in fact, as long ago as 1536, when the Brotherhood of Trinity House was granted a charter to build lighthouses at North Shields.

Trinity House had started life as a medieval guild of sailors which was re-formed in 1514 and eventually given a virtual monopoly over the control of navigation in England. They had three separate houses or headquarters – one in London about which we northerners show no interest whatsoever, so don't ask – one in Hull and one in Newcastle. Both of these still survive and both are outstandingly interesting places.

Trinity House, Hull, is the more impressive from the outside. It has owned, over the years, substantial chunks of Hull's Old Town on streets like Whitefriargate, Posterngate and Princes Dock Side and built splendid buildings on all of them. Its own entrance on Trinity House Lane has a long pedimented front built in 1753 with really excellent and lively carving in the pediment. There's a fine Royal Coat of Arms and assorted anchors and Neptunes and things, much as you'd expect. Inside this building is the Courtroom which is spiffing, grand Georgian stuff with chandeliers and lots of plasterwork, a high coved ceiling and beautifully carved door surrounds. The other key building is the chapel which was rebuilt in 1839 and has a smashing interior including an astonishingly rich ceiling, a brilliant design of interlocking curves and geometric shapes.

Trinity House, Newcastle, is more hidden away, not so demonstrative from the outside and not, to be honest, so grand inside either;

but it is a wonderful place, making up in intimacy what it lacks in grandeur. You have to dive into it off the quayside streets into a little warren of tiny lanes and little squares, the lanes burrowing under and through the buildings. The Hall at Newcastle is grand but not so grand as Hull, the chapel is smaller but beautiful too. It's Tudor, with a beamed ceiling and richly polished Jacobean furnishings and old stained glass. Everywhere, on all the buildings huddled around these tiny lanes, the former masters of the Corporation have left their mark in quaintly lettered and dated stone shields.

Both of these places are close to their particular river and were, and to some extent are still, surrounded by the trappings of sea-borne wealth. The Quayside at Newcastle changed hugely in Victorian times but there are still fine merchants' houses which date back to the 17th century. At Hull, the legacy of 18th-century merchants' wealth is even more apparent. There are magnificent merchants' houses like Maister's House and Blaydes House, richly decorated, and hundreds of others, less impressive but still testaments to the city's maritime wealth. It's easy to forget nowadays, when most shipping is banished away to impersonal container ports near the mouths of rivers, how important places like Hull and Newcastle were to shipping in the past. Newcastle, for example, was so important that the financial year for marine insurance worldwide begins (or began, there was a Brussels attack on this recently) on 28th February, which just happens to have been the first day on which ships leaving the Tyne could guarantee to get into any of the Baltic ports without being troubled by ice.

But if Newcastle and Hull were important, if the east coast as a whole has provided all the material so far for this survey of the coast as a working place, there are at least two places on the west coast which can't possibly be ignored.

Whitehaven

The first is Whitehaven in West Cumberland which started life as a fishing village belonging to the Abbey at nearby St Bees. In 1630 it was bought by a chap called Sir Christopher Lowther (big posh Cumbrian family) who built a small harbour there. His son, Sir John Lowther, made the harbour bigger. He built the Old Quay in 1687 and started to develop the coal deposits which he'd found on his land all around the harbour and indeed under the sea as well; Whitehaven was the first place in the world to have pits that went out under the sea and if this chapter was about the history of mining I could go on to tell you about the important developments that took place here, especially under the ingenious control of several generations of mining engineers called the Speddings. In 1731, it was a Spedding, Carlisle Spedding, in fact, who sank the shaft of the Saltom Pit (an unprecedented 456 ft) and improved the drainage and ventilation to a level which made it possible to mine beneath the sea bed. He introduced Newcomen atmospheric engines into mines to improve the drainage. He was the inventor of the 'steel mill', a means of providing a dim light into the mine without risking gas explosions. It was done by revolving a steel disc over a flint and if the light it produced was indeed somewhat dim it was at least more agreeable than using the phosphorescent light given off by rotting fish, which is what they had used up till that point.

At the same time as developing his harbour and coal industry, Sir John also started to build a new town.

It's an odd place this new town of Whitehaven ... I've got to be careful here because my mother came from here so I don't want to offend anyone ... but it *is* an odd place. It has lots of good buildings, Georgian buildings, but it's not beautiful and it has rather faded over the years despite attempts to fight back, but it is very interesting. It is the first planned town to have been built in England after the Middle Ages and it is laid out in a regular rectangular grid – like New York but just a touch smaller ... well actually quite a bit smaller. It was started in the 1680s and building continued on into the middle of the 18th century.

My mum's friend, Nancy, had one of the original houses facing on to St Nicholas Church in the middle of the town, which dated, if memory serves me right from about 1727. It was a typical Whitehaven house, plain and roughcast Georgian on the outside; not posh, but quite big – three storeys high plus a basement kitchen. The kitchen, I recall, still had an 18th-century built-in pine dresser, but it is the staircase I remember best because my mum's friend Nancy decided, when she was in her seventies, that she was going to strip the Georgian banisters down to the natural pine. It was a tremendous staircase with two well-turned banisters to each stair, climbing from the ground floor right through to the top of the house. Night after night she would sit on a stair sanding away. One banister at a time, at least 36 stairs altogether. I don't know whether she ever finished, but her noble effort was one of the things that inspired my love of architecture when I was a boy.

The growth of Whitehaven was fuelled by coal, exported in vast quantities from the harbour, mainly to Ireland at first; the whole of Dublin and most of the rest of Ireland got its coal from Whitehaven. Later the trade extended to America as well and ships returning from America brought tobacco with them so the town became important for that trade as well. Shipbuilding started and the town started to export coal to the Baltic and to Wales and Scotland so that the ships could bring timber back for the shipbuilders. All of this continued on into the middle of the 18th century when Whitehaven grew to be really quite an important town, in fact in 1744 the harbour actually handled more tonnage than Liverpool. New quays were built at various times through the century and it looked as though the town could really take off, especially by the 19th century when West Cumberland's tremendous reserves of iron ore became important as well.

But 'twas not to be. Alas. Glasgow snaffled the tobacco trade. Liverpool snaffled almost everything else. Whitehaven was probably the first new town and the first purpose-built port of the Industrial Revolution but it had one major problem – those damn Lake District hills. Got in the way. Still do. If Whitehaven, instead of having a few bleak and unprofitable hills behind it, had had the whole wealth of the Lancashire cotton towns as its hinterland, who knows what might have happened.

But it didn't and Liverpool did …

Liverpool

What can you say about Liverpool's maritime heritage? This week, the week I'm writing this, I read in the paper that Liverpool's waterfront area has been put forward, along with the town's commercial centre, as a World Heritage Site. And rightly so, is all that I can say, for it is a remarkable place.

There are two remarkable things about it – the huge commercial offices on the Pierhead and along the waterfront from which its business was controlled, and the docks and warehouses where the real work was done.

The huge offices are fairly recent, only built between 1907 and 1913. The famous Liver Building, the Cunard Building and the Mersey Docks and Harbour Board Offices (a snappy little title) are the ones that you see on all the pics and they look particularly fantastic because Liverpool has an advantage that no other British city shares as far as I can think – it has a really broad river in front of it so you can go across to the other side and take advantage of the vastness of the view.

There's nothing in that view which isn't Victorian or later because though Liverpool has a long, long history, you have to look pretty carefully before you find much evidence of it and that's because this city, as I said in the first chapter, owes its greatness to the 19th century.

That's true of the docks as well. There were docks built as early as 1709 and they continued to be built for the next hundred years but the ones that you remember, the docks that hit you like a sandbag, the unforgettable ones, are the ones built by Jesse Hartley.

Jesse Hartley was Liverpool's Dock Engineer between 1824 and 1860 … 36 years in the same job, and in that time he more than quadrupled the area of the city's docks. He needed to, because those were the years when the Lancashire cotton industry was booming and Liverpool was its main port. Passenger travel to America was booming too and the tobacco industry as well. The Liverpool economy was on a roll and the docks were the key to all of the wealth. Liverpool didn't *make* all that much but it certainly knew how to move things about.

When I start to think about these docks I get confused. There are so many of them. Some are older and just added to by Hartley, others he built from scratch. There's Canada Dock and Huskisson Dock, Sandon Dock and Wellington Dock, Collingwood Dock, Salisbury Dock, Stanley Dock, Clarence Dock, Trafalgar Dock, Victoria Dock, Waterloo Dock, Canning Dock and Canning Half-Tide Dock. There's Wapping Dock and Brunswick Dock, Toxteth Dock and Harrington Dock. That's an awful lot of docks isn't it, boys and girls, and I've probably forgotten a few others.

I certainly haven't yet mentioned the greatest of them all, the one he's best known for, the one that environmentalists like moi went apoplectic about when they thought it might be demolished after long periods of neglect. And that's the Albert Dock, begun in 1841 and completed in 1845, right at the beginning of the Victorian period. It's his best. It's the greatest dock in the world, surrounded by the greatest warehouses in the world. It is all so great because it has immense power. The masonry of the dock walls is done in massive blocks of granite and the scale is cyclopean, epic. The warehouses also have an unparalleled solidity and dignity. They're five storeys high and they rest on short stubby Greek Doric Columns of tremendous strength and weight and every now and then the plainness is relieved by an arch, an elliptical arch. Elsewhere in the docks it is Hartley's details which are so exciting. The dock gates at Stanley Dock, for example, have massive battlemented gatepiers, like giant chesspiece castles. They have ingenious mechanisms so that the door is concealed in one of the piers when it's open and slides out and into a groove in the other pier in order to lock the gates. Extraordinary objects designed by an extraordinary mind.

It seems an odd thing to say about buildings which are so solid and so plain, but Jesse Hartley's dock buildings are enormously romantic, their massiveness is quite sublime. In my opinion they are among the most memorable things in the whole of Britain.

Which is more than you can say about the seaside village of Allonby on the Cumberland coast where I used to go for my summer hols when I was a little boy. One day I set off from our little cottage to go for a walk, wearing nothing but my bathing trunks, but it started to rain so I came back home to put my school cap on before completing the journey. I think I must have been a very odd little boy. All of which is not relevant at all except that I loved it and I wanted to mention it as a representative of all the other seaside places that haven't got a look in in this chapter. People did go sea bathing there (as early as 1748 apparently) but left no legacy behind them. There are no docks or picturesque harbour, no fishing at all. There's just a long row of cottages, a green and a glorious view of the Scottish coast opposite – and a memorial in the church to a man called Joseph Huddart who was born here in 1741 and went on to invent a new and safer ships' cable, chart many of the most dangerous seas in the Far East, and suggest the improvement that would lead eventually to the invention of the plimsoll line on the side of ships which prevented them from being overloaded – yet another of those unsung northerners who turned out to be such good chaps.

The Railways –
a peculiarly northern
triumph

I used to be a passionate trainspotter. When I went to Carlisle Grammar School, the school day finished at 4 o'clock and if I got on my bike and pedalled like mad I could get to the station in time to see the Thames-Clyde Express at 4.08. I did that often. I used to sneak into the engine sheds at Kingmoor too, and get chased by the gadgy. I even used to come over to the North East on special train-spotting trips – that's how passionate I was.

One of the reasons I used to come to the North East was to see the great A1 class of engines – those beautiful sleek express trains with the slopey fronts – because we didn't get those on the West Coast line. I saw several of them on one trip to the engine sheds in Gateshead but I never saw the Holy Grail of trainspotters. I never saw the most exciting of all British railway engines. I never saw *Mallard*.

I did a programme about trains and railways on TV recently and illustrated it with some grainy but beautiful shots of *Mallard* steaming up the East coast line and to give the shots extra oomph we super-imposed the train's whistle as a sound effect. Knowing what trainspotters are like we did our research and were careful to use a genuine A1 train whistle on the film … only to receive a bag full of letters pointing out that *Mallard* was the only train in its class to have an American-style whistle. My producer wept.

Tiny places – big stations

I stood and told this story on a tiny village station between Newcastle and Berwick … I'll re-phrase that. I stood and told this story on the station of a tiny village between Newcastle and Berwick. It's a small but significant difference, because Chathill, the station where we filmed, couldn't really be said to have a village at all – a station, a post office and half a dozen houses, that's all, and yet the station itself is quite a splendid affair – stone-built in an elaborate Tudor style with pretty windows and big fancy chimneys. It doubles as a private house now but it used to combine its function of station-master's house with ticket offices and waiting rooms and all the usual panoply of stationness. It has a nice rain canopy over part of the platform with five wooden pillars and carved wooden brackets, and there are platforms on both sides of the lines. On the far platform is an equally pretty little wood and glass shelter-cum-waiting-room for passengers heading towards Newcastle. Beside the station there's a level crossing with all the desirable lamps and gatey things and a big and spiffing signal box. (It's one of the unfulfilled dreams of the Grundy life to visit a signal box and pull – I hardly even dare think about this – a lever.)

Chathill has, in fact, all the things you'd expect a station to have – except a caff selling unnecessary carbohydrates and any sort of community to actually get on the trains. It was built in 1847 for the York, Newcastle and Berwick Railway and I think it's worth remembering that only about ten years earlier there were no railway stations at all, that platforms had only just been invented and only ten years before that there weren't even any railways.

So in its beauty and scale and isolation it seems to me to be a good example of the way that railways spread across the country like a rash the moment they were invented.

But where did the rash start? Where was the point of first infection? The north, of course. If you want to see the finest prehistoric remains in the world you could go to Stonehenge, for example. If you want to see the oldest and the finest classical architecture in the world, you might go to Athens. The world's finest Gothic cathedrals – Chartres? Salisbury? But if you want to get back to the absolute beginning of railways, the prehistory of railways even ... you come to the north of England ...

... or Wylam as we call it, that's as good a place to start as any

Wylam's a village in the Tyne Valley, a few miles west of Newcastle and it's one of the stops on the Newcastle to Carlisle Railway which if I might be allowed to say, as one who knows, is a very beautiful railway line. From end to end nothing mars the interest of its views and travellers on it have the satisfaction of knowing that it was opened in 1835 and is therefore one of the oldest lines in the world. Building began in Newcastle and headed west and the line broke new ground in lots of ways. It was the first line to cross the country. It was by far the longest line in the world at the time. It was the first line in the world to use exclusively what has become standard gauge (lines four feet eight and a quarter inches apart to be precise – exactly the same width, I might add, as the Romans used for their carts) and it was the first railway anywhere which provided proper passenger facilities at intermediate stations along the line. Wylam station was one of the first stations to be built on the line and it is therefore quite possible the oldest country station in the world still to be in passenger use. Isn't that something!

When railways were invented no one had any models to tell them what stations were supposed to be like (stagecoaches didn't need them) but from the absolute beginning railway stations have been more or less like Wylam – some sort of shelter or waiting room, offices and a platform all stretched out along the track. Industrial archaeologists call it 'lineside style' and nowadays we take it for granted but it was invented here, on the Newcastle and Carlisle Railway. Sadly no one knows who came up with the idea. There's lots known about who proposed the line and put the money up and so on, but no one knows for sure who was the architect who invented country stations.

But Wylam, for the railway explorer, is more than just one historic station. If you cross the bridge to the other side of the river you move out into a railway world which makes even the station look young ... you move out into the prehistory of the railways.

Nowadays the village is a pretty, prosperous dormitory village for Newcastle but at the beginning of the 19th century it was a mining village and in 1805 the pit was inherited by a man called Christopher Blackett.

Colliery wagonways

The great problem with Wylam Colliery was that it was a long way from Newburn, the nearest place where coal could be loaded onto ships. Up to this moment wagons of coal were hauled by horses along wagonways which led from the collieries down to the shipping points on the rivers Tyne and Wear. These wagonways attached to North-East pits were among the very oldest railways in the world. They started to appear early in the 1700s and they used wooden rails for the coal wagons to run on, making it easier for the horses to haul heavy loads. Scores of these wagonways can still be traced. My wife, foolish woman that she is, goes jogging along one in South Gosforth in Newcastle which is a footpath still. Another one in County Durham ran from Tanfield Colliery to the River Tyne and at one point it has to cross a deep ravine of the Tanfield Beck so it includes a bridge called Causey Arch which was built in 1727 by a local mason called Ralph Wood. When it was built it was the largest single-span arch in the country and it can reasonably be called the oldest railway bridge in the world.

Tanfield was later converted into a proper railway but as far as I know there's only one wagonway still actually working as a wagonway – it's part of the Bowes Railway run by volunteers at Springwell on the outskirts of Gateshead. Normally the old wagons on the Bowes Incline, as it's called, are hauled by a stationary steam engine but from time to time they have special events with horses hauling the old chauldrons or coal wagons. Nowadays the rails they use are made of iron and it was thought for ages that none of the old wooden rails had survived anywhere until extraordinarily, in 1997, while an old pit heap was being removed at New Herrington in County Durham, a set of surviving wooden rails suddenly emerged from underneath the slag. It was a sort of pre-railway marshalling yard where lines intersected and there were even sets of movable points – all in wood. Amazing.

At Wylam, Christopher Blackett replaced his wooden rails with iron ones but the problem was that, even with iron rails, the horses couldn't haul enough coal economically so he became interested in the possibility of using steam engines instead. The first (economically unsuccessful) steam locomotive had been built in 1804 by a Cornishman or southerner called Richard Trevithick but several of the earliest railway locomotives in the world and several of the most important names in railway history came from Wylam.

One of them was William Hedley. He was manager at the colliery and he gathered a team of engineers around him including another exceedingly famous railway pioneer called Timothy Hackworth and they started to experiment with steam locomotives.

One of the key questions was whether an engine with smooth wheels running on smooth rails would have enough grip to haul any sort of load and Hedley apparently laid a test track in the grounds of Wylam Hall, Christopher Blackett's home, and experimented at dead of night to see if it could be done. Evidently it could because Hedley went on to design and build the world's first technically and economically successful locomotives. The only building from the Wylam Colliery to have survived used to be part of the blacksmith's shop. It's been nicely restored recently and it's lovely to see it still in active use because it's the building in which Hedley built the railway locomotives Wylam Dilly and the even more famous Puffing Billy round about the year 1814.

Wylam's greatest claim to fame

But that's not the end of Wylam's railway significance. The village's final and greatest contribution to the history of the railways was born in 1781 in a simple stone-built Northumbrian cottage right alongside the Wylam wagonway. His name was George Stephenson and he grew up to become the most famous railway engineer of all time (OK, I know there's I.K. Brunel as well, but was he northern? Hm? Was he? I rest my case).

If you're looking for a northern hero (and if you're not I'll want to know the reason why) then it seems to me that George Stephenson fits the bill. Born to a working-class family, he had no proper schooling and worked in pits – but he trained himself, educated himself and when Killingworth pit, where he worked as a brakeman, was threatened with flooding he proved his ingenuity by improving the pumping engines and saving the mine. Within a couple of years this local chap had become one of the country's leading advocates of steam travel. At one point he was called before a full parliamentary enquiry which was looking into his ideas and he was questioned by a gaggle of the finest barristers in the country. One of the stories I love is that they had to bring in a translator to help them understand his Geordie dialect! But he stuffed them. He won the day and went on to design the two earliest proper commercial railway systems in the world, the Liverpool and Manchester in 1830 and before that, the oldest of them all, the ultimate grand-daddy of the transport revolution, the Stockton and Darlington Railway of 1825.

The S & D

The Stockton and Darlington Railway ran about 25 miles from Witton Park, through Shildon and Heighington to Darlington and finally Stockton. All along it there are mementoes of its earliest days. At Stockton is the world's first ticket office, at Darlington the first architect-designed railway bridge (Skerne Bridge by Ignatius Bonomi), over Northgate in Darlington the world's first railway viaduct (designer G. Stephenson himself). The world's first iron railway bridge has been taken to the National Rail Museum at York but it was originally over the River Gaunless at West Auckland. There are nicely carved milestoney things all over the place and cottages with S & DR datestones on them but the two things I like best were added just a little bit later.

In Darlington there is North Road Station which replaced the original station in about 1842. It's really nice. How about that for an architectural comment. It is though. It's like a Georgian house with a low-pitched roof and satisfyingly wide eaves. Inside it's spiffing because it has become a museum and so has retained all of its old fittings and gained a whole heap of superb railway bits and pieces as well. The most famous bit and piece is one of G. Stephenson's locos – not the hugely famous 'Rocket' of 1829 which achieved the stupendous average speed of 37 miles an hour – but the equally important 'Locomotion No.1' which on the 27th of September 1825 hauled a load of 90 tons for 18 miles, to gasps of astonishment I have no doubt. But there is another, less well known object in North Road Station that I like even more because it really brings home to me how long ago these early railways were built. It's a passenger carriage, one of their earliest passenger carriages but it doesn't look like a railway carriage at all. It looks exactly like a stagecoach ... no, I'll say that again ... it is a stagecoach ... on rails. When the S & DR was opened, nobody trusted steam locomotives to haul human beings, so at first only coal wagons were pulled by steam, passenger trains used the same lines but were pulled by horses and it wasn't until the 1830s that passenger traffic and steam were allowed to come together.

The other thing I like especially on this historic line is a museum as well. It's at Shildon which was born as a railway town in the 1820s and went on in later days to become one of the great railway engineering centres in the country until the industry was pathetically allowed to die in the second half of the 20th century. But it still possesses loads of little fragments of its early railway history including a two-part museum. First of all there's a nice little Georgian house which was the home of Timothy Hackworth who was, if you recall, a key member of William Hedley's team involved in building Puffing Billy at Wylam. He went on to become Resident Engineer for the Stockton and Darlington in 1833 and his house is a really simple and attractive late Georgian house with a lovely late Georgian atmosphere inside ... and real coal fires in the grates on the winter's day when I was there.

In those pioneering railway days, industry was still exciting enough to live with and Hackworth was quite content to live next door to his works. They were called the Soho Works and the main bit of them to have survived is the engine shed which was built as late as 1855 but it's a terrific place with a tremendous atmosphere. There are fires in here too, working fires used in the restoration of old engines and they took me straight back to the sneaky visits to train sheds in my trainspotting youth because this museum is full of the noise of beaten iron and the smell of burning coal and hot iron and rust – the humdrum beauty of the railways.

The L & M

This chapter is rapidly turning into a guide to museums because by far the best place to see the surviving structures on the Liverpool and Manchester Railway, the other great pioneering railway, is at the

Museum of Science and Industry in Manchester. This museum is in the Castlefields area, just south of the city centre, which in my opinion is, apart from Liverpool Docks, the most dramatic historic industrial landscape in the country. There are several canals, including the Rochdale Canal and the 18th-century Bridgewater Canal which was the first industrial canal to be built in the country and it's rich in commercial and industrial buildings of every sort including a terrific range of buildings from the Liverpool and Manchester Railway and its successors. Castlefields is an area which fell into terrible decline in the middle of the 20th century but which, in the 1980s and 1990s, was dramatically and wonderfully rescued and restored.

What's it got? First of all a whole host of 19th-century bridges across the River Irwell and the canals and nearby roads. They make a marvellous collection. The earliest and most traditional is a stone bridge of 1830 by Geordie Stephenson himself (only one of several possible derivations of the word 'Geordie' incidentally), the most recent two steel footbridges from the 1990s, but the most memorable are the various iron bridges, in particular a beautiful brick and iron bridge of 1849 over the Rochdale Canal which has cast-iron arches and parapet all with delightful Gothic details. But the real reason to come here is the restored station. Liverpool Road Station, which is now part of the museum, was built in 1830 and it's a really nice building. It looks more like an early bank or a gentlemen's club than a station because it's very classical with rusticated stone on the ground floor and stucco up above. There are two doors, one rather large and elegant for the first-class passengers, the other smaller and plainer for the rest of us, which I think is appropriate, don't you? One likes to know one's place.

Railway Architecture

Well, so far in this chapter we've had a certain amount of history and a tiny little bit of engineering, the odd humble little shed, but apart from Liverpool Road Station, not a great deal of architecture – a situation which is about to change because in the great railway frenzy which gripped Britain from the 1830s onwards, architecture became one of the expressions of pride for each of the new companies and one of the key advertising tools they used to attract customers. They fall into two main categories – posh and not posh.

Posh but first of all – not posh

I'm not going to talk a lot about the *not posh* because there are just too many of them. Most of the stations in the north, like in the rest of the country, are *not posh*. These *not posh* stations used a cottagey and comforting feel to appeal to travellers. Sometimes they look like small manor houses instead but they are first and foremost pretty. They're built in local materials and often in local styles. In the Vale of York and on Humberside they're all built in a gentle yellow brick, simple and cottage-like, vaguely Georgian. In Northumberland every station is built of sandstone and the vast majority of them are in the Tudor style. All over the north each railway company had its own style and so you come to them like old friends every few miles or so down the line, little clones of each other. I have a favourite line actually, the one which ran from Alnwick, across the moors to Coldstream on the Scottish Border. It only opened in 1887 and it was closed down in 1965, in the first wave of Beeching butchery but all of its stations survive. They're lively and festive, with fancy ironwork and pretty roofs with elaborately carved bargeboards and they just look so darned decorative against the plain green of the Northumberland hills.

It's a paradox that the best preserved of these *not posh* stations, on the whole, are on the lines that have closed down. On loads of the stations that are still open the irresistible tastelessness of railway officials has successfully obliterated much of the charm, but the abandoned stations survive as time capsules imaginatively remodelled for new uses. I've seen platforms blocked off at each end and turned into swimming pools, ticket office grilles used as serving hatches, signal boxes as guest bedrooms, drinking fountains as flower planters, accommodation arches as sheep shelters. In the countryside nothing gets wasted.

A few of the *not posh* have, of course, been kept alive in the most enjoyable way by enthusiasts of one sort or another. Beamish Open

Air Museum near Stanley in County Durham has a gorgeous reconstructed station from Rowley near Consett in upper Weardale. There's a tremendous little station museum at Norham, right on the Border (the Berwick to Kelso line) but Grosmont, in the middle of the North York Moors, and more importantly on the Esk Valley Railway, is *the* great example. The railway arrived in Grosmont in 1835 and its engineer was none other than the great Geo Stephenson himself. The approach to the station was through a tunnel (bypassed now and used by pedestrians) which is almost certainly the oldest railway tunnel in the world. Nowadays ordinary diesel trains follow ordinary timetables on the whole line as far as Whitby, and under ordinary circumstances that would be quite enough because the line runs through gorgeous country, but there are also steam trains that run from Pickering as far as Grosmont and to satisfy the taste of all the people who travel on the special trains the station has been kept going in tip-top nick, not posh of course, but charming and entirely complete.

Posh

So the *not posh* dominate the scene, but the *posh* are wonderful too. These are the poshest in my opinion, the ones to seek out for architectural reasons:

1. Newcastle Central Station was designed by the Newcastle architect John Dobson in 1845 though the building wasn't finished until after his death. This is one of the best stations in the whole country. It's big, stone, classical and fab on the front but inside, like in all the great 19th-century stations, the inspiration changes and engineering takes over from pure architecture. It has a tremendous train shed with long curved platforms and wonderful sweeping, curved roofs. Both of these things, the curved platforms and the arched glass roofs on curved wrought-iron ribs became almost commonplace later but both seem to have been invented here. Dobson specifically claimed that he invented a way of curving the iron roof ribs during the manufacture process. His longest platform is over 400 metres long.

She was not amused

Newcastle Central Station was officially opened by Queen Victoria in 1850 and afterwards she was taken to a celebratory banquet at the newly opened Station Hotel next door. Unfortunately the manager, who was new to the job, wasn't hot on etiquette and knowing only that he had provided loads of comestibles and not knowing who was going to pay for them, made the mistake of giving the bill to the Queen who was far from amused. In fact she avoided the City from then on and it's said that when she passed through it in the Royal train on her way to Balmoral, she had the blinds in her carriage pulled down.

The approaches to Newcastle Central Station from north and south are both entirely remarkable:

To the south trains have to cross the Tyne which flows through a deep and steep-sided valley as it passes through Newcastle. Now if there's one thing railway engines are really weedy about it's steep-sided valleys so the engineers were left with two choices – (a) develop some sort of hoist system to lower the trains down the slopes and up the other side (the first choice) and (b) build a bridge to cross the valley at high level. They chose (b) and quite originally, I think, called the resultant bridge 'The High Level Bridge'. The High Level is one of the masterpieces of British engineering. It was designed in 1845 by Robert Stephenson, son of the sainted George. It's a double-decker with a roadway on the lower deck and a railway on the upper. It has massive stone piers and the rest is made up of a complicated geometry of cast-iron and wrought iron, too complicated for a little brain like mine. The effect is stupendous, not pretty but overpowering.

To the north of the station the trains had to get through the city which included getting past the castle and crossing a very, very steep-sided road called Dene Street. The castle was easy-peasy. They knocked it down, or at least they drove the line through the middle of it, between the Keep and the Gatehouse. (Berwick is another town where they demolished most of the castle for the railway.) Is that amazing? Can you imagine what would happen if it was proposed today. It seems so unbelievably arrogant and insensitive to think of now and yet, in Newcastle certainly, the effect is ... I don't know ... interesting. There are lots of castles in this country but how many have railway lines running through the middle of them? It is an extraordinary experience to stand on the roof of the castle keep and watch trains sweeping past you on both sides. Taking the trains across Dene Street meant building a viaduct of brilliant drama. It soars above your head as you swoop down towards the river bank and all of this soaring and swooping is one of the most exciting visual experiences in present-day Newcastle – and that's saying something.

2. York Station. Not half as impressive as Newcastle from the outside, though it makes a fine sight when the huge and splendid Royal Station Hotel is part of the scene, but the train shed is superb. It's not as old as Newcastle and it is of exactly the same type (curved platforms, arched roofs) but it is absolutely stunning. The cast-iron columns which support the roof are splendid Corinthian columns and the roof has a noble and sweeping simplicity which is really beautiful.

3. Darlington (Bank Top Station). 1887. Red brick, quite grand and more of the same inside.

4. Durham. Shouldn't be listed here really because it's *not posh*. It's nice and Tudor with attractive iron and glass canopies but it's not on the same scale as the previous three. But the view from it! The greatest church in Britain towering over the town; a magnificent railway viaduct striding over the roofs of working-class terraces. It's like a dream of the best of the urban north.

5. Monkwearmouth Station, Sunderland. This is a little pearler, built in 1848 by a local architect called Thomas Moore. It isn't large but it's one of the most beautiful railway stations in the country. It's in an absolutely splendid Greek style. There's a portico with giant Ionic columns and an elegant (but short) drive leading up to it. It looks more like a miniature British Museum than a station, to be honest, and in fact it is another station which has become a museum in recent years; but behind it there's a new station

belonging to the Tyne and Wear Metro system which now shares the old railway lines and this is another little gem – from the end of the 20th century – hi-tech, utterly contemporary, steel and glass. It's so satisfying to see these two pieces of totally different architecture so boldly and successfully juxtaposed.

6. Carlisle. I couldn't miss out Carlisle. Not when the Thames Clyde Express went through it (at 4.08). Anyway it's the only Gothic one in my list of poshies, and it's pretty. It was built in 1847 by Sir William Tite and it opens into an attractive forecourt with a big Victorian hotel on one side and the mighty Carlisle Citadel on the other. Very nice.

7. Liverpool Lime Street. Hugely impressive from outside because of the former Station Hotel which is now offices. Impressive, but not quite so from inside. It is of a different type to Newcastle and York because instead of a series of arched roofs there are just two parallel and enormously wide iron and glass roofs. When the first was built in 1867 it had, at 200 feet, the widest span of any in the world.

8. Manchester has loads of stations and used to have others. I've already discussed the redundant Liverpool Road Station. Central Station is now the G-Mex centre and has a terrific roof structure even wider in span than Lime Street. Victoria Station was opened in 1844 and extended often since. Piccadilly Station has a hugely successful 1960s office building in front of it with unbroken horizontal rows of windows snaking sinuously up the hill towards the entrance of the station. But the one to go specially to see is Oxford Road Station which somehow doesn't feel English at all but has a curiously northern European feel – Dutch possibly or Danish, though to be honest I've never been to either of those two countries so what would I know. I would know, however, that it is my favourite 20th-century station. It was built in 1958 by the Midland Region Architectural Team and has a lovely shell-shaped roof, like one of the arches of the Sydney Opera House except on a small scale and made of wood.

9. Huddersfield. 1846. From outside the poshest of them all. Its entrance is a giant portico of Ionic columns. It's a temple, no less, a Greek temple and not a titchy one either but grandiose, a remarkable reminder of how these early Victorian railway builders saw themselves, of the huge scale of their vision and ambitions.

Beyond architecture – engineering

But though Huddersfield is vast and magnificent, the real scale of early railway achievements is not to be found in the architecture they dressed the railways in, but in the engineering that kept it up and running. It's astonishing how much engineering went into building the railways. Cuts, tunnels, embankments, bridges, accommodation arches, viaducts ... they're wonderful things all over the country, but the north, because of the nature of its landscape, is particularly rich in viaducts. Where there's hills, there's valleys, and where there's valleys there's viaducts, as they say. Actually they don't say that at all, I just made it up to sound wise, but it is true.

My friends Steve and Mary, wise in lots of ways but not so hot on railways, chose to drive back from Manchester to Newcastle by a pretty route over the moors and along the Pennines. They stopped for lunch (and knowing them probably a snooze) in a bleak and beautiful, but above all deserted spot in upper Ribblesdale, north of Settle. Imagine their chagrin and surprise when suddenly their peace was invaded by literally hundreds of cars out of which leapt middle-aged men festooned in anoraks and cameras with long lenses, and complacent long-suffering women bearing flasks. For a quarter of an hour Steve and Mary sat mystified and mildly oppressed and the massed hordes stood around sucking tea – until suddenly a steam train appeared and crossed the long, high, many-arched viaduct at the head of the valley, of which S & M had been aware as an item of pleasantly picturesque interest but less than aware of its railway significance. The multiple men were galvanised into action, cameras whirred, flasks topped, anoraks zipped, the train disappeared and the massed cars roared off in a convoy to their next photo opportunity. Steve and Mary, puzzled but pleased to be alone, went back to sleep.

By accident they had, of course, hit upon *THE RAILWAY ENTHUSIAST* who is drawn to steam like a Geordie to chips and where more dramatic to see it than the Ribblehead Viaduct on the Settle to Carlisle Railway. It is one of the great set pieces of the railway landscape – stone built, round arches, gradually increasing in height towards the centre as the valley deepens, it's wonderfully sited and wonderfully satisfying but no more so than dozens and dozens of others around the region. I expect you have your favourite viaducts but this is my book so these are my mine:

1. Corby-Wetheral on the Newcastle and Carlisle line. 1830 by Francis Giles. Beautiful red sandstone viaduct, enhancing an even more beautiful setting.
2. Penshaw, County Durham. The Victoria Viaduct over the Wear on the East Coast Main line. 1836. Modelled on the Roman bridge which still stands at Alcantara in Spain. High on the hill above it is the Penshaw Monument, a monumental Greek Doric temple erected in 1844 in honour of George Lambton, the First Earl of Durham and First Governor of Canada. Nikolaus 'rough' Pevsner wittily asks, 'Is there any other place where one can stand beneath a "Roman" viaduct and see a "Greek" temple nearby?'
3. Hownes Gill, near Consett, County Durham. 1858. Twelve tremendously impressive arches, 50 feet wide and 150 feet high.
4. Yarm. Sweeps very excitingly over the roof tops close to the centre of town, rather like …
5. … Durham
6. Knaresborough. Another thrilling bridge over a thrilling gorge, through the middle of a fascinating town, leading into an eminently sweet *not posh* station. Pevsner doesn't like this one. He described the way the Viaduct cut through the middle of the town as 'one of the most notable railway crimes of England.' JG, of course, does not agree.
7. Berwick. 1847 by Robert Stephenson. The grand-daddy of them all in my opinion. Twenty-eight splendid arches.

Grovel

Mention of Berwick brings me to the end of what I'm going to say about railways in a spirit of some shame for all the things I haven't found time to mention and an even greater sense of shame for all the other, non-railway engineering experiences that have been pushed to one side. Berwick has a wonderful 17th-century stone road bridge as well, for example, where am I going to mention that properly; or the first suspension bridge in Europe to carry traffic – a few miles upstream from Berwick at Loan End, built in 1819 by Capt Samuel Brown. Or all of the medieval bridges; John Carr (of York)'s beautiful road bridges in the North Riding, for example, they deserve consideration. And what about canals! The Bingley five-rise; John Rennie's extraordinarily powerful 'Roman' aqueduct of 1797 at Caton near Lancaster. What about reservoirs? Lead mining?

What about the Middlesbrough Transporter Bridge?

So many monuments, so much to see. Getting close to some of them, patting their cyclopean stonework and mighty iron beams, seeing the astonishing variety of solutions that designers have come up with, can be a profoundly moving experience. Aren't we lucky that the north, with its bleak and inhospitable hill tops and steep-sided valleys, has proved such a rich and challenging terrain for engineers so that nowhere else can such a variety of mighty works be seen in such a small area.

And aren't we proud, we little northerners, that we provided the world with this splendid mode of transport, inventing the engines themselves and developing the forms and buildings that surround them, trying them out first of all in the northern landscape before exporting them to the whole of the rest of the world. The railways … are they the most important of all of our building achievements? I think they may well be.

chapter **e i g h t**

Towns and Cities

Does the north have a capital?

In the past it definitely did and there was no doubt where it was.

York

York was the capital of the north in Roman times. It was literally the capital because the Romans divided the island into a number of provinces. London, for example, was the capital of Britannia Superior while York was the capital of Britannia Inferior. I bristled grumpily when I discovered that and went out looking for a Roman to shout at but calmed down when I was told that 'inferior' and 'superior' merely referred to distances from Rome. Several Roman Emperors lived in York and one of the greatest, Constantine, the first one to accept Christianity into the Empire, was declared Caesar in York in AD 306.

It was also the capital of the north in Saxon times. It's a deservedly little known and unremarkable fact that I am writing these words on Easter Sunday 2003, exactly fourteen hundred and six years *to the day* after Edwin, King of Northumbria, was baptised into Christianity at York by the Bishop Paulinus on Easter Day AD 627. Spooky! Because of Paulinus, and at the desire of the then Pope, Gregory the Great, York became the ecclesiastical capital of the north. Its church, the Minster, is officially called 'the cathedral and metropolitical church of St Peter in York' whatever that means, but the connection with St Peter in Rome was a deliberate sign of its importance. It became the seat of an Archbishop and the second church in England after Canterbury. It still is.

It was definitely the capital of the north in Viking times. The Vikings took the city in 866, called it Yorvik and made it the capital of their Kingdom in the north.

York had tough times for a few years after the Norman Conquest but pretty soon it was emerging as the capital of the Norman north as well. The Normans rebuilt the Minster and made it for a while the largest building in Europe north of the Alps. The town soon ranked fourth in England and by the end of the 14th century it was second only to London in terms of wealth and size of population. Quite often, when kings were on the move to sort out problems in the country, York became the temporary capital of England. By the end of the Middle Ages it was mega in terms of the church, political power and trade. Capital of the north in fact.

Vestiges of greatness

All of these periods of power have left glorious remains in the city. I was there last week for a couple of days and I have to tell you that I didn't know where to look. I kept tripping over old things ... but let's leave my wife out of this and concentrate on buildings.

You have to search a bit to find the Roman remains but in fact they're more substantial here than in almost any other town in the country. Significant chunks of the medieval city walls incorporate Roman masonry including the lower half (20 feet or so) of a tower called the Multiangular tower which is to be found in the Museum Gardens and beside it there's a stretch of wall which stands to about 17 feet high and gives a real impression of how well defended the Roman fort must have been. The fort itself, at least its HQ building, the Principia, was on the same site as the Minster and it was huge – its main hall was over 225 feet long. Intriguing bits of it are visible in the Minster undercroft.

Anglo-Saxon and Viking remains are harder to find in the real world of the city. There's no sign at all of the Saxon cathedral and in fact nothing visible at all outside of museums, except that most of the main streets in the city were used by the Vikings as you can tell by their names which all seem to end with the word 'gate' (Petergate, Gillygate, Stonegate, Goodramgate) which is really the Viking word 'gata' meaning a road. 'Snicket' as well: York is a warren of little snickets which sounds rather like an insult (you 'orrible little Yorkshire snicket, you) but is in fact a Viking word for an alleyway or lane. So walking around York is to tread where all the little Olafs and Gudruns have trod before you.

Medieval magnificence

But if really early York has to be searched for or imagined, medieval York is everywhere. It's surrounded by an almost complete set of medieval walls – a more complete set than anywhere else in Britain and inside them there are dozens and dozens probably hundreds of surviving medieval buildings, far more than in any other town or city in the country. I said that really boldly as if I knew, and yet I made it up. But I bet it's true.

There's the Minster of course, which would be enough on its own for most towns. I don't actually think that York Minster is the greatest building in the north, it isn't as great as Durham and I find Beverley Minster more beautiful, but it is a wonderful building and bits of it are unforgettable. The north transept is unforgettable and the beautiful west window, the chapterhouse, the stained glass and the Norman crypt; and above all it towers in a totally medieval manner over the narrow streets and the jumbled roofs of the town. Stepping out of the claustrophobic narrowness of Stonegate, for example, into the space around the Minster, is to be biffed over the head with scale and grandeur. You're immediately right up against its walls and you're forced to gaze upwards towards the sky as the Gothic builders hoped you would.

Apart from the Minster there are still 14 other medieval parish churches. There used to be more. There used to be 25, which seems a lot, but I suppose that you have to imagine that the vast majority of the population would have gone to church in those days and since the population in the later Middle Ages was about 15,000 it still means

Cragside, Northumberland. Lord Armstrong's country cottage.
Victorian romance married to Victorian inventiveness.

left The Temple of Piety, Studley Royal, near Ripon, north
Yorkshire. Grecian simplicity 18th century style.

right Belsay Hall, Northumberland. Grecian simplicity
19th century style.

Grundy's fantasy. A typical 17th century
Lake District farm, Hartsop, Westmorland.

Laithe farms in Swaledale. Plenty of room
to swing a cat should you want to.

First prize for greenness. Fields and
fieldhouses near Muker, Swaledale, north
Yorkshire.

Northern grit – millstone grit near Sowerby Bridge
in Calderdale, west Yorkshire.

Simple but big. A typical Northumbrian farmhouse
at Old Bewick near Alnwick.

top Newcastle-upon-Tyne: 1. Early Victorian elegance. William Gladstone described Gray Street as 'Our finest modern street.'

bottom left Newcastle upon Tyne: 2. Medieval power and wealth. The (new) Castle. 12th and 13th centuries.

bottom right Liverpool. 19th century civic pride. The Picton Reading Room. 1875.

Northern grit – millstone grit near Sowerby Bridge
in Calderdale, west Yorkshire.

Simple but big. A typical Northumbrian farmhouse
at Old Bewick near Alnwick.

The Farne Island. Grace Darling's Longstone
Lighthouse, 1826 – and lots of seals.

Tiny village, big station. Chathill Station,
built in 1847 by Benjamin Green.

The High Level Bridge, Newcastle (and Gateshead
of course). Robert Stephenson's masterpiece.

Cuthbert Broderick's magnificent Grand Hotel
in Scarborough. 1863.

bottom left York: 1. Medieval power and wealth. The city walls.

bottom right York: 2. 18th century wealth. Fairfax House,
by John Carr. 1760.

top Newcastle-upon-Tyne: 1. Early Victorian elegance. William Gladstone described Gray Street as 'Our finest modern street.'

bottom left Newcastle upon Tyne: 2. Medieval power and wealth. The (new) Castle. 12th and 13th centuries.

bottom right Liverpool. 19th century civic pride. The Picton Reading Room. 1875.

top left The Albert Dock, Liverpool. Jesse Hartley's cyclopean masterpiece.

top right A temple to industry. Marshall's Mill, Leeds. 1838.

Titus Salt's alpaca mill at Saltaire. It's big, it's very big and amazingly it has found new uses.

top left Sunderland Cottages. Sunderland's unique single-storey
version of the terraced street.

top right Industrial charity. Workers' housing at New Earswick,
York, built by the Rowntree family.

bottom left Industrial Might. Mid-19th century mill
on Marshall Street, Leeds.

bottom right Flying freeholds in Hebden Bridge, west Yorkshire.

that there were about 600 people for every church. They're all beautiful, these churches, but most visitors who come to see York's parish churches have a favourite and for most people it's the same one. Holy Trinity is hidden away in a secret churchyard behind a row of medieval houses on Goodramgate. Its architecture is mainly from the 14th and 15th centuries but its appeal is not just architectural, it's loved because the church almost totally escaped being restored in Victorian times so it is a gorgeous, untidy jumble of old-fashioned fixtures and uneven floors. There's no electricity and some of the windows are still filled (like so many other York churches) with beautiful old stained glass which was paid for by a vicar called John Walker and since he forked out his own dosh for the pictures he's had himself painted into the corner to make certain that people wouldn't forget who'd paid. To understand medieval stained glass you've got to have far more knowledge of the Bible and medieval mythology than I've got. The East window at Holy Trinity has pictures of loads of Marys for example, including Mary the wife of Cleophas and Mary the wife of Zebedee. I bet you hadn't even realised that Zebedee was married, had you. There's also a wonderful picture of the body of Christ which is here because John Walker was a member of the Guild of Corpus Christi, which my vague memories of schoolboy Latin tell me means the Guild of the Body of Christ.

York had all the usual medieval Guilds and they've left some remarkable things behind including a marvellous cycle of Mystery plays and one of the greatest surviving Guild Halls in the country. The Merchant Adventurers Hall was built, probably about 1357, by a group of merchants who were also, not to put to, fine a point on it, Adventurers. They practised overseas trade and they set themselves up as the Guild of our Lord Jesus and the Blessed Virgin Mary. The hall that they built is the finest of all York's many timber-framed buildings. There was a hospital on the ground floor and a main hall up above which is 12 metres wide with a magnificent oak roof – a space so wide you couldn't get trees long enough to cover it so it's covered in two spans with a row of oak pillars down the centre of the hall. The room is pure wood. The walls are wood and so is the roof, the floor is made of exquisitely polished medieval pitch-pine planks. It's all gleamy and weathered and wonderful.

But if the Merchant Adventurers is the best of the wooden buildings, there are scores of others. The streets in the central area of York are lined with medieval timber-framed houses. Some of them shout their presence at you with their dramatic black timbers set against the whitewashed walls between, others have been sneakily disguised by later centuries, their timbers plastered over and their sticky-outy bits sawn off so that you have to get inside or round the back to see their real age. By sticky-outy bits I mean 'jetties'. *Jettying* is when each floor sticks out a bit over the floors below it. The sticky-outy bit is called a *jetty* and there seem to have been two reasons why they built houses like that. First of all, it gave you a little bit of extra space. At street level you were restricted by local by-laws as to how far you could come forward into the street, but higher up you could snaffle a bit of extra room. But the main reason, I'm sure, is that it looks good – top heavy – impressive. These houses seem to be saying, 'I'm really big I am'. None of them had jetties round the back, just on the front. They were just dirty showoffs, and between them they have created some of the most picturesque and best loved streets in the country. The Shambles, Petergate, Stonegate are so utterly charming as the houses lean out towards each other. Go to see them on a winter's afternoon when the shop windows are bright in the gloom at street level and the gables stand out against the darkening skies. You'll turn medieval and start saying 'odds bodikins' ere lammas-tide.

Post-medieval magnificence too

At the end of the Middle Ages, York fell into a bit of a slump where it remained until the end of the 17th century, at which point it took off once again towards the dizzy heights of northern Capital. What happened was that it became the centre for regional government and in particular the place where Yorkshire's legal system was based. In the 18th century justice and local government were administered by means of a number of courts. There was the sheriff's court and the quarter sessions and twice a year crown judges came up from London to hold the assizes. These legal events (and especially the assizes) were major biggies on the social calendar and attracted all the local country gents and gentesses into town – and there were lots of them in a big, rich county like York. They poured into town for fun and frolics and days out at the assize courts and because they were rich they built splendid town houses for themselves to stay in while it was all going on. One example that you can visit is the house on Castlegate built for the Fairfax family by John Carr (of York) in about 1760. It's magnificent outside and has one of the most sumptuous interiors I remember seeing. There are at least six superb plaster ceilings in the rococo style, stunning staircase, fab fireplaces and dramatic door surrounds, the whole Georgian works and, while Fairfax House probably represents the best there is, there are loads of others, almost any one of which you would drool over in most towns.

As well as private town houses they built equally sumptuous public buildings. The various court buildings, for example, make up one of the great architectural set pieces of Georgian England. It's on the site of the medieval castle – in fact the 13th-century keep, Clifford's Tower, still takes up one side of a square with 18th-century legal buildings making up the other three sides. The grandest of them … there's a bit of a paradox here I'm sure, is the early 18th-century County Gaol which is a stunning building in the Baroque style and that's flanked on either side by the Assize courts and the Female Gaol which are almost as grand. The Assize courts were built in 1773 by John Carr (where from?) and they contain two of the most beautiful courtrooms in the country. It would almost be worth committing a crime in order to be tried there amidst the plasterwork and the mahogany furnishings. Almost, but not quite. Anyway they weren't made beautiful for the benefit of the poor unfortunates in the dock but for the ladies and gentlemen who thronged the public galleries to see and be seen and for the entertainment value of it all. A lovely way to spend the day before a late afternoon stroll along the newly laid-out New Walk beside the River Ouse followed by an evening of cards, dancing and genteel flirtation at the splendid Assembly Rooms in the centre of the town. Hard to beat.

Some towns got rich and powerful because they made things or traded with other places. But 18th-century York was different, it was rich and powerful because a lot of rich people lived there. It was the classic example in northern England of an aristocratic town but that wasn't enough to keep it on top for ever. Other towns, making money in different ways were sneaking up on it and York's star began to fade. There was still some later development and it has the usual rings of 19th- and 20th-century housing that's found in all English towns, but its essential character, the character of its centre, froze sometime towards the end of the 1700s and we've been left with a town that mingles wonderfully the medieval and the Georgian.

Old towns galore

York might be the best known, but it certainly isn't the only example of such a town in the north. In its little way Carlisle's a bit like that and so is Alnwick ... Hexham, Warkworth, Berwick – all Northumberland's best country towns share the character. Durham too – superlatively Durham, the old town of Durham crushed up around the castle and the cathedral and surrounded on three sides by the great incised meander of the River Wear. Whitby's similar, a marvellous mixture of the Georgian and the medieval and nothing much else. Thirsk and Ripon. Helmsley ... In the North West, Appleby, Kirkby Lonsdale and Kirkby Stephen are good examples and Lancaster's another very special one. Like York, Lancaster was a county town, the centre of regional government in the North West and also like York its courthouse and prison are in the castle, except that here they're still locked away behind the medieval castle walls and still perform their ancient legal roles.

And especially Beverley

But the other *great* example of such a town, in my opinion, is Beverley. I love Beverley and think it's one of the very greatest towns, not just in the north, but in England ... a hint of York, but without the tourists, and with charms all of its own. Its Minster, of course, is sublime. I've already written about it briefly but it is worth re-asserting that it is one of the very greatest churches in the whole country. John Betjeman, in the introduction to his *Collins Guide to English Parish Churches* introduced a test of quality for a church – is it worth cycling five miles against a stiff wind to see? Well, Beverley's worth pogo-sticking thirty miles in a snow storm ...

naked. The purity of its interior vistas and the breathtaking quality of its details are unmissable. Carvings like those on the canopy of the 14th-century Percy Tomb show extraordinary virtuosity while the carved grotesque figures of townsfolk and medieval musicians around the nave walls are by turns touching, informative and down-right chucklesome.

The Minster doesn't stand alone. At the other end of the town is the Parish Church of St Mary which in any other context would be worth at least 17.2 Betjeman miles in its own right and yet it gets overlooked in the shadow of the Minster. It's a noble church, largely of the 14th and 15th centuries. Its tower collapsed in the middle of evensong on Sunday the 29th of April 1520, with some loss of life. The disaster would have been greater apparently if a large part of the congregation hadn't gone to watch a bear baiting instead. If that isn't an argument in favour of blood sports I've never heard one, I'm surprised the Countryside Alliance haven't used it in their advertising.

Between these two churches, the town follows the most simple line. A single twisty line of road (apparently following the line of an ancient stream) runs its whole length, passing alternately through wide open spaces and narrow intimate ones. The two main open spaces are called the Saturday Market and the Wednesday Market. Both of them have existed since medieval times. The Saturday Market has a beautiful market cross in a light-hearted and playful Queen Anne style. It was designed in 1711 by a local architect called Theophilus Skelton, which is a nice name, I'm sure you will agree, but one you're glad your parents never thought of. Saturday Market also has the distinction of hosting the oldest surviving cinema in Britain which seems to me to be a fact worth celebrating.

On either side of this main drag through the town there's a whole series of really marvellously attractive Georgian houses. Some are in rows and terraces, some in little groups but there are loads of big splendid ones which stand alone in their own grounds. Some of these would be worth selling your soul for to be honest, or possibly your granny's soul if you would rather hold on to your own. They're all built of warm red brick with white painted doors and windows and lovely weathered orange-y pink pantiles on the roofs. Lots of them are

Queen Anne-ish in date and so have broad eaves and deliciously swept hipped roofs.

If you did sell your granny's soul and acquired one of these lovely Beverley houses you could sneak out in the evenings and go to Nellies – not a naughty lady, I hasten to add, but a pub, more properly known as The White Horse, which has retained inside all of its old character in a way that we hairy old Real Aley chaps yearn for. It is a welter of little rooms and old furnishings, fires and gas lights. Buxom barmen pull foaming pints and the barmaids are nice too. It's the least altered pub I know and well worth cycling a few miles to get to, but you'll almost certainly need a taxi home.

A profound sense of shame accompanies me as I head away from Beverley (cycling against a stiff breeze) because of the number of wonderful small towns I have had to shovel, hugger-mugger into a few brief paragraphs. But by the end of the 18th century there were changes afoot in the world of the northern town, changes that were to leave the old (and beautiful) country towns far behind.

Newcastle upon Tyne

In the Middle Ages, when York was the second most important town in the country, Newcastle upon Tyne was a measly ninth. It was still a very impressive measly ninth, mind you. Its defensive walls were among the most powerful in the kingdom, there was a mighty castle and a clutch of fine churches and all the medieval trimmings but in terms of population and taxable income it was definitely well behind York. However, by 1700 Newcastle had done a sneaky overtaking manoeuvre and had leapt into the lead. When the traveller Celia Fiennes (who got about a bit and has already had a few mentions in this slim vol.) visited the town in 1698 she wrote: 'it most resembles London of any place in England, its buildings lofty and large of brick mostly or stone, the streetes broad and handsome'.

Ere long the 'streetes' were destined to get even more broad and handsome because at the very end of the Georgian period, Newcastle was one of those towns that quite deliberately began to set out to re-invent itself as a regional capital. Actually, 'ere long' is pushing it a bit because, though the place developed considerably throughout the 18th century, and there were quite a lot of nice new buildings put up in that time, the really big change didn't happen until the first half of the 19th century – but when it did the architectural results were startling.

The first signs that a change was taking place were a few bits and pieces of development. Newcastle had started its life down beside the river and on the steep bank immediately to the north of it. In 1700 it was still a tightly packed medieval city surrounded by defensive walls, but in the course of the 18th century it began to grow and to drift north and west, away from the river and the old centre. Early in the 19th century two big new developments took place outside the city walls which encouraged the drift. There was a big, posh urban square called Eldon Square and a big (if anything) even posher block of terraced houses called Leazes Terrace. Both of these were built in a new style of architecture for Newcastle. They were very classical, very pure and noble and built of the sort of perfectly cut sandstone which had been introduced a few years earlier into country houses in the area. They were sophisticated – not provincial, but rather metropolitan in feel. Newcastle was beginning to feel its oats as an important place.

But the big problem that Newcastle had was the route into town from the only bridge over the Tyne. To be honest it still is a problem for this fat little writer because even unto this day it is exceeding steep and goes on a long way, but in those days the available roads were narrow and difficult, as well as steep.

Newcastle's Regency new town

There were a few plans put forward to improve access and to redevelop the rest of the town but the one that won the day was devised by a property developer called Richard Grainger. It was an incredible plan. It involved demolishing the newly built Butchers' Market and the newly built Theatre. It meant pulling down loads of streets and knocking down loads of houses. Grainger also had to acquire the massive house and grounds of the Blackett family which was called Anderson Place and which had the reputation of being the finest house in England inside city walls. He bought it for £50,000, which was a pretty tidy sum in those days (still wouldn't go amiss today) and he demolished it. His plan would never have happened nowadays, of course. Nowadays there would have been 13 different planning inquiries. Three subsequent Home Secretaries would have overturned the findings of their predecessor. Traditionalists like me and the Civic Trust would have jumped up and down in an excited manner. The man himself would have died of old age and his successor would have ended up by building some ghastly half-hearted, watered-down version of the plan in tame, safe materials in order to fit in with what was there already.

What actually happened was that he presented the plan to the City Council in June 1834. They accepted it there and then and work started straight away. Less than a year later the biggest building in the plan, the massive new indoor market now called Grainger Market, was up and running, and by 1840 the city of Newcastle had a new planned centre ... boom boom!

Grainger's new town centre wasn't necessarily the best choice of the various plans on offer. It failed to address the real problem of access from the river bank, and at least two of the alternative plans were grander in concept; his plan doesn't even integrate all that well with the old town round about it. But it was Grainger who was the go-getter. He was the one who got it done and his is the plan that Newcastle has lived with ever since and for all its weaknesses it has given the place a centre to be proud of.

The style is classical and rather grandly monumental, the material is beautifully dressed sandstone. If you don't know Newcastle you should think of Edinburgh or the splendid terraces around Regent's Park in London in order to picture the style but Newcastle is smaller and more compact and much less formal than either of those places. Grainger was lucky to have at his disposal a clutch of really talented local architects and different bits of the scheme were given to different architects so there's quite a lot of variety – but only within the overall classical framework.

The centrepiece is called Grey Street and it's a very beautiful street indeed. It's now the main route up from the river so it climbs steeply which gives it fine distant views. It also curves, so the view unfolds as you climb and though it's very grand throughout, the best buildings are at the top – the splendid porticoed Theatre Royal and the monument to Earl Grey, the celebrated tea bag and politician, who was responsible for the 1832 Reform Act. The Monument, as locals call it, as if it were the only one in the world, is a Roman Doric column, lots of feet high, which acts as focal point for Grainger's two main streets and is the single most important landmark in Newcastle today (apart from St James Park, home to the mighty Magpies, obviously).

Newcastle: 20th-century attacks and rescues

Grainger made Newcastle the only city in England with a planned centre and are we grateful? I think we are. There was a time in the 1960s when Grainger's go-getting spirit was re-kindled by a raft of politicians, architects and planners who, like their predecessors in Grainger's day, but without their genius and vision, were once again determined to make Newcastle a modern regional capital. T. Dan Smith, the leader of the city council at the time, wanted to make Newcastle 'the Brasilia of the north' and in pursuit of this unlikely dream great sweeps of the old town were hoyed away, to be replaced by things which even at the time seemed like a backward step and which hindsight has learnt to despise. But luckily the wave of destruction ended before the core of the planned early 19th-century town could be affected and I think Geordies, to a man and to a lass, are grateful for that.

In recent years the planned town has begun to see a renaissance and massive urban renewal schemes both there and on the river bank have pulled the life of the city back towards the river where it started from. The Gateshead bank of the river, which lost any distinction a couple of hundred years ago, has become the scene of extraordinary changes. Alongside new housing and a hotel complex, we've had the creation of the hugely effective and successful Baltic Centre for Contemporary Art, next to it a huge hi-tech music centre in sweeping curvy glass and steel, and between them both the new and exquisitely graceful Gateshead Millennium Bridge all drawing huge crowds back to a riverside which by the last quarter of the 20th century had become decayed and abandoned. In fact all of these dramatic changes on the south bank of the river have allowed a hideous possibility to sneak into the minds of dedicated Novocastrians – that a time might come when people will come to Newcastle in order to look across the river at Gateshead.

So these are pretty good times for Tyneside townscape, on the whole, but returning to the 1830s and the dreams of Grainger and his contemporaries, Newcastle never did become more than a very local capital. Despite the industrial wealth generated throughout the Victorian period by men like George and Robert Stephenson and Lord Armstrong, Newcastle was being left behind in the Northern-Capital-Stakes by events further south.

Victorian super-cities: Liverpool and Manchester

By the middle of the 19th century, Manchester and Liverpool had become the new super-cities. They were bigger and richer than many of the capital cities of Europe. Because they dealt in cotton and therefore with America they had become global cities, open to influences from the new world as well as the old. All of this shows in the architecture, including those buildings already referred to elsewhere in this book. Liverpool Docks are the greatest docks in the world, it's no accident that Manchester and Liverpool were the first cities in the world to be connected by a railway, and no accident either that the innovative use of new building materials, of iron and steel, concrete and glass, is a feature of both cities as well.

I think that Liverpool has the best buildings. Beyond the docks and the Pierhead offices, the whole commercial centre is chock-a-block with terrific Victorian buildings. There are huge confident insurance offices and banks, all in stone, all richly carved – the palaces of a capitalist culture.

But there are also splendid civic buildings. I said earlier in the book (desperately trying to justify my passion for country houses) that most of the beautiful buildings were built by private individuals – but in the 19th century that situation began to change. Bear this date in mind.

Before 1835

Before 1835 towns were run mainly by corporations which had existed more or less unchanged since the Middle Ages. The members of the corporation often started off as the leaders of the great medieval merchants' guilds and gradually went on to rule whole towns. Nobody ever got elected – you just took over from your dad, or you were invited to be on the corporation by your friends, so as the centuries passed, corporations tended to be just a cosy little circle of the well-to-do; but then in …

After 1835 …

… things began to change in a big way because that was the year that the Municipal Corporations Act was passed. After 1835 councils were elected and the new councillors were very different from the people who had run the old unelected corporations. They were go-getters, empire builders. They brought aggressive new blood into local government and in town after town they were driven by fierce pride in their new empires to create a whole new landscape.

In the years that followed 1835 a whole raft of new legislation was introduced that allowed town councils to make changes. The Health of Towns Act (1848), The Burial Act (1852), The Recreation Ground Act (1859) these and loads of others let councils raise rates to build things. Towns spent a fortune on improvements. They bought up gas companies and set about making towns brighter and safer. They built hospitals, public cemeteries, public baths, sewage works and water pumping stations to improve the cleanliness and the health of the population. They built parks, wonderful municipal parks and art galleries and libraries, civic halls and concert halls to improve the minds of the people. They built law courts and police stations, prisons, workhouses. They built schools and public markets. And at the heart of this expanding empire they built themselves grand new Town Halls.

Acropolis on the Mersey

Except that Liverpool didn't … build a town hall, I mean, because it already had a beautiful 18th-century one. It did however build a remarkable collection of public buildings on a raised area called The Plateau, just outside the old city centre. They include the Walker Art Gallery, the Sessions House, the William Brown Library and Museum, the College of Technology and (best of all) the Picton Reading Room. They were built between 1857 and 1902 and all but one of them are splendidly Neo-classical, oozing Corinthian columns and impressive pediments – which is odd because they were all being built at times in the 19th century when this style was really out of fashion elsewhere in the country.

So in clinging on to old-fashioned styles, was Liverpool being behind-the-times and stick-in-the-mud, despite everything I've been saying about innovation? Oh, no, no, no, no, no, certainly not. This tremendous group is determinedly classical for two reasons. Firstly, Liverpool was consciously creating a sort of Forum for itself, suitable for a great and leading city such as Liverpool longed to be, connecting itself in a way to ancient Rome. But secondly, they were built in classical style because they were trying to fit in with the St Georges Hall which lies in the centre of the group and which is one of the greatest public buildings in the country. It looks like the Parthenon or some other equally great Greek temple. It stands high and proud on a podium with broad flights of step leading up to the various entrances. There are more Corinthian columns than you could shake a stick at, even if you wanted to. I think I counted 58 in case anyone's interested. One end is pedimented like a temple, the other has a rounded apse with attached columns all round it. On each of the long sides there are gigantic colonnades of columns. It's magnificent, the finest Neo-classical building in the country and it was begun in 1836, within a year of the Municipal Corporations Act. The first architect, H.L. Elmes, was only 22 when he won the competition to design it, but the strain of bringing it to a conclusion proved too much for him. He died of consumption at the age of 33 before it had been finished, so the job was taken over by one of the masters of 19th-century architecture, C.R. Cockerell. The interior is Cockerell's and it's unbelievable. It contains a massive public hall of the utmost grandeur, two splendid Court Rooms and an amazing Concert Room. Now you might suspect that one *massive*, one *utmost grandeur*, two *splendids* and an *amazing* is rather too many superlatives to use in one sentence and I'm sure you'd be right but I find myself unable to care. Cockerell's interior is much jollier, much less severe than the rather chilly splendours of the exterior. The Corinthian columns in the hall are in red granite and the floor is a brilliant mass of coloured and patterned tiles. And the Concert Hall … ah … oooo … eeee. It has a wavy-fronted balcony all the way round, which is supported by beauteous classical damsels in diaphanous robes. They're not real women if you get my drift, but statues with sort of plant pot things on their heads to support the balcony. It might sound odd but they are so elegant – I'm sure if I were to go to a concert there I wouldn't be able to keep my eyes off them. Many Liverpool men, I'm told, have tried (unsuccessfully) to chat them up.

So, with all of this innovation, all of this commercial wealth and all of this civic splendour, is Liverpool the capital of the north? I don't think it is.

You think you know where I'm headed? You think I'm going to choose Carlisle, or Keswick because my Auntie Bessie lived there, or some equally sentimental choice, but no …

… it's Manchester.

Frank Musgrove in *The North of England: A History from Roman Times to the Present* writes:

The nineteenth century was a triumphant age for the north of England. Its greatest triumph was Manchester: shock city of the 1840s, international symbol of the new industrial age.

He goes on to quote a contributor to the *Cornhill Magazine* in 1881:

London is now isolated in the midst of the agricultural south … if Britain had now for the first time to choose a capital, its choice would naturally fall upon Manchester.

When I go to Manchester from Newcastle (this seems such a disloyal thing to say. I hope my North East friends don't ostracise me for saying this) I always feel as if I've arrived in the big city. The scale of everything is different. The streets are bigger and the buildings are bigger and the city centre is bigger too. Manchester doesn't have as many historic buildings of superlative quality as Liverpool, it's not planned and it lacks the steep hills that make Newcastle such a wonderfully varied experience. It certainly doesn't have the range of ancient buildings to be found in York. Sheffield has a more exciting situation and better views. Leeds has a more enjoyable shopping centre ... but Manchester has a bit of everything. There's a superb medieval cathedral (originally a collegiate church) and in Cheethams Hospital and Baguley Hall a couple of absolutely top-notch medieval domestic buildings. It has historic industrial architecture, as we've seen and it has the finest Town Hall in the country bar none.

The Town Hall was designed by Alfred Waterhouse who was born in Liverpool in 1830, first practised architecture in Manchester, but then went south to London to acquire a national reputation. His best known building in London is the Natural History Museum but his best building of all, designed in 1867, is Manchester Town Hall.

By contrast to Liverpool's public buildings in the Neo-classical style, Manchester's Town Hall is Gothic, gloriously Gothic outside and even gloriouser Gothic inside and the Gothic style is indeed a feature of Manchester. One of the other truly great public buildings, the John Rylands Library is Gothic too – a wonderful freer Gothic of the 1890s. This is another marvellous interior with the most theatrical and exciting staircase. The original Manchester University building is Gothic too (Waterhouse again), and there are the Crown Courts and the Reform Club and the Albert Memorial and a whole host of others. But Manchester has classical too (the Theatre Royal springs to mind) and there is wonderful Italianate stuff from the middle of the century (the City Art Gallery and the Free Trade Hall) and there's Arts and Crafts and Edwardian Baroque and Free Renaissance. In fact Manchester has everything and one of the things that makes it a capital city is that it was, and has remained, open to new influences throughout its history. Nowhere in the north, for example is there a wider range and a more exciting range of buildings from the 20th century.

Manchester's 20th-century adventurousness

The sequence starts in 1903 with the First Church of Christ Scientist by Edgar Wood. This was the most original church of its date in England (St Andrews, Roker in Sunderland by E.S. Prior gives it a run for its money). The sequence ends for the time being, at the very end of the century with three extraordinary new museum buildings. The Lowry Museum at Salford Quays and the Imperial War Museum in the north at Trafford Park – both utterly startling with bizarre free-form shapes – and Urbis, a shimmering glass building rising high above Manchester. In between virtually every decade is represented with bold and successful buildings in every 20th-century style.

20s There's a terrific Midland Bank by Lutyens from the 20s

30s I bought a car a year or two ago from a man who worked at the Daily Express Building of 1939 – a tour-de-force of smoothy 30s design with a skin entirely made of glass with sweeping rounded corners – the building, that is, not the car.

40s I can't think of anything from the 40s

50s I've already mentioned Oxford Road Station but the Cooperative Insurance Society's Tower of 1959 is the city's first and best skyscraper.

60s Loads. Some ghastly (Piccadilly Plaza, yuck), some superb (Chemical Engineering Pilot Plant ...)

You get the idea. Manchester has the scale and the wealth to think big. Of course, at times this means the scale and wealth to think ghastly. It's extraordinary, for example that the city has allowed the wonderful Free Trade Hall (where I once touched Ray Charles' hand, I'll have you know) to be so utterly banjoed and the city has been diminished, like all other British towns and cities, by the bland taste-lessness of the 20th century, by globalised shopping and the impossible demands of the car, but despite this, all the time it has held on to this spirit of urban adventure. In the last 20-odd years it has grasped the concept of re-use and re-development, not just of individual buildings but of whole neighbourhoods (suburban 60s nightmares like Hulme, Victorian industrial districts like Castlefields and Canal Street). It has re-introduced the tram and it has begun to embrace new architecture in a way that makes most places seem positively fuddy-duddy. That's why, in my opinion, it's safe to call Manchester the capital of the north.

All of which is fine if you're talking about town and city centres ... but what about the back streets?

Terraced houses, flats and cottages

Call me a cantankerous bad-tempered old git but I've got to moan. You see, I have something to moan about now which is as bad as any of my moans in the opening chapter. I could have included it then but I've been saving it up, lulling you into a false sense of warmth by describing lots of nice things, hoping you will have forgotten the view that outsiders have of us northern folk, so that this mega-moan will fill you with a suitable level of ferocious northern wrath.

I have got another book about English Houses, one that I haven't mentioned so far, which is filled with hundreds of beautiful photos of lush houses. It won't surprise you to learn that there are barely any photos of houses in the north, but among the very few there are, there's one showing a terrace of houses in Newcastle.

Now, I have to admit that this book was first published in the 1960s which is a bit of an excuse for what follows, but my glossy paperback edition was put out by a major national firm of publishers in the mid-1980s, so it's not that old, then …

… Unlike the photo of Newcastle, which looks very old. There's only one car visible in this photo and that seems to be pre-war if not prehistoric. There are a few old-fashioned children playing in the background and an old-fashioned doll's pram on the pavement. There's a gaslight, for heaven's sake, and in the foreground are two women standing in the middle of the road gossiping, wearing pinnies and head-scarves, their arms folded under their bosoms like

Les Dawson's granny or Andy Capp's Flo. It's a Newcastle, in fact, that died sometime in the early 1950s if not before, but I wouldn't mind that so much if it weren't for the caption that goes with it, which says:

> 'This characteristic example of the 19th century speculative builders' housing shows none of the flamboyance and individuality of the Victorian mansion or villa. It is a mean and diminished version of the Georgian terrace composition.'

Opposite it on the page is another Victorian terrace, a slightly posher one with bay windows, which honesty forces me to have to admit is an example from the south of England. This time the caption says that the bay windows ...

> '... impute a spurious vitality to the grim mechanical rhythm of the repeating units and accentuate the stark monotony with which the bays project one after another directly on to the drab street ... [they are] ... designed to impart an air of respectability to this last degraded and distorted phase of the noble architectural theme of the terrace ...'

I was cross when I read that. I don't know whether I was more cross at the way Newcastle was only being represented by something which the writer thinks of as 'mean' and 'diminished' or by the fact that my house was being described as 'the last degraded and distorted phase' of something ... because I live in a terrace house very like the one in the photo.

Now I know that terraced houses are not a specifically northern type of building, they are a specifically British type of building, but I want to include a chapter on them for three reasons. Firstly, when people think of the north, they think of terraces. They do. I've heard them. Secondly, we have so many of them, they make up such a vast part of our built environment, that it would be criminal in me to ignore them. And thirdly, we in the north have some of the most interesting terraced houses in the country including, of course ...

My house, my terraced home

Like hundreds of thousands of northerners, I've always lived in a terraced house. I was born into one, my family moved into another when I was seven. My student digs at college in Durham were in terraces, my first married flat was half a terraced house and since 1970 I've lived in the one I'm in now. I'm going to stay there too, until death or the bailiffs drag me out. I love my terraced house, including the bay window, despite the fact that it has 'a spurious vitality' and 'a grim mechanical rhythm'. I love sitting in it in the early evening or on a weekend morning watching the life of the street pass close in front of me, just beyond my tiny front garden.

My terraced house was built in about 1906 – so it's not quite Victorian – but it *was* built by speculative builders who put up the street a few houses at a time, as and when there were buyers. Each buyer had a certain amount of freedom of choice. You could have a one- or a two-storey bay window, for example, and you could choose to have one big bedroom at the front on the first floor or two smaller ones. You could choose to add an attic with a dormer window if you wanted one, or you could do without. Rumour has it that the first buyer was even given the choice of naming the street and because he was a keen cyclist, decided to name it after his bike.

There were limitations as well as choices. There always are. According to the deeds I am not allowed to keep pigs in my backyard or brew beer and I'm not allowed to put up any erection higher than 12 feet which, as you can imagine, has been something of a restriction to me.

Considering that it's 'mean' and 'diminished' my house seems to me to be quite rich in facilities. My backyard used to have an outside toilet and a coalhouse, though both have now gone, but because my house was built as late as 1906 it has always had an inside toilet and a separate bathroom as well. There are four bedrooms, which is very generous, and a breakfast room as well as a kitchen. It has a little internal porch with a glass door which helps to keep the winds and the door-to-door salespersons at bay. There's a cupboard under the stairs and the staircase itself has nicely turned wooden balusters.

I suspect that my house was originally built for lower middle-class families. I think this partly because lower middle-class people like myself have continued to live in the street ever since – teachers, tradesmen, nurses, people like that. It always has a few younger people in better paid professions who stay for a while before moving on to something more impressive. I also think it was for this class of people because it looks as if it was. It doesn't have proper gardens – just a backyard and a tiny front garden; there are no architectural frills which might have been added if the house was aimed at slightly posher folk. Inside there is the same simplicity. There don't appear to have been facilities for servants and, though it is very nice, there aren't many decorative bits or any expensive finishes.

In the area of Newcastle where I live there are thousands of terraced houses. A lot of them are quite like mine, some are smaller and even plainer, some are bigger and considerably posher. A few are absolutely splendid and palatial but what they've all got in common is that they are terraced houses built in the Victorian era or shortly after and that they're still doing very nicely a hundred and odd years later, thank you very much.

It is quite amazing how resilient and adaptable this class of houses has turned out to be. Take my house again. One of the bedrooms is now the study where I am typing these words. The breakfast room and kitchen have been knocked into one room to suit our particular form of family life. The coalhouse has gone but we've got lovely snuggly-snuggly central heating and loads of those clever imitation gas fires which look convincingly like coal, feel convincingly warm but don't tread dirt all over the carpets. The backyard has lost its toilet and become a patio instead, awash with potted plants and decks and things as if we were living in Majorca instead of Newcastle. Far from being the 'last degraded and distorted phase' of its architectural type it has turned out to be a living, changing, constantly desirable example of a housing form which is peculiarly English and, to be honest, absolutely typically northern.

Slums?

In talking about terraces, I need to say, I think, that I'm not talking about slums. My dictionary defines a slum as 'a squalid overcrowded house ... a squalid section of a city characterised by inferior living conditions and usually by overcrowding'.

There was a time in the middle of the 1900s when planners and architects seemed to think that almost all terraced houses were slums so they pulled them down in vast quantities and replaced them with tower blocks. The photograph of the Newcastle terrace that caused me so much grief was, I think, taken in the suburb of Byker where a whole community of terraced streets running down the hills towards the Tyne almost defined the character of the city in many people's minds, until the terraces were pulled down at the end of the 60s to be replaced by something more modern. But the Byker terraces were not slums. They were working-class houses, part of a vibrant Tyneside community, and what caused them to be pulled down was not desperate need, or overcrowding or extreme poverty, though there might have been pockets of all of those things, but a new planning philosophy which saw terraced houses as outmoded.

As a way of illustrating how planners and architects thought at that time, I've got a photograph which I tore out of an architecture magazine back in the 1960s. It shows a Tyneside terrace and behind it, lots and lots of storeys high, there are three tower blocks in the Shieldfield area of the city, newly built by the city architect. The caption praises the tower blocks in the following terms:

In contrast with the old-fashioned and dingy buildings of yester-year we illustrate here the modern way of living that comes from modern design and constructional methods.

I bet I don't need to tell you that the 'old-fashioned and dingy' buildings 'of yester-year' are still there and actively sought-after nowadays as desirable homes. The flats are there too (though modified by new approaches and security access systems) and generally regretted.

There really were slums all over the north, of course. They were the result of bad housing, or of good housing which had been allowed to go bad by a lack of proper control. The conditions placed on me by my deeds (no pigs, no beer and especially no substantial sticky-uppy bits) are there to stop me using my house for unsuitable purposes. They were written into the original building permissions to stop my street turning into a slum. But in lots of places this never happened. Older houses were badly used and allowed to become overcrowded, or unscrupulous builders got away with putting up houses without adequate safeguards.

At my mum's friend Nancy's house in Whitehaven, for example, and in the streets all around her, the back gardens had long ago disappeared, eaten up by uncontrolled development in the 19th century which squeezed meaner houses and jerry-built workplaces into whatever space they could find. The result was overcrowding and unsuitable living conditions – a problem which, very properly, the 20th century had to sort out.

This happened everywhere. Bad houses got squeezed into the gaps behind better houses. The worst examples were known as courts. They were really narrow lanes or small yards surrounded by houses. They were cut off from the street, and the way into them was usually by a tunnel through a building fronting onto the street. There are still lots of courts about, I can think of several in Newcastle, but none of them is now used to live in, they all seem to have cheap premises for small business use nowadays, but in the past they were often pretty terrible places to live.

Here's a description of a court in Manchester which was written by Friedrich Engels in 1845. I probably wouldn't read this while eating my dinner if I were you.

'… Right and left a multitude of covered passages lead from the main street into numerous courts, and he who turns into thither gets into a filth and disgusting grime, the equal of which is not to be found … and which contain unqualifiedly the most horrible dwellings which I have yet to behold. In one of these courts there stands directly at the entrance, at the end of the covered passage, a privy without a door, so dirty that the inhabitants can pass into and out of the court only by passing through foul pools of stagnant urine and excrement …'

Hm!

Well, I'm certainly not talking about housing like that when I'm praising the terraces of the north. The sort of terraces I'm talking about weren't perfect. I know that; they were built fast in order to house the vast numbers of people needed for the new industries, but they were also built to *replace* the sort of slum housing seen by Engels. They were built under the influence of a series of Acts of Parliament designed to improve working-class housing and, sometimes even more importantly, they were built under the influence of local council by-laws, which laid down even stricter controls than the ones imposed by Parliament. And sometimes they were built under the inspiration of philanthropists who were aware of the horrible conditions that currently existed and wanted to do something about it.

Saltaire and a few other model workers' villages

The West Riding of Yorkshire has a terrific crop of towns, villages and estates which were laid out by Victorian factory owners for their workforces with rather more care and charitable concern than normal.

The earliest was done by a Halifax mill-owner called Colonel Akroyd. He had a mill at Copley just south of Halifax and in the 1840s he put up some streets of back-to-back houses for his workers and he built a few other bits and pieces – a school and a library and a canteen where they were guaranteed a nice dinner of meat and potatoes each day for a penny halfpenny. It's all still there, still nice and distinctive, nice 19th-century feel.

A few years later Colonel Akroyd built another village for the workers at his other mill on the far side of Halifax and with commendable modesty he chose to call it Akroydon, after himself. A nice touch, I thought, and made even more touching by the fact that he built himself a mansion on the hill above his workers' cottages with a stable block which is about 32,000 times posher than the humans' houses. But nevertheless, I like Akroydon. The houses are pretty, though small, the views must have been lovely once, before the town expanded beyond it, and the accommodation was much better than the workers would have found elswhere.

I don't like it as much as I like Saltaire, though.

Saltaire is the most famous of all of these philanthropic model villages and it deserves to be. I went to have a look at it just three days before writing this and really liked it again, as much as I have done every time I've been there.

It was built between 1851 and 1876 a few miles north of Bradford by a Bradford mill-owner called Titus Salt. They certainly knew how to name a lad, those old Victorian families. His mill was for manufacturing cloth from alpaca, or llama wool, which produced a very posh and luxurious product which was made into upmarket ladies' dresses (or indeed dresses for upmarket ladies). The mill is gigantic and hugely impressive as well and round it he built a model town of 824 houses with shops and a church, schools, parks and all the proper institutions for a town at that time. Each of these institutions is a very beautiful place in its own right but it is the houses I want to talk about now.

When Saltaire was being built, Bradford was the world capital of the worsted industry, making loads of dosh for the factory owners and constantly growing bigger and more powerful. In the first half of the 19th century its population had increased from 13,000 to 150,000 and it was having a really bad time housing all of those people. Conditions seem to have been similar to the ones that Engels saw in Manchester. Sanitation was appalling, overcrowding terrible, pollution was rampant. There was cholera, smallpox, anthrax, TB, terrible infant mortality. It really sounds a horrible place to have been a working-class family in. This was the world that Titus Salt moved into.

He chose to build his model town on a greenfield site away from the pollution of the city and he built nice houses – not great houses but nice houses. Even by today's standards they seem nice. Actually, to look at, I think they're beautiful, built in fine stone with lovely Italianate architectural details. A lot of them have got nicely round-arched doors and windows, boldly framed, with keystones to each arch. The streets are laid out in rather a systematic grid pattern with slightly taller and posher houses at the ends of each row, which gives the streets an extra touch of distinction. The back lanes are narrow, no more than a walkway between very small backyards, but even here there is a sense of intimacy rather than meanness.

So even today they seem fine, but at the time they were a revolution. There were no nasty enclosed courts, no foul smelly bits, no shared houses and gross overcrowding. On the contrary, each of the backyards had its own private privy which was emptied regularly, and even the smallest houses had two, sometimes three, bedrooms along with a kitchen and a living room.

Of course, Saltaire and the other model villages were exceptional places. They were put up by men with highly sensitive social consciences who believed that their great wealth (because they were very rich) carried social responsibilities along with it and men like that, I think a cursory glance around the world will back me up on this, are pretty few and far between, but nevertheless, if there aren't a lot of Saltaires, there are still plenty of other extraordinarily interesting developments of terraced houses throughout the north.

Variety

That quote, that irritating quote that I gave at the beginning of the chapter, talked about the Newcastle terrace as a '*characteristic example*' and I suppose it is possible, if you just have a casual glance, to think that a terraced house is a terraced house is a terraced house – that they're all more or less the same. But this is not the case. Nay, nay, lad. Far from it. There's an excellent book called *The English Terraced House* by Stefan Muthesius which first opened my eyes to the extraordinary variety of style, plans and patterns of terraced houses around the country.

Most books on architecture make the claim that by the mid-1800s local and regional styles had disappeared from English architecture because, by that time, railways were able to deliver identical materials to any part of the country. Welsh slate had become so common that everybody everywhere was using it. Brick was everywhere. Travel was easy too, so it wasn't really possible for places to remain behind the times. Builders everywhere knew what the rest of the country was building and so everybody ended up using the same style. That's what most of the books say and it all makes sense, but Stefan Muthesius was the first to point out to me that in fact it isn't true, that even Victorian terraced houses have regional styles; that towns in the West Riding built different sorts of working-class terraces to towns in Lancashire; that Hull has highly unusual layouts for its terraced streets and that a blindfolded visitor to Sunderland would know where he was, the instant the blindfold was taken off, so utterly distinctive are its terraces.

The moment I read about the variety, it became obvious. My terrace house, for example, is built of brick with sandstone surrounds for the windows; all Newcastle terraces are like that. South Shields where I work – a mere eight miles down the road – is quite different. There are no stone surrounds in South Shields, they use wood instead, brightly painted wood, and very pretty it can look too, the long terraces with the repeated patterns of the bay windows all painted in different colours.

In South Shields there are a number of other specialities. It used to be an important shipbuilding town, especially in the time of wooden ships and it's really common in the town to find the old ship-builders' carpentry skills transferred to the houses. You get carved wooden brackets on the door surrounds as fancy as ships' figure-heads, elaborate and bulging with carved fruit, flowers and faces (though too few bosoms for my taste). One street near the college where I work has a distinctly nautical feel. There are high triangular gables, wood panelled and painted white, which look like sails and above the doors there are oval windows that look for all the world like portholes. This street was known locally as Honeymoon Row because the houses were small and quite cheap, but pretty and romantic, so they were popular with Edwardian newlyweds.

In Carlisle where I was brought up, many of the earlier terraced streets, the ones built in the middle of the 19th century, have a really attractive feature. They're built of two different colours of brick – a nice rosy pink one and a paler whitish one and the two colours are laid alternately to create a lovely checkerboard pattern. It doesn't seem to make any difference whether they're cheaper working-class houses opening straight onto the street or larger middle-class ones, they share this quality.

I suspect that wherever I went I would find this variety and I could spend the next 30,000 words describing it to you, but there are a number of particular variations which will do to express the range of possibilities offered by this one, common but often overlooked, house style.

The Flying Freeholds of Hebden Bridge ...

... and probably a number of other places in the steep-sided valleys of the West Riding.

Hebden Bridge is in Calderdale between Halifax and Rochdale.

The Rochdale Canal runs through it. The valley is narrow at this point and the valley sides quite painfully steep. When I was walking up them I found myself admiring the view more often than I normally do. That was my excuse, anyway. The valley bottom is filled with the town centre and the mills and other industries that needed the canal, so any housing had to make do with the hillsides. Almost all of the houses are built in terraces which run along the hillside, following the contours. Because the hills are so steep, in many cases the houses have no entrance at the back, or even no openings at the back because they're built directly into the hillside – but the really extraordinary thing is that in order to save on space, the houses in the next street further up the hill are built on top of the ones below. That means, of course, that they look like ordinary two-storey houses from the front but at the back they look like flats, three and four storeys up in the sky. On the opposite side of the street the arrangement starts again, so every street you walk along appears to have two-storey houses on one side and four-storey houses on the other. It really is amazing.

I gather, though I have to admit that I've done no detailed research into this, since I find studying contracts and things as interesting as watching *Hollyoaks*, but I do gather that wholly original forms of ownership and responsibility have had to be devised to cope with the bizarre relationships that must exist. It's known as 'flying freehold'. It doesn't bear thinking about, does it. It's bad enough being responsible for an ordinary house but I wonder who's responsible for the roof or the foundations? What if damp at the back downstairs threatens the stability of both houses? What if a runaway lorry demolishes part of downstairs house? I wonder if there are advantages too, though. Perhaps the two houses help to keep each other warm. Maybe you are only responsible for half the roof. I wish I knew the answers to questions like that. I bet you wish I did too. But I don't.

Back-to-Backs in Leeds ...

... and of course lots of other places in the West Riding.

People down south, I suspect, think that all northern terraced houses are back-to-backs but *real* back-to-backs have always been rather limited in their geographical distribution. In the North East, for example, there have never been any, but there was a time when they were pretty common in lots of of other places – in Birmingham and Nottingham and in Manchester, for example, but for reasons which I'll come to in a minute, they were abolished in most areas a long time ago and nowadays they are pretty rare except in the West Riding of Yorkshire.

But what were they? you impatiently demand to know. They were ... they are ... houses with no rear access, no back door and no back windows. Usually they share their back wall with a house in the next street so they are literally *back to back*, but there are a few half rows which just end in a blank back wall. Those ones look odd, I have to admit.

Because they've got no light or ventilation at the back, it's fairly obvious that they can only be one room deep. You couldn't have rooms at the back of the house with no natural light at all, so as a result they are one room deep but quite tall. They're usually two storeys high with a basement and an attic making them four storeys in all. The examples I know best are in Leeds, just off Roundhay Road, and those are the ones I'm describing now – not necessarily the way they *are* now, but the way they *were* when they were built.

The basements are provided with natural light by little half-windows which peep up above the pavement and originally they would have had a pantry and a coal shed which could be filled directly from the street via a low door beside the window. On the ground floor you entered straight into a small scullery and a door from there led into the main room – the kitchen cum living room. The staircase was in the corner of this room, probably not shut off in any way. Upstairs there were two bedrooms, a tiny one and a bigger one. The attic was quite big, usually with a dormer window and was probably used as bedroom space as well.

Notice anything missing? Nee lav and nee bath, as we might say in Newcastle. They've all got lavs and bathrooms nowadays of course, fitted into the basements or into the smaller of the first-floor bedrooms, but originally there were only outside toilets grouped together in gaps in the terrace – one block of toilets for every eight houses. The gaps are still there but they're used to hold the wheely bins now. Presumably, if people bathed at all they bathed in tin baths in front of the fire or went to a public bath house.

(An old man from Blyth, in Northumberland, told me a story about tin baths. He had a new girl friend and she took him back to her house where he sat beside the fire and was introduced to her dad. As they chatted, his girlfriend started messing about with tin baths and hot water and stuff and it became obvious that she was getting ready to have a bath in front of the fire. My friend said that he got nervous and made a move to leave before anyone could be embarrassed, but her father stopped him and said, 'Diven't worry, son, she'll niver splash you.')

I filmed in these streets of back-to-back houses in Leeds recently and I found them very interesting. I can't exaggerate and say that I would like to live in them because the houses are small and the area relatively poor and there are no gardens and no private back yards, and yet they are still obviously useful because they're still being lived in – in fact the area had quite a vibrant feel to it. One of the features of streets of back-to-back housing is that you get larger buildings built across the ends of the rows and these often have shops on the ground floor. So the area of Leeds where I filmed is rich in corner shops, lots of greengrocers and newsagents and butchers, ladies' hairdressers, video shops and so on, and that gives the streets a real sense of life.

Nobody is absolutely clear why the West Riding towns kept on building back-to-backs so long after other places banned them but at least one answer is that they continued to be popular. Leeds tried to ban them but had to relax the ban because people wanted them. They were finally banned under a National Town Planning Act in 1909 but even after that, development schemes which already had planning permission continued to build back-to-backs right up to the 1930s. Why? Well, they were fairly cheap to build and they've stayed cheap to buy – and they must be quite warm, sharing party walls with other houses on three sides and having comparatively few rooms to heat. You can understand it.

When I was filming, I got talking to one lady who lived in the street we were in and she told me she'd moved there from near Barrow-in-Furness and that she loved it. She'd been there 30 years and she'd always loved it. It was cosy, she said, and the neighbours were friendly and, good grief, how she'd decorated it – stuff and knick-knacks, flowers in pots. It was really homely, just what you'd want a back-to-back in a Yorkshire town to be like.

The Avenues in Hull

Sounds posh that, doesn't it? The word 'avenue' suggests tree-lined streets of middle-class housing but that's not what the word means in Hull. In Hull, an avenue is a street of houses at right-angles to the main street. There are long main streets with houses along them in the usual way except that they are broken up by the avenues running off at right angles. The avenues have no roads running down the middle of them, they have footpaths instead, and short gardens and very often brightly painted wooden bay windows as well. You can get to the back of the house in the avenues either by a back lane or by another pathway behind each row which you've got to reach by a tunnel through the houses on the main street ...

... a tunnel! Thinks. Doth that sound like the entrances to the Manchester courts as described by Engels? Indeed it doth. It seems that at one time Hull had loads and loads of courts of the old-fashioned and thoroughly nasty variety and when they got to be rebuilt in Victorian times the people of Hull hung on to the old patterns and built houses which were rather court-like, not stretched out along normal roads in the traditional way – except of course, that they built them much nicer than the old courts had been. They tended, on the whole, to avoid doorless and overflowing privies and in fact the avenues in Hull are lovely little streets and must have been ever since they were first built. They're nice because in 1852 and again in 1875, the city introduced strict by-laws which controlled how they should be built – how far apart they must be, how big the gardens had to be, that at the front they must have direct entrance to the main street (not through a tunnel in other words), that there must be access to the back of the house as well as to the front.

What Hull did was to take an old-fashioned and traditional form and adapt it to new use and they did it so successfully that these streets have been a key feature of the town ever since – distinctive, affordable and attractive. Which is more than you can say for most of us.

The Tyneside Flat

On Tyneside we have very few of these avenues, no flying freeholds and no back-to-backs. What we do have is terraced flats, hundreds and thousands of them. Two storeys high with one flat on the ground floor and one flat on the first floor. They're not quite unique. London has some and there are said to be a few elsewhere, though I've never seen them and I've just, to my absolute shock and horror, seen a photograph of a street of them in Sunderland of all places, which was demolished a number of years ago; but there is almost no doubt that they were invented on Tyneside much earlier than they appeared anywhere else and they are also much more common there than anywhere else.

They seem to have first appeared round about 1850 and in about half a century, by 1911, as much as 44.5% of the population of Newcastle lived in flats – in Tyneside flats of course. Elsewhere in the country only 3.7% of the population lived in flats. That's a remarkable difference, I am sure you'll agree. I am now going to offer you an explanation as to why that should be the case ...

?

??

???

... to be honest I can't. People mutter about closeness to Scotland where folk have lived in flats for centuries but there's nothing else about Tyneside which is especially influenced by Scotland. Stefan Muthesius has a load of ingenious suggestions but none of them are really convincing. He suggests that on the steep banks of the Tyne people were used to living in tall houses which were subdivided horizontally. He says that early in the 19th century, overcrowding was worse on Tyneside than elsewhere so people got used to sharing houses. He points to a local by-law which said that all cellars had to have areas in front of them to provide more light and ventilation and that may have led to basements becoming ground floor flats. All of these seem to be reasons that could have happened anywhere and therefore they seem to be rather weak explanations as to why flats only appeared on Tyneside. They also seem to contradict each other a bit. So JG is not convinced.

I have another explanation which is my own tragically unscientific thought.

Perhaps someone invented them and they caught on! There's a thought. They appear mainly on the estates laid out by the big industrialists, men like the great Lord Armstrong, whose huge factories on the Tyne employed thousands of men, all of whom needed housing. It just seems possible that he (or one of the other big employers) said to his builder, 'See if you can come up with something fairly cheap that'll house lerds and lerds of people (this is Tyneside after all) in not too much space.'

'Cos that's the effect. You get two houses for the price of one piece of land. Dashed cunning, if you ask me.

You can always tell if a street has Tyneside flats instead of ordinary houses because each house has two separate doors side by side – one of them leads into the ground-floor flat, the other opens straight onto the stairs to the upper flat. You can tell from the back lane as well, because the outshuts, the rear extensions at the back of the houses, always have a staircase down from the upper flat and the backyards are divided in two by a wall so that each flat has its own little private space at the back. This little piece of privacy contained a privy, of course, or 'netty' as it's called on Tyneside. This is another thing that people argue about. Why 'netty'? Is it from the French 'nettoyer', to clean? Or is it named after the 'necessarium' which monks had in their monasteries? But whatever it's called and wherever the name came from, all of these Victorian working-class house types that I've been describing were built with outside toilets.

Back Lanes

Most backyards had two doors in the backyard wall: one door for shovelling out the nasties and another door for pouring the coal into the coalhouse, and though the doors themselves have often gone, their position is almost always visible from the back lane because of the newer brickwork where they have been filled in.

I love back lanes. Mine is a typical Tyneside back lane – 20 feet wide and nicely cobbled still, perfect for footie, challenging for cricket (because of the cobbles) – but it has lost most of its old privy and

A lavatorial interlude: a brief visit to the netty

Did you know that, on average, we spend a year of our lives on the toilet? Actually I didn't know that either. I've just made it up, but we do spend a jolly long time. It's a very important place to us and yet it is almost an invisible place. People use toilets almost constantly I believe, but nobody seems to notice them, so I intend to detour for a moment or two, opening the door on the toilet ... after knocking discreetly first of course.

I said a few moments ago that my terraced house, built in 1906, was provided with an indoor toilet from the start. Let me introduce you to it ...

It's a water closet of course and much to my wife's chagrin it still has its high level cistern that releases a mighty torrent of water when you flush it, making so much noise that it notifies people as far away as South Africa that you have just been to the lavatory. Its chain has a cunning way of hiding behind the curtain which catches out the unwary. Our Gran once disappeared for some time on a visit upstairs and it became clear that she couldn't find the chain and was mystified as to how our new-fangled loo worked. Eventually she fell back on older technology and got a bucket of water from the kitchen to flush it. Our loo has got a nice high pan, boldly emblazoned with the Edwardian maker's name – PURITAS – a strong Latin name to suggest quality and tradition and of course to emphasise how utterly clean the whole process is. It has an S-bend to provide an impenetrable barrier to any lurking smells. The room was provided from the start with an outside window and a separate drain all to itself.

The point about my little toilet is that it represents the level of sanitation that was available to most people in the north by the beginning of the 20th century and that was a very high level by comparison to earlier times. A generation earlier the situation was very different indeed. Go back a couple of generations and ordinary people had hardly any sanitary provision at all.

My great-grandfather, who was a Lake District labourer, was reluctant to use a toilet at all, right up to the end of his life. He apparently used to say, 'It's far sweeter ahint the dyke' but as Engels pointed out in Manchester, there were no dykes to hide ahint in big cities and as the population increased, so did the lavatorial horror.

Some places employed 'night soil men' to take the stuff away, but they didn't take it very far, not far enough. In Newcastle they just hoyed it over the wall and in 1620 a dunghill 98 yards long, 32 yards wide and 10 yards high caused part of the city wall to collapse. By the first half of the 19th century the situation reached crisis point. There were cholera outbreaks in 1831, 1848 and 1853 and as many as one child in seven was dying from lack of proper sanitation.

So they started building drains, and by 1865 it was a legal requirement that every house should have a drain connected to a common sewer under the road. That didn't mean, though, that by that time every house had a proper water closet like my lovely little indoor lav. That was to take another half century to achieve. For a long time the situation was quite varied.

For example, in 1885 in Newcastle, only 22.8% of houses had an indoor water closet (i.e. flushing lav). Almost 41% had an outside WC but there were still 35% of all houses which had outside privies. These weren't flushing loos but ash closets in which the oojah was mixed with ash and cinders from the fire and emptied out every now and again by the old night soil chappy who came round with his bin and poured the contents of the privy through a door in the backyard wall. What a lovely job that must have been ... but as the old joke (almost) goes, it might be oojah to you but it was bread and butter to him.

Anyway, that means, if my maths have stood up to the strain, that until the end of the Victorian period, over three quarters of houses had to make do with outside toilets ... the wonderful netty.

Of course it was the smaller and poorer houses that were the last to be provided with indoor facilities and many of us from such backgrounds who are a bit older will still have memories of outside loos – the icy dash – the fear of lurking spiders – the darkness – the paraffin lamp left burning on cold winter nights to keep the temperature above freezing. It used to be a way of life.

Yer had ter gan ootside, pet, whativer the weather. It made yer canny tough, like.

One elderly lady I talked to blamed the gradual disappearance of outside toilets (or netties) for the rise in vandalism in late 20th-century England. She said that children were bored because they could no longer pass the time by leaping along the back lane from toilet roof to toilet roof ... or as she put it: 'Wey, there's noot for them ter dee, nooadays, yer knaa. In wor day, yer could gan nettie lowping.'

coalhouse doors; people have punched garage doors into the walls and there have been all sorts of changes so it isn't quite as nice as some. But when you find a smasher ... oh, I could take you to some beauties ... in Durham, for example, unaltered, with nice granite runners down the middle of the cobblestones and hooks set periodically into the walls to hang washing lines from; where the backyard walls are capped with brown terracotta coping stones and the drain covers are solid and Victorian. It's like stepping back in time. I love it when you still see washing hanging out in the back lane. I know a terrace in Morpeth where they still hang their washing out, crisscrossed across the lane. It looks odd with the parked cars, mind you. I feel that there might be some arguments.

I heard the artist David Hockney tell a story about back lanes. He was born in Bradford which is awash with back lanes but lives in Los Angeles which isn't, and one day he went to collect his mum from the airport when she had come for a visit. As they were driving through poshest Beverly Hills, or somewhere, she went thoughtful and said, 'Look at those houses. All of that garden and not a bit of washing out on a beautiful drying day like this.'

I read another story about back lanes and backyards and Yorkshire ladies and things. Apparently, in the 1990s, there was a mysterious rash of injuries to elderly West Riding, working-class ladies. It coincided with the arrival of wheely bins on the scene, and it turned out that lots of respectable old ladies, desperate to maintain their lifetime's grip on the evil dirt, were breaking limbs by falling in to the wheely bin while trying to wash it out.

What I'm saying, I suppose, in telling stories like those, is that part of the appeal of terraces and back lanes is to do with nostalgia for a well-ordered northern working-class past, for a time when millworkers in clogs trudged down to the tram and mothers in pinnies washed their steps and small Bobby Charltons played football with their brothers in the back lanes of pit villages like Ashington.

Ashington

I have a weakness for pit villages, for simple red-brick pit-village churches and the unadorned grids of pit houses. They're not pretty of course, though they're sometimes in pretty places and their names can be quite extraordinary. 'No Place' and 'Co-operative Villas', near Stanley in County Durham are my two favourite pit village names. Though I'm equally fond of some of the street names you find in other villages. The 'Brontë' streets in Felling (Charlotte Street, Anne Street and Emily Street) are narrow, gardenless and abut up against the railway line and are about as far removed from *Wuthering Heights* as it's possible to be. I like Electric Avenue and Voltage Crescent in Shiney Row as well.

The name Ashington, in the south-east Northumberland coalfield, is another which sounds a bit pit villagey as well – a town made of ash, though in reality it's a much more ancient name and means 'the settlement among the ash trees', which is nice – especially as the town really is a pit village and is often described as the biggest pit village in the world. Like Saltaire, it was the product of one single company, in this case the Ashington Coal Company; but unlike Saltaire there doesn't seem to have been much charitable intention in creating the place. The company just needed lots of houses to put the workers in, so there's nothing very architectural about it and the houses are of a type which is familiar in hundreds of other pit villages in the North East … except that the rows are bigger. The terraces are gigantic, they go on for ever and their length makes them seem remarkable; but they're also laid out in a way which is quite unusual. There are just pathways between the houses and quite substantial front gardens, so superficially they're a bit like The Avenues in Hull. The back lanes have pretty well all been altered nowadays, unfortunately, because they were really distinctive. They're my reason for giving Ashington a special mention because they are very, very wide and at one time they all had little tramways built down them to sort of automate the process of taking away the rubbish and the contents of the ash closets. Isn't that a modern sort of idea.

... a little worry ...

OK, I've been zooming round the north enthusing about a variety of different terraced house types and I want to finish with the type that impresses me most … but I have a worry. I come from Newcastle, you see, the Toon, as they insist on calling it in the local paper these days, and I'm not sure how my neighbours will take to me choosing a favourite of any sort, which comes from Sunderland. And yet that is what I must do, for I am a great admirer of ...

The Sunderland Cottage

I seem to recall, many pages ago, saying that a blindfold traveller, suddenly exposed to Sunderland, would know instantly where he was, because only Sunderland among the towns and cities of England has terraces of single-storey cottages.

Once again, like with the Tyneside flat, I don't know why this is. I have seen lots of suggestions but none that is entirely convincing so instead of talking about where they came from I'm going to tell you what they're like.

Single storey. Terraces. Unique. Actually within that rather narrow description there are lots of variations. Some were obviously intended to be for poorer families but others are distinctly lower middle-class in feel. Some are tiny, single-fronted and open straight onto the street. Others have small gardens and are as big inside as normal two-storey houses. The rooms in fact are often surprisingly large. Living rooms 16 feet by 14 feet are common and they can have good size parlours, bedrooms and kitchens.

They first began to appear in the 1840s and they were still being built early in the 20th century. They are still very, very popular today for the same reasons that they were always popular. They are not very expensive and they give their occupants a place of their own. Privacy is the great selling point of the Sunderland cottage. They all have a private yard and their own front door and you don't have to share it with anyone. Angela Long, who writes with pride about her home town in a book called *Northumbrian Panorama*, says this

'To the worker, the early cottage allowed privacy and space to bring up his family, and the growing pride of the working-class artisan could be expressed by moving into an estate, either as a tenant or as owner of one or two cottages.'

Because there were cottages of all different sizes, she points out, a family, through its lifetime, as children came along and the family got larger, could change houses several times without moving more than a few streets. And because they were fairly cheap and Sunderland's shipyard workers were relatively well paid, a surprisingly large number of working-class families could even own their own houses. Angela Long points out that, in 1890, 27% of the population of Sunderland owned their own home while in Birmingham the figure was a measly 3%. The town had a lot of Building Societies too, including one called the Working Man's Building Society, so there seems to have been a strong independent feeling about the people of Sunderland in the 19th century which is reflected in the sort of splendid, sturdy little houses they built. Perhaps the independent feeling was partly created by the cottages themselves on the principle that where you live is what you are.

chapter ten

The Back Streets

Around the centres of northern towns and mingled with the terraced streets there was a whole world – the world, you might call it, of the Hovis advert – a world of factories and pubs, chip shops, Victorian churches and chapels. That's the world I want to visit now. The only question is what order to visit it in and the answer, to be honest, is as obvious as life itself, the daily rhythm. You go to work first and then you come home (to your terraced house). You slip out for a jar or three at the local down the road, buy a bag of chips on the way home, sleep it off and go to chapel next day to say you're sorry. That's just the way it is.

The mill

The first job I ever had (except for being a juvenile charperson at my Auntie Martha's house) was in a factory.

When I was 17 … hmmm, thinks … Like Frank Sinatra I could sing that … when I was 17, it was a very good year, it was a very good year for small town boys. It *was* a very good year for me because I got a summer holiday job at a factory in Carlisle called Dixon's Mills.

I was in the despatch department, well actually, I *was* the despatch department that summer, because the chap I was supposed to work with fell ill just after I arrived. What I despatched was wool, high-quality woollen thread. Some of it was despatched no further than Linton Tweeds in the weaving sheds on the other side of the mill yard who made – and still make – material for the Paris fashion houses. And a lot of it went to Jaeger and Pringle at Hawick up in Scotland because we at Dixon's Mills only despatched the best.

My temporary seat of power was on the ground floor, obviously enough – you can't despatch things out of upstairs windows and hope to get away with it – but one of my jobs was to go upstairs to the spinning floors to collect batches of wool for despatching purposes. I loved going up there; the vast floors were completely filled with great rows of spinning machines with spinning bobbins all along the top. The noise was tremendous. Rows of mill girls looked after the machines, shrieking at one another over the din, watching for broken thread, putting on new bobbins, removing full ones and tossing them into barrows behind them.

All of this was happening in the 1960s, but they were scenes that couldn't have changed much since Victorian times and I'd like to tell you that I was excited because I was aware of being part of all of this living industrial history, that I was aware that it was soon going to change, but no, it was the girls who excited and scared me when I went upstairs. Bye, they were tough and unpredictable, capable of unspeakable acts with woollen thread and barrows. And they were fast. You quickly learned never to turn your back on a Carlisle mill girl.

I've been describing Dixon's Mill as a woollen mill but actually, like all of the Carlisle Mills, it was built originally as a cotton mill. It was built in 1836 and for a brief period of time it was the largest factory in the world, in fact, when I was 17, it was still the biggest building in Carlisle, apart from the new Civic Centre, which was taller but not so bulky.

It's seven storeys high

225 feet long

and it's got 391 windows

And then there's the chimney. Dixon's chimney always seemed a more important Carlisle landmark to me than the castle or the cathedral. The brim of the chimney was wide enough to ride a mini round and 305 feet high – I think it has lost a bit off the top in recent years – but at 305 feet it was one of the tallest chimneys ever built (the tallest ever was the Blinkhorn chimney at Bolton which was 366 feet, but that has been demolished).

The engineer responsible for Dixon's Mills was a very impressive Scottish engineer called Sir William Fairbairn who worked for a while in Newcastle, but then went on to become a major bigwig in the development of the Lancashire cotton industry. The method of construction he used was fairly recent and quite revolutionary at the time. The outside walls were conventional stone walls but inside he used something called 'fireproof construction' which meant that all of the materials used in it were supposedly fireproof. The ceilings were made of brick arches supported on cast-iron columns. The floors were made of sheets of iron. It was a system devised initially for the cotton industry where inflammable cotton dust made the risk of fire particularly high. In Lancashire it first appeared in 1792, in the Yorkshire woollen industry ten years later. As a system, to be honest it sounds better than it was in practice because, if the textiles did catch fire, the cast-iron columns were just as likely to fail as if they had been made of wood and it wasn't until mills started using concrete for their construction towards the end of the 19th century (Manningham Mill, Bradford, 1871 might have been the first) that the danger from fire began to go away.

A whole world of mills

I've been a bit naughty starting off stuff on mills in Carlisle which was a very minor player in the industrial revolution, instead of Lancashire and Yorkshire where the whole thing got going but, to be honest, it doesn't really matter where you go. The factory system started with the textile industry – it really got going in Lancashire in the 1760s but in architectural terms it followed a very similar pattern wherever it appeared.

First of all, the mills had to be beside a river. In the early days they needed water because the spinning machines were driven by water wheels, so the first mills were built in the steep-sided valleys of the Pennines where, I am reliably informed, a good head of water can always be guaranteed. But even when steam power took over (1770 it was first used. The first purpose-built steam mill was built in 1791) a good water supply was still necessary to feed the steam engines – it just didn't need to be running so fast, so the mills were able to come down out of the hills onto the plains. But wherever they were, the mills tended to look more or less the same – tall, multi-storey, rather narrow with big windows to provide as much natural light as possible. Before gas lighting arrived they were always quite narrow so that each workroom had rows of windows along both sides and even after the arrival of gas (first gas-lit mill, Lodges Mill, Sowerby Bridge, West Yorkshire, 1802) a lot of mills continued to be built narrow because natural light was cheaper than gaslight. As well as the main building there was always a big chimney to make the steam engine as efficient as possible, and to house the engine there was a smaller engine-house at one end. If it was a big factory complex then there were single-storey weaving sheds as well and perhaps a gas plant for making the gas to light the mill. The offices were sometimes separate or sometimes they made an entrance, a sort of frontispiece, to the main mill.

I don't need to tell you that mills like this are to be found all over the West Riding and all over Southern and Eastern Lancashire. Because they needed to be beside rivers or canals they're often found stretched out in long rows along the river banks, mill after mill forming formidable cliffs of stone. In town after town you find them dominating the valley bottoms and leaving the steep hillsides for people to live on. Pretty well everywhere you go you find that everything was built in the same style – a simple, stripped down, classical style with hardly any fancy bits at all.

Salts Mill at Saltaire is typical, though it's a particularly good example. It was another design by Sir William Fairbairn, done in 1853 and much bigger than my Dixon's Mill. It's 550 feet long and the whole complex is gargantuan with a vast T-shaped six-storey main block dominating the whole town. There are a few architectural details which add some interest to the building – long rows of tall arched windows in places and Italianate turrets and quite a powerful entrance to the offices – but what makes it so impressive is not the architectural touches but the scale and the solidity and the plainness.

Marshall's Mill in Leeds – not quite so plain!

There are exceptions of course. There always are. A few owners wanted factories with more architectural oomph and among these, the great example is the mill in Leeds which belonged to a man called John Marshall who is far too little known.

Marshall's dad owned a linen shop in Leeds and this seems to have pushed John towards spinning flax instead of wool which was much more usual in Yorkshire. He opened his first mill in 1787 and later built a complex of mills in a street which is now named after him. He made a fortune out of flax, employed almost 10,000 people and became one of the first industrialists to go into Parliament. Like Titus Salt and Colonel Akroyd he had a liberal background and strong religious beliefs and used some of his money to provide baths and changing rooms and schools and things for his workers. On the other hand he was utterly against factory reform so we shouldn't get too carried away praising him for his charitable and liberal nature.

We can praise him, though, for his final mill, which is amazing. It was built between 1838 and 1843 and it's unusual in lots of ways. For a start, instead of being multi-storey like most mills of this date, it's single storey, top lit by sixty-five glass domes – a great open plan space (over two acres) which allowed the production processes to be organised in a more flexible way. It wasn't until the 20th century that other factories adopted this approach. And then there was his artificially controlled environment. Flax needs to be kept damp and warm so there was a form of central heating with humidity created by water evaporating in underfloor channels. The roof was made of brick arches and it was insulated with layers of plaster, tar, earth and grass. Apparently the grass was kept under control by having sheep on the roof.

The mill was designed by an engineer called James Combe but he was working with an amateur architect, Joseph Bonomi, the brother of the Durham architect Ignatius Bonomi, who gave this innovative building a remarkable architectural character. He built it as an Egyptian temple, which is a style that is very rare in England but became briefly fashionable after the Napoleonic wars when

Europeans had the opportunity to visit the pyramids for the first time. The office block is astonishing. It's supposed to be a copy – and I'm quoting here since I've never been to Egypt myself – of the Great Ptolemaic Temple of Horus at Edfu which was built in 257 BC. It has six giant papyrus-shaped columns along the front and the walls are 'battered' which means that they all slope slightly inwards. The same papyrus columns, but in cast-iron instead of stone, support the roof of the mill.

I may be missing something but I don't think any other mill comes close to Marshall's in architectural elaboration. There are vast ones – Dean Clough at Halifax, for example, or the mills along the Rochdale canal at Ancoats in Manchester but none as elaborate as Marshall's.

New uses for old mills

Virtually none of these mills is still actively milling (though Marshall's is). The textile industry has faded away under attack from globalisation and you would have thought, well, I would certainly have thought, that massive great buildings like these which were not built for prettiness on the whole, snaffling as they so often do the best land along the valley bottoms, weighted down by the memories of the drudgery and hardship that went on in them, visually dominating the towns around them, would all have been pulled down and replaced by something else.

But they haven't. It is one of the most astonishing things about northern architecture and townscape in the last ten or twenty years that communities have been prepared to go to almost any lengths to avoid pulling down their mill buildings and have shown massive ingenuity in finding new uses for them. Salts Mill for example has everything. Bits of it have been taken over by other more recent industries, bits have been converted to housing. It has wonderful galleries full of wonderful art by Bradford's David Hockney; it has cafés and restaurants and book shops. Instead of being an abandoned monument to a dead industry it's become an absolutely marvellous day out. Dean Clough's the same – extraordinary variety – drama, music, opera, art, high-tech industries.

Other mills all over the north have been converted to classy contemporary housing. I have a picture in front of me of a loft-style apartment to die for. It's in Chorlton New Mills in Cambridge Street in Manchester, which contains a collection of mills that go to the heart of the Industrial Revolution. They were built from the 1790s over a period of about 20 years and they were owned for a while by the great visionary Robert Owen before he took himself off to found New Lanark on the Clyde. In the 1820s and later, they were owned by a man called Mackintosh who invented a way of waterproofing material. He patented his invention and introduced Mackintoshes to the world and where would we be without them? Wet is where we'd be. I really enjoyed discovering that Mackintoshes were invented in Manchester. The Cambridge Street Mills are a terrific group and they were converted into housing in 1998–2001. The flat I'm looking at is made remarkable by the space ... oh I'd love all of that space ... and by the elegant simplicity of the original fireproof construction which has been retained and exposed – the beautiful sweep of the shallow brick arches supported on slender cast-iron columns.

Whole areas of industrial townscapes, abandoned by their original users, have found new uses and become among the most exciting parts of our northern towns and cities. Along the Aire and Calder Canal in Leeds, for example. I had a tremendous walk along it the other day when I was photographing Marshall's Mill (OK, I got lost). It's been turned, even without most of its industry, into a wonderful place – a vibrant post-industrial cityscape of the old canal along with all of its mills, old but beautifully restored, surrounded by exciting new urban housing and the gleaming tower blocks of central Leeds in the background. Places like this are a rare testimony to the power of identity. It seems obvious that these mills and the life they supported have become so deeply rooted in our affections and our sense of what we are that we refuse to let go of them. Good on us, is what I say.

You might feel grumpy with me that in talking about factories I have restricted myself to textile mills as if there have been no other sorts of works dominating the back streets of northern towns. What about other industries? What about the heavy engineering and iron and steel, what about coal mining and shipbuilding and the railway industry, because all of these exist or existed on a vast scale and created around them the same sort of working class worlds as the mills.

A few individual examples of these historic factories survive, still dominating and giving life to their neighbourhoods. One lovely example is the group of late 19th- and early 20th-century factories in York which nowadays is part of the international chocky, sweety group Nestlés whose products I have been told, though I have of course no personal experience of this, are very nice. They used to belong to Rowntrees, makers of the incomparable fruit gum and winners, in my mind, of the important prize for factory owners with a conscience.

We tend to think of factory owners in the past ... well, to be honest we tend to think of them nowadays as well ... as fat cats, living in t'big house and grinding t' face of workers into t' dust. But right from the beginnning of factories, while there has been no shortage of nasty face-grinders, there have been plenty who have had a very different agenda, including of course Titus Salt, and Rowntrees which was founded by a man called Joseph Rowntree who was not only a spiffing chocky maker but also a Quaker with a very nicely sharpened social conscience. He funded schools and he set up a variety of charitable trusts which are still important today, 150 years later, in areas of education and poverty and so on. His son Benjamin conducted pioneering surveys into poverty in York and wrote books on the subject. But he didn't just write books. He did solid, real, practical things which altered the lives of his workers.

Benjamin set up a trust called the Joseph Rowntree Village Trust which in 1903 began to build one of the most important housing estates in Britain, one of the very earliest Garden Villages in Britain. It's called New Earswick and it was never limited just to Rowntrees' workers though most of them did live here. It was built as a model type of housing for ordinary working families and it was meant to be 'artistic in appearance, sanitary' but above all affordable ... and it succeeded wonderfully. One hundred years later it's still beautiful.

But the interesting thing about Rowntrees is how many aspects of people's lives they thought important. Body and soul were important so, as early as 1912, they provided dining facilities for the staff, but it wasn't just about survival, they served adequate food. In the same building there were lecture theatres, a school, and a night school, so that workers could improve themselves. There were even sports facilities. And Rowntrees spread out into the community as well ... always with the same concerns – enriching people's lives. So there's the Joseph Rowntree Memorial Library, the Joseph Rowntree Memorial Theatre, Rowntree Park which was given to the city in 1919, enriching the leisure time of the people of York in the most charming way.

When you see all of these things which seem to have nothing at all to do with making chockies it just makes you feel so glad that there have been, and still are I hope, factory owners with the conscience and the vision to look beyond the narrowest definition of what their responsibilities are to their workers and their community.

But historic factories like Rowntrees are an exception and in most cases the works themselves have either gone or been so changed that there's nothing historical left. The times when you looked down the terraced streets of Wallsend on Tyneside and saw vast ships towering above the roof tops have gone. In Middlesbrough only tragic fragments survive of the great ironworks which gave rise to the town and which led Gladstone to describe it as an 'Infant Hercules'. All over the north the pit villages are still lived in but the works and the pithead gear has all disappeared. The vast works of the Don Valley have been removed or rebuilt. Huge factories remain of course, but rarely in their historic form.

So that's a day's work over ... just time for a swift half on the way home.

Pubs

A Swift Half ...

I love pubs, I really do. When I lived in America temporarily, northern pubs were one of the things I missed most ...

Good grief, I can't believe I said that. Don't tell my Auntie Martha (my first employer if you recall) or my Auntie Bessie ... or even worse my Auntie Margaret. They were good chapel ladies, my aunties, Plymouth Brethren actually, and they disapproved of pubs and the evil drink absolutely. I was brought up in a world of nice, respectable cafés and other rich and exotic sources of tea and sticky buns, but alas, I have fallen. I have quaffed the beaded liquor and sunk into the gutter. I blame my father-in-law who used to recite at the dinner table:

I have no pain, dear mother now,
But, Oh, I am so dry;
Connect me to a brewery
And leave me there to die.

The 19th century, the period when our great northern working-class back streets were taking shape, was a period of great warfare in the world of the pub. There were two battles going on: the battle between the brewers and the Temperance movement, and the battle between the rival breweries for the soul and loyalty of the drinking man.

The Temperance battle seemed to be partly won in 1872 when the Liberal government, encouraged by chapel folk like my aunties, first introduced Licensing laws into England in a bid to control excessive drinking. Temperance organisations, not unlike my aunties, loathed drink and preached its evil in lurid tales about the death of drunkards:

Five cents a glass! How Satan laughed
As over the bar the young man quaffed
The Beaded liquor, for the demon knew
The terrible work that drink would do;
And before morning the victim lay
With his life-blood ebbing swiftly away.
And that was the price he paid alas!
For the pleasure of taking a social glass.

They persuaded landowners to open Temperance hotels which would provide a wholesome alternative to the pubs. It was the Victorian equivalent of trying to persuade youths to go to church youth clubs instead of beating up grannies. It was doomed to fail as a movement – and it did. I can't think of an example in the middle of a town off the top of my head, but in the village of Matfen near Hexham there's a Victorian pub next door to a Victorian Temperance Hotel. Guess which one is still a drinking establishment and which has given up the ghost and become a house?

At Matfen the pub won that particular battle hands down. The Temperance Hotel, like almost all temperance hotels, settled comfortably into a domestic life, its name the only memory of its worthy moral role.

But pubs went on from strength to strength, sapping the morals no doubt, not only of the labouring classes but, I'm afraid, Auntie Margaret, of me ... because I do love me swift half.

But in 1872 the battle between the brewers was just hotting up. Until the middle of the 19th century, most pubs were small. Often they were just converted houses, or corner shops that sold beer instead of bacon. You still see them everywhere. They've usually smallish late Georgian houses with ordinary house-y windows upstairs, frosted or chased glass windows downstairs. Often there's a corner door and always a nicely painted fascia board with the pub's name on. Inside, just a simple little room with a bar at one side, pumps for the hand-pulled beer along the top of it, bottles on the nicely carved mahogany back bar behind it, a few tables and simple benches around the walls. The lights are quite low and behind the bar a buxom barmaid ...

Wake up, Grundy, you've been dreaming, lad. Such places don't exist, or if they do they're as rare as well-kept real ale and harder to spot. Nowadays that pub has a karaoke night on a Thursday, a quiz night on a Tuesday. There's a gig by a thrash metal band on Saturdays, of course, but the band has to compete with three assorted games machines and an in-house music tape which the staff refuse to turn down because they've always liked Agadoo. And there's no real ale.

Pubs change, that's the nature of them. There's a pub around the corner from me which I used to like – I won't tell you its name because I'm going to be a bit rude about it and I value my kneecaps. All of my friends and I used to like it. It was much as I described up above except that there were two rooms, a slightly larger front bar with a pool table and a small back room which we went into on a regular basis. There was also a dart board, which is what drew us to the place because we liked big complex games of darts. And there was a jukebox which some might see as a disadvantage but in the 1980s and early 90s this particular jukebox still had 'Wimaweh' by Karl Denver and 'Big Noise From Winetka'. It had Brenda Lee and Fats Domino and as if that wasn't enough it was neatly placed in its own niche in the corner, framed by chintz curtains made doubly attractive by tie-backs. The overall décor of the bar was undoubtedly unusual. There was a flight of plaster ducks on one wall which gave a pleasingly domestic image, we thought, but behind the bar, among the postcards from Benidorm and the quaint notice telling you that there was free beer available to all customers aged 70 or above (accompanied by both parents) there was an attractive collection of small, plaster statues with mirthful messages and enormous penises.

It was friendly though and it did sell draft Bass which was enough to compensate for any number of shortcomings in its decorative regime. One Christmas I took my American friend Celia there for an evening out. She, having a strange idea about English inns, had come to stay in a Yorkshire country hotel to experience a good old-fashioned Dickensian Christmas. The experience turned out to be so depressing that she came to Newcastle instead and I took her to my pub to see a real English hostelry. She lasted about 20 minutes and decided to go home saying that she preferred typical English pubs. I pointed out that my pub was typical of about 97% of the pubs available in England and she said in that case she'd stick to the other 3%. I thought she was a bit terse about it. Perhaps she objected to the plaster ducks, I believe many people do.

Anyway, I was talking about change and the English pub, including this favourite pub of mine, underwent a transformation. Its two rooms were knocked into one, destroying in one single dazzling stroke all of the intimacy that had existed before. The dart board was retained (amazingly enough in modern times) but placed unusually in a sort of waist-high corridor at one end of the bar against which seats were placed – thus cunningly combining two disadvantages in one architectural feature. On the one hand the waist-high barrier made it impossible for players to gather round the game and interact in any meaningful way, but on the other hand, being only waist-high, it couldn't stop rebounding or errant darts from slaying bar staff or impaling customers sitting on the adjacent seats. 'Wimaweh' has long gone, of course, to be replaced by wall-to-wall football and MTV on large TV screens.

Since then, since we have been driven, my friends and I, to roam the streets pathetically in search of somewhere more acceptable to a gang of ageing chaps, it's changed again and no doubt it will continue to reinvent itself for as long as it survives. That's the nature of pubs. They've been doing that since the beginning so there's not a lot of point in expecting to find many back street pubs which have retained their historic features.

They were certainly changing in the second half of the 19th century when the mills and factories were going full tilt, and especially in the 1890s when there was a Tory government which was opposed to trade restrictions and beer licences. At that time, wages were comparatively high in the north and there was a terrific explosion of new pubs as the big breweries battled with each other for the loyalty and the lolly of the working man. Lynn Pearson, who wrote a book about Northumbrian Pubs, records that in 1882, in Newcastle, there were 446 fully licensed houses, 324 beerhouses, 36 breweries and 77 off-licences – a total as she says 'of 883 places at which alcohol could be bought'. Ever a woman for a startling statistic, she goes on to tell us that in the late 1870s beer production was more than 30 million barrels a year 'with weekly consumption averaging out at over five pints per head for every man, woman and child'. Working on the assumption that many children didn't take up their full statistical allowance, that means that a lot of chaps were drinking a lot of beer and the breweries started a battle to persuade them to drink it in their pubs.

What they did was to build palaces. You see them everywhere and, however much they've been altered inside to take account of changing tastes, from the outside they are obviously palaces still. If you'll bear with me I'll just describe one, a random and fairly typical example of one in a working-class suburb of Sunderland. It's called The Mountain Daisy … can I resist a sideways leap into the weird and whacky world of pub names? I can, I think, for the time being at least, though I may find myself drawn irresistibly back to it later. It's called The Mountain Daisy which, to be honest, is about the least appropriate name you could make up in this very towny setting. It was built in 1902 for a local brewery called W.B. Reid and it towers over the surrounding terraces of single-storey Sunderland cottages like a palace – which of course was a very deliberate impression because its size and its architectural splendour was an advertising ploy to pull in the punters. It's got a big corner tower to act as a sort of beacon and the façade is enriched with marble and brick and terracotta. There are big glowing, Art Nouveau stained-glass windows to make it look fab at night. Who could resist it?

Well, not me evidently, because suddenly there I was – inside.

Its long front bar has been altered, but the little back room is far from typical. I was misleading you when I said that. It's a survival, which is amazing. It is entirely tiled. Every inch of the walls and the whole of the bar is covered with richly decorated ceramic tiles. The bar is awash with classical patterns, the walls awash with local scenes, all done in ceramic tiles made by a firm called Craven Dunhill from Ironbridge in Shropshire. It was a sensible material to use in a pub in some ways – we housewives know that it's always sensible to use easy-to-clean surfaces in a busy area – but the taste for tiles and other forms of ceramic surfaces was mainly a late Victorian delight in new materials and brilliant finishes.

What the late Victorian drinker found when he went into almost any of these beer palaces was … a palace. A jewelled palace, a finely wrought and delicately made palace. You might have expected them to be tawdry and brash but the surviving examples suggest not. In Sunderland there's another untouched interior called the Dun Cow which I think is just a beautiful room. The bar itself is original and so is the back bar, the shelves that hold the bottles behind the bar are just delicious – a delicate filigree of mahogany fretwork. The shapes are sinuous and half way between Gothic and Art Nouveau and the same shapes are picked up in the curved glass screen which divides the room in two.

The most remarkable thing about these gigantic and exquisitely decorated turn-of-the-century pubs is that they were palaces specifically built for the working man. Pubs sometimes tried to attract the middle classes by dividing themselves up into different rooms like snugs and saloons and so on but it didn't really work. On the whole they tended to be avoided by the middle classes. The 1901 edition of the international travel guide, *Baedeker*, for example, advised all tourists to avoid taverns and public houses. They were for the working man. They were fantasies to draw the ordinary man away from home to experience luxuries he had no chance of seeing in any other way. They were dream factories.

The best surviving example, by far, is not actually in a working-class suburb but in a fairly central part of Liverpool. The Philharmonic is a gloriously decorative froth of an interior, rich in glass and tiles, plasterwork and beaten copper. I accept no legal responsibility for this statement, but it's almost worth changing your sex to see the gentlemen's urinals which somehow manage to be nobly sturdy and manly and yet at the same time prettily attractive. This is not a feat achieved by many gentlemen's urinals nor indeed by many gentlemen. Most of us can't achieve either.

I say that The Philharmonic is the best surviving example but, to be honest, I don't know many others. There are obvious dangers in trying to become too much of an expert in the interiors of pubs and three factors have stopped me from trying. First of all, as I've been saying, change is so rapid and so widespread that you can get discouraged awfully quickly. Secondly, it's almost impossible, without detailed local knowledge, to spot the difference between an interesting pub and a dreadful one. You visit one turn-of-the-century half-timbered pub called The Queen's Kneecap and it has fine food and a range of fine ales, friendly locals, a cheery manager and an aged and rather smelly dog dozing by the fire. You visit another which looks identical from the outside, but the moment you walk in your feet stick to the carpet, preventing you from escaping the malevolent sniffing of the manager or his wall-eyed alsatian.

But the third reason I have for not being too specific about the pubs of the north is that in themselves they are not really northern. There doesn't seem to me to be a northern style. They are English pubs, Victorian pubs, usually altered a dozen times since they were built. They just happen to be such typical features of the sort of northern back streets I have been describing here. And I would like to point out that though I may have seemed a touch apoplectic in my comments about them (put it down to my age) I am off now to sample a few swift halves before stopping off, on the way home, at …

The Chippy

The embarrassment in Leicester and the incomprehension in Edinburgh

I was in a chip shop in Leicester once and I asked for some batter with my chips. The woman looked puzzled, said she'd ask the manager and disappeared. She was gone for some time and people in the queue behind me muttered darkly. I was embarrassed and eventually she came back, looking pleased, with half a pound of *butter* in her hand. I said, 'No, I wanted *batter*,' and pointed to the little pile of bits in the corner of the range.

'Oh!' she said, 'You mean scratchings!'

Another time I was in Edinburgh (for I have travelled far in pursuit of gastronomic delights) and a chip shop owner said to me, 'D'you want some qwnklerknsls on yer chups?'

I hadn't a clue what he'd said so I nodded and he poured this thick, brown, glutinous stuff all over them. It was like crushed monkey. I still don't know what it was.

You see, the amazing thing about chip shops is that they're different wherever you go in the country – batter here, scratchings there. Some parts of the country serve cod, in Yorkshire it's nearly always haddock. In London they seem to serve anything as long as it could swim once and my experiences in Edinburgh suggest that they prefer fish which died a long time ago. Sometimes you ask for fish and chips, sometimes for a paper. Some places boast about vegetable oil, others insist on good old-fashioned dripping.

Why? In this standardised age, when most other takeaway food is just about identical, why is every chip shop unique? Where did they come from? Who invented them and when, and how, in this day of the takeaway explosion – hamburgers, pizzas, kebabs, curries, sweet and sours – how on earth does the humble fish and chip shop survive?

The first mention of fried fish, I hate to have to tell you, is in a London context. In chapter 26 of *Oliver Twist*, published in 1837, Dickens writes about an alleyway off Holborn Hill:

'Confined as the limits of Field Lane are, it has its barber, its beer shop and its fried fish warehouse.'

It also has filthy shops with huge bunches of second-hand silk hand-kerchiefs purchased from London's pickpockets, so it has to be said that the fish half of the fab pair burst onto the scene in rather disreputable circumstances. Within a few years, and certainly by the time Henry Mayhew wrote *London Labour and the London Poor* in 1861, there were more than 300 fish fryers in London. Most of them were cooking dabs, dipped in batter to hold them together and fried in shallow pans on open-air barrows. They were sold around the pubs accompanied by slices of bread.

Fried potatoes arrived in a more respectable way. They first began to appear in recipe books in the early 1700s and by the 1860s were described as potatoes à la mode, 'cut into square shapes about the length and thickness of the little finger' – chip in fact.

But who brought the wondrous duo together for the first time? Nobody really knows but there are a number of claimants. There is an amusing little suggestion that it might have been a shop in London's East End called Malins which opened in the early 1860s, but I think we northerners can snigger behind our hands at that. Another claimant is a shop opened by a man called John Lees in 1863 in Mossley near Manchester. He'd set up originally in a hut to sell pea soup and pigs' trotters, a rare delicacy I'm sure, and perhaps not rare enough, but fortunately he gave that up at some time in the 1860s to sell fish and chips instead. And then there was an Oldham Tripe Dresser (his trade, not a comment on his sartorial taste) called Dyson who is said to have had a range built specially to fry fish and chips in 1866.

But, wherever it started, the fish and chip trade grew fastest in the fertile ground of northern working towns, especially the mill towns of the Pennines where there was a large working population which was rich enough for most of the 19th century to buy a few treats and where there were lots of women working in the mills with too little time to cook. The Pennine towns were also close to two seas and by the 1860s they were well served with railways so that there was a plentiful supply of fresh fish.

Fish and chip shops also look best in the back streets of northern towns. I'm not suggesting that they're architecture of course. Chip shops are nearly always tatty little shops with tatty little signs, but that doesn't mean that they're not worth looking at. They're an important part of the northern townscape. At night they gleam irresistibly in the darkness of terraced streets, and even if they're not architecture, they do have a style of their own.

They have grown rather than been designed, though they all have a few key things in common. They have to have a high counter of course – high enough so small boys have to gaze up at it and small girls have to be picked up by their dads to see over it. I prefer those shops where the counter is also the back of the range where the food is cooked so that the queue snakes along the back of the range and the customers snuggle against its wamth for comfort on cold winter nights. The range has to have a warming tray along the top so that the tempting goodies are doing their tempting job as you wait to be served.

The décor is always minimal – an easy-to-clean plastic menu board, a few adverts and posters from the Federation of Fish Friers and a fish identification chart from the White Fish Authority. There should be handwritten specials on little dayglo stars stuck to the walls with Blu-Tack.

Lovely places. It pleases me that they have managed to survive the onslaught of alternative nosh and that they haven't followed the American line and gone glossy and well packaged and that they have stayed little and individual and suitable for the back streets of our northern industrial towns. I say *suitable* because, though the north is home to an extraordinary range of wonderful buildings, it is also full of ordinary ones. This region is poorer on the whole than most parts of the country, its towns are more thoroughly working class and more extensively Victorian and chip shops, which were probably invented in the north, are still typical of its identity

It's probably a shocking thing to say, but for all the beauty of the hills, and the majesty of the cathedrals, there's nothing gives me a warmer sense of being northern than the sight of a cobbled back street, a mill in the distance, a pub on the corner with the promise of pints of draught bliss and a fish supper on the way home.

So, I'm going to end this book on chip shops, because there are few better ways to end anything than with a bag of chips ... but not with scratchings.

Postscript

I have to apologise. These are some of the places I have to apologise to: Leeds, Sheffield, Bradford, Wakefield, Harrogate, Darlington, Preston, Bolton. I've hardly mentioned any villages by name and there are small towns all over the north I'll hardly dare show my face in. I've said nothing about canals, or the Middlesbrough Transporter Bridge. I haven't mentioned the lead mining landscape of West Durham or the thrilling skyscapes of Tyneside's shipyards. Parks and gardens barely got a look in so there's no mention of Studley Royal or Duncombe Park, or Bramham Park or the marvellous 17th-century topiary at Levens Hall in Westmorland. Chapels! I can't believe I haven't said anything about chapels. My Keswick aunties will be turning in their graves that I haven't found time to explore the extraordinarily rich legacy left by all of their beloved nonconformist chapels. And as for individual buildings, I haven't mentioned even a fiftieth of my own personal favourites ...

But then again, do you know how many cities and towns, villages and individual buildings there are in the north? Lots. There are lots of them and the measly allotment of 75,000 words to talk about them would have given me an approximate 2.3 words per settlement if I had attempted to be even-handed in my approach. So if you want to know about the ones I haven't mentioned you'll have to give yourself some of the pleasure I've had and potter off around the north seeking them out for yourself.

But on the other hand, perhaps a pre-emptive apology might be in order to deflect criticism away from some of the many mistakes I am sure to have made. An irritated reader recently wrote a letter in response to an article I had written and said words to the effect that he wasn't sure that Mr Grundy was notable for his accuracy. There is much truth in this. Many years ago there was a wonderful series of books by Michael Green about The Art of Coarse Sport. *The Art of Coarse Rugby* was the first but my favourite was called *The Art of Coarse Acting*. In it Green defines a coarse actor as 'one who knows his lines … but not the order in which they come'. Well, I'm afraid I'm a bit of a coarse historian and if I have made errors I hope you'll pass them on to me in a spirit of sweetness and light because I am a very sensitive flower and brood a lot if criticised.

Right. Summy-uppy time. After all of these words and after all of the travelling and thinking about the buildings of the north have I found a northern style?

No, I don't think I have – but there are things which seem worth saying.

Castles, inevitably, are a theme. The north quite simply has more and of more variety than anywhere else. Among them are the bizarre bastlehouses which are to be found nowhere else at all.

Innovation is a theme. A willingness to embrace new technologies in the 18th and 19th centuries transformed the north and the rest of the world followed. Where would we have got to without railways or without factories, without all the brilliant inventivenss that the north offered to the world. Salt and vinegar crisps. They were invented in the north. Where would we be without those? Thinner, probably.

I think I've spotted a tendency towards plainness, though it's a tendency which breaks down at the drop of a hat. There's precious little plainness about the great Baroque houses of late 17th- and early 18th-century Yorkshire or about the Elizabethan and Jacobean great houses along the Pennine flanks; and the builders of Victorian town halls and office buildings in the north wouldn't have recognised plainness if it had been presented to them on a plate with watercress round it. But solidity and plainness is commoner than not. It is present in the beautiful farmhouses of all six counties, and the villages, however pretty they are in their locations and arrangements, are filled with plainly beautiful cottages. The castles are plain and workmanlike, the churches are simpler and plainer than many down south and all the better for it, the many ruined abbeys have a self-conscious simplicity which is more beautiful than any decoration could be. The north, as a whole, seems to me to lack the obvious and blissful beauties of other regions but its solidity makes its buildings a match for any in the world.

And finally, I've realised, or re-realised because I've known it all along, that the north is filled with wonderful buildings and doesn't deserve in any teeny, weeny little way, the scabby treatment that's been meted out to it by so many writers. I've just remembered one more such quote. Thirty years ago there was a celebrated tug of love case involving a North East mother and a French father and *Paris Match* did a profile of the area. In French, which I haltingly translated, it described Newcastle as 'a small mining town in the North East of England, still locked in the horrors of the Industrial Revolution.' Wait till I do my book about France.

Bibliography

Addison, Sir W. *Local Styles of the English Parish Church* (Batson, 1982)

Biddle & Nock *The Railway History of Britain* (Michael Joseph, 1983)

Brooks, P.R.B. *William Hedley: Locomotive Pioneer* (Tyne & Wear Industrial Monuments, 1980)

Brunskill, R.W. *Vernacular Architecture of the Lake Counties* (Faber & Faber, 1974)

Caffy, Lucy *Workers Housing in West Yorkshire* (RCHM) (HMSO, 1986)

Clayre, Alasdair (ed) *Nature and Industrialization* (OUP, 1977)

Colls and Lancaster (eds) *Newcastle upon Tyne* (Phillimore, 2001) Charlton, Beryl *Upper North* (Beryl Charlton, 1987)

Denyer, Susan *Traditional Building and Life in The Lake District* (Gollanz, 1991)

Dixon and Muthesius, *Victorian Architecture* (T & H, 1978)

Faulkner and Greg *John Dobson: Architect of the North East* (Tyne Bridge Publishing, 2001)

Faulkner, T.E. (ed) *Northumbrian Panorama* (Octavian, 1996)

Fawcett, Bill *A History of North Eastern Railway Architecture: Vol 1 The Pioneers* (NE Railway Association, 2001)

Girouard, Mark *The English Town* (Yale UP, 1990)

Grouard, Mark *Life in the English Country House* (Yale UP, 1978)

Grundy, J. *Robert Anderson* (unpublished dissertation, 1967)

Hall, I. & H. *Georgian* (Sessions, 1978)

Hall, I. & H. *Historic Beverley* (The Beverley Bookshop, 1973)

Hammond and Powell Douglas *Leeds: Three Suburban Walks* (The Victorian Society, 1987)

Hartwell, Clare *Manchester* (Yale UP, 2002)

Hoskins, W.G. *English Landscapes* (BBC, 1973)

Jenkins, S. *England's 1000 Best churches* (Allen Lane, 1999)

Lefebure M. *Cumberland Heritage* (Arrow, 1970)

Musgrove, Frank *The North of England: A history from Roman Times to the Present* (Blackwell, 1990)

Muthesius, S. *The English Terraced House* (Yale UP, 1982)

Pearson, L.F. *Building the West Riding* (Smith Settle, 1995)

Pearson, L.F. *Lighthouses* (Shire Pubs, 1995)

Pearson, L.F. *The Northumbrian Pub* (Sandhill Press, 1989)

Pevsner (revised Neave) *Yorkshire: York and the East Riding* (Penguin, 1995)

Pevsner (revised Radcliffe) *Yorkshire: West Riding* (Penguin, 1967)

Pevsner (revised Williamson) *Durham* (Penguin, 1983)

Pevsner and Richmond (2nd edition revised Grundy et al) *Northumberland* (Penguin, 1992)

Pevsner *North Lancashire* (Penguin, 1969)

Pevsner *South Lancashire* (Penguin, 1969)

Pevsner *The Buildings of England: Cumberland and Westmorland* (Penguin, 1967)

Pevsner *Yorkshire; The North Riding* (Penguin, 1966)

Quiney, A. *Traditional Buildings of England* (T & H, 1990)

RCHM and W.Yorks Archeological Service *Yorkshire Textile Mills 1770-1930* (HMSO, 1992)

RCHM *Houses of the N Yorks Moors* (HMSO, 1987)

RCHM *Rural Houses of the Lancashire Pennines 1560-1760* (HMSO, 1985)

RCHM *Rural Houses of West Yorkshire 1400-1830* (HMSO, 1986)

RCHM *Shielings and Bastles* (HMSO, 1970)

Rollinson, W. *A History of Cumberland and Westmorland* (Phillimore, 1978)

Sheeran, G. *Brass Castles* (Ryburn, 1993)

York: Historic Buildings in the Central Area (RCHM HMSO, 1981)

Index